About the Auth

Born and raised on the Indian reserve at Morley, Alberta, west of Calgary, Chief John Snow was elected Chief of the Nakoda-Wesley First Nation from 1968–1992 and again from 1996–2000. The first ordained minister of the United Church from the Stoney Nation, Chief Snow holds an honorary doctorate of laws degree from the University of Calgary (1981) and an honorary doctorate of divinity degree from Cook College and Theological School, Tempe, Arizona (1986), as well as numerous achievement awards. Chief Snow is a trailblazer and a nation builder; he is a spokesman, ambassador, statesman, lecturer, writer, author, and spiritual leader for his people.

Chief Snow has been the featured speaker at many events—from school graduations to treaty conferences, elders' think-tanks to constitutional meetings and treaty rights symposia. Chief Snow has also been the leader in many groundbreaking events and establishments during his career since the first edition of *These Mountains Are Our Sacred Places* in 1977. He hosted the North American Indian Ecumenical Conference held from 1971 to 1985 on the sacred grounds within Stoney Indian Park; established the Nakoda Conference Centre in 1980, the Chief Goodstoney Rodeo Centre in 1982, and the Nakoda Hotel built in 1988 and 1989; implemented local control of community education and the Morley Community School in 1985; successfully negotiated two precedent-setting land claims in 1990 and 1999; and, in 1999, invited the sixth triennial World Indigenous Peoples Conference on Education (WIPCE) to Morley (WIPCE was held on the sacred grounds of the Nakoda People in August 2002).

Since his retirement from political office in December 2000, Chief Snow has suffered the personal loss of his wife, Alva, in 2000. However, he takes great pleasure from his nine grandchildren and continues to advise and mentor his seven adult children in their professional careers.

This book I dedicate to my wife, Alva, and my sons and daughters, John Jr., Rachel, Terry, Tony, Gloria, Billy, and Teresa, without whose encouragement, understanding, and help this book would not have been written.

I would like to acknowledge my family—my brother Wallace Snow and my sister Glenda Crawler—who encouraged and helped me in recalling the legends and traditional teachings we received when we were growing up in the little log cabin we called home. I want to thank Ian Getty, with whom I worked for many years, for his assistance and for writing the introduction to this edition. Also thanks to Terry Munro and his staff for typing and reviewing the epilogue. Finally, thanks to my grand-children, who were very supportive and brought pop, tea, coffee, cookies, cakes, and sandwiches to me while I wrote the epilogue.

These Mountains Are Our Sacred Places

THE STORY OF THE STONEY PEOPLE

CHIEF JOHN SNOW

FIFTH
HOUSE

Cover and interior design by Cheryl Peddie / Emerge Creative
Cover photograph by Darwin Wiggett
Interior photographs provided by the Stoney Tribal Administration, except for noted exceptions from the Glenbow Museum and Archives
Copyedited by Joan Tetrault
Proofread by Ann Sullivan
Scans by ABL Imaging

The publisher gratefully acknowledges the support of The Canada Council for the Arts and the Department of Canadian Heritage.

**Canada Council
for the Arts**

**Conseil des Arts
du Canada**

We acknowledge the financial support of the Government of Canada through the Book Publishing Industry Development Program (BPIDP) for our publishing activities.

Printed in Canada by Friesens

05 06 07 08 09 / 5 4 3 2 1

First published in the United States in 2006 by
Fitzhenry & Whiteside
121 Harvard Avenue, Suite 2
Allston, MA 02134

Library and Archives Canada Cataloguing in Publication

Snow, John, 1933-
      These mountains are our sacred places : the story of the Stoney Indians / John Snow.

(Western Canadian classics)
ISBN 1-894856-79-1

      1. Assiniboine Indians—Alberta—History. 2. Assiniboine Indians—History. I. Title.
II. Series.

E99.A84S65 2005   971.23004'97524   C2005-902381-3

Fifth House Ltd.
A Fitzhenry & Whiteside Company
1511, 1800-4 St. SW
Calgary, Alberta T2S 2S5

1-800-387-9776
www.fitzhenry.ca

Contents

Foreword

It is both an honour and humbling to write this foreword. As an Indigenous woman and a teacher, I am a committed believer in preparing new generations of transformational leaders in the political, social, and science sectors. Hence, I am always in search of good resources to use at our First Nations College. Dr. Snow's oral literary research is important in aligning and promoting Indigenous grassroots history and knowledge for use in places of higher learning. For too long we have relied on western interpretations of our history. *These Mountains Are Our Sacred Places* identifies who we are and impacts on prospective students by validating their contexts and authentically transforming the past into the present. For students questioning their place in modernity, Dr. Snow's book is a gentle reminder that our spiritual lands, our Mother Earth, beckons and embraces all.

In his writing and teaching, Dr. Snow works humbly within an Indigenous paradigm. He shoulders the responsibility of interpreting the oral teachings, and this takes great skill and knowledge of self. As an intermediary, he eloquently interprets the elders' knowledge, thus positioning it in time and honouring the traditional way of passing knowledge. He poignantly captures in print the time-honoured ways of servant leadership and situational leadership, traditional organizational structures and perspectives on relationships (including our human responsibility to each other and our relationship with the land, elements, and the cosmos). *These Mountains Are Our Sacred Places* acknowledges our interdependence and the holistic nature of the world. The book highlights the structures that work for First Nations peoples, including decision making through consensus and equal voice rather than through power, authority, and control, which are elements of linear thinking.

I continue to honour and encourage people to walk the path forged by trailblazers such as Dr. John Snow. *These Mountains Are Our Sacred Places* gives me hope that we can make effective changes within our spheres by drawing on the foundations left for us by our ancestors. Like a warrior of old, Dr. Snow deftly secures this knowledge to share with the world.

Dr. Leona Makokis
President, Blue Quills First Nations College
St. Paul, Alberta

Preface

This is a narrative that tells the story of my people, the Stoney people, from before the coming of the whiteman down to the present day. It describes our cultural beliefs and values, how these have been preserved in oral tradition and historical records, and how they have affected Stoney attitudes toward modern life and aspirations for future Stoney generations. It explains why my people's thinking does not separate the political and the economic from the social and the religious, and how threads of each are interwoven throughout all Stoney reasoning. It describes Indian reverence for and association with nature.

The year 1977 marks the centenary of the signing of Treaty Number Seven. This agreement was made one hundred years ago between representatives of the Queen of Canada and those Indian people who were native to the Saskatchewan River country in what is presently known as southern Alberta. It was an exchange of promises in perpetuity—as long as the sun shines, the rivers flow, and the grass grows.

Unfortunately there is a suspicion today among the Indian people that those governments directly responsible for honouring the terms of the Treaties will attempt to play down the real significance of the centenary, turning it into a mere ceremonial show. The Stoney people, on the other hand, insist that everything possible be done to accentuate its importance and bring the real meaning of the event to the attention of the Canadian people.

Throughout my lifetime the promises of Treaty Seven have never been far from my mind. As far back as I can remember, the Stoney elders have reminded me of the importance of the agreements contained in Treaty Seven and the promises made to my people at Blackfoot Crossing one hundred years ago. My people have told me that they prayed, burnt the sweet grass, smoked the peace pipe, and observed our sacred ceremonies before they attested their signatures to the treaty parchment. The Treaty is a Sacred Covenant made before the Great Creator. Therefore, it should never be broken by either of the parties concerned. But whenever I have heard an interpretation of those agreements and promises from government officials, I have been made aware of how different the officials' view is from that of our tribal elders. The difference separating the two versions is as great as the difference that separates night from day.

It was with the view of attempting to clarify and explain my

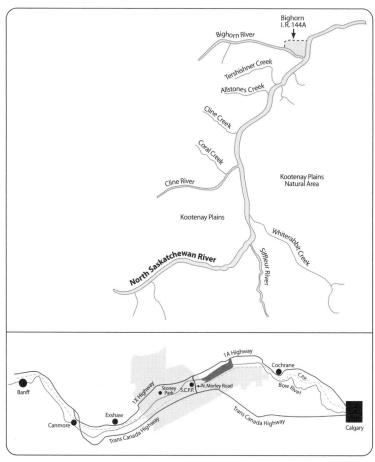

Much of this book deals with our reserve at Morley (below) and our still-unsuccessful efforts to claim our ancestral lands in the Kootenay Plains, which had been promised at treaty (top).

people's understanding of the Treaty—and of relations between themselves and the whitemen in the hundred years that followed its signing—that I began doing research in 1969. I looked at archival material—documents, letters, memoranda, maps—and I listened to the recorded stories and recollections of Stoney elders. Many people helped me with this research and many things have grown from it.

Not the least result of my labour is this book, in which I will try to point out what has happened in the past hundred years, and how restrictive government legislation plus public indifference have constantly threatened the survival of traditional Stoney beliefs, values, and lifestyle. But the reader may be surprised to find that a note of hope enters the later pages, as I try to explain our new belief in and hope for survival in a bicultural society.

The narrative begins with the stable social, religious, political, and cultural state of my people in the period prior to contact with the immigrant Europeans.

Part Two begins by developing the theme of the destruction wrought by the whisky traders and the introduction of new technology and values. The acceptance by the Indian people of the missionaries and the North West Mounted Police as a means of regulating the new problems is explained.

The period of treaty-signing is dealt with thoroughly, and the significance of this event continues like a thread throughout the succeeding chapters. Misunderstanding, misconceptions, and failure on the government's part to hold to treaty agreements, coupled with the immigrants' greed for and arrogant exploitation of the land, are viewed from the Indian perspective.

The period 1885 to 1948 is dealt with in detail in Part Three, and every attempt is made to explain why my people view themselves as having been dispossessed of those very things which are essential to our survival as a people.

The years 1948 to 1965 are passed over quickly. It was a period when the Indian people were forgotten because the dominant society became too involved with the economic development boom and its own growing affluence.

Part Four brings us to 1969, a year of special significance to the Stoney people because of the introduction of self-government following the granting of citizenship to Indian people across the nation. The same part introduces the theme of biculturalism, the most important goal of my people today as we seek a path that will allow us to live in the best of the dominant culture and our own, rather than slip between the two.

It is in this section that I try to bring out the challenges of the modern age, the loosening of ties of the Department of Indian Affairs, and the planning of our own development.

The religious theme returns in the last pages of Part Four to draw the book to a climax. The Indian Ecumenical Conference is held each summer at Morley with the Rocky Mountains providing an inspirational sight for more than 7,000 delegates from Indian tribes across North America. A description of its effect on Indian religious thought is essential to the theme of the book.

Hereditary Chief of the Nakoda people, the late Chief Jonas Goodstoney and his wife, Mary. He is the elder sage who gave me my name, Walking Seal, according to our tradition. Mary was always proud of my Indian name and told me many times how I received it.

The final chapter is softer in tone. The harsh reality of the past century must be written in harsh fact. The future of the Indian people is one of hope. I look to the coming century with confidence, and this is reflected in the ending.

In conclusion, I want to thank all the Wesley Band members who have helped me during my years of leadership, in particular the elders for the wise advice they have given me when I needed to make important decisions on their behalf. I also would like to acknowledge the people who encouraged me in completing this book: the Stoney Tribal Council, the staff of the Stoney Cultural Education Program, Mac and Audrey Newman, Ian Getty, Chief Bill McLean, Felix Poucette, former Chief Willie Goodstoney, George Ear, Peter Wesley, Bill Fraser, and Warren Harbeck. Thanks are also due to Dr. Joan Ryan and Dr. Hugh Dempsey for reviewing the manuscript; to Donna Dewaard and Lenora Brooks for typing it.

Stoney Reserve
Morley, Alberta
May 1977

Walking Seal Has Come

I was born on 31 January 1933 in a one-room log cabin on the edge of a beautiful evergreen forest on the Stoney-Nakoda Indian Reserve at Morley, Alberta. I remember during the warmer seasons we lived in teepees and tents, as we often went on camping trips along the foothills country. I also experienced living in teepees during the cold winter months. I always enjoyed living in a teepee with a fire in the centre to keep us warm and to light the place at night. I heard many legends within teepees while sitting around the sacred fire. It seems that I was living in a dream world, learning our traditions. The forest, animals, birds, and all of nature seemed to come alive in the stories. My world view was from an Indigenous perspective until I was sent to the Morley residential school operated by the United Church of Canada. I was the fifth child of eleven in our family, born to Cora Bigstoney and the late Chief Tom Snow, who served as one of the Nakoda Chiefs during the 1950s.

In the first edition of *These Mountains Are Our Sacred Places*, I wrote briefly about my Native name but I do not explain the meaning it carries. My mother told me that a few days after I was born, a pow-wow was held at a large schoolhouse near the northeast corner of the reserve, where community functions and tribal gatherings were held. My mother told me how she was informed that at the pow-wow I was given the traditional Indian name *Intebeja Mani*, or Walking Seal, by the hereditary Chief Jonas Goodstoney. She said: "He gave you the name without seeing you, as though he knew you and knew that you were coming." She said that the old Chief announced my name at the community gathering. Neither my parents nor I were at the pow-wow hosted by the tribe. Perhaps my parents thought I was too little or too young to be taken out into the cold winter night to a large gathering only a few days after I was born.

Chief Jonas had heard via the moccasin telegraph among the tribal members about the baby boy born to Tom and Cora Snow just a few days before, and he told some of the people, "His name is *Intebeja Mani*." Then, he announced to the pow-wow gathering, "Walking Seal has come."

Mary, the Chief's wife, loved to tell me the story of my naming. She would say, "Your grandpa announced your name, saying, 'Walking Seal has come,' to the people at the pow-wow and everyone was curious about who this Walking Seal was." The people looked around the audience to see if a new person was there. They were thinking that a visitor from another tribe had come to the pow-wow. Some even said, "I hope he is a good medicine man and not a bad one." The old Chief kept the people in suspense for most of the pow-wow. People kept asking, "Who is Walking Seal and where is he?" Near the closing of the event, the old Chief announced, "A baby boy is born to Tom and Cora Snow and his name is *Intebeja Mani*, Walking Seal."

My traditional name was conferred upon me by an elder sage who knew the Nakoda traditions and was one of the keepers of wisdom. He was a ceremonial leader, an oral historian, and a hereditary chief of the Nakoda people. I have often wondered why Chief Jonas passed this name on to me without having seen me or my parents beforehand. There were eleven children in our family and the old Chief named only one of us.

As I look back over the years, I have come to realize the significance of this traditional naming ceremony. Chief Jonas was a hereditary chief. His father was Chief Jacob Goodstoney, who signed Treaty Number Seven with the British Crown at Blackfoot Crossing in 1877. I believe that by conferring upon me the name Walking Seal, this wise sage placed upon my shoulders the responsibility of leading the Nakoda people into the modern age. Even though I was only a few days old, Chief Jonas Goodstoney, through his intuition and through the wisdom of the sages that preceded him, anointed me with a traditional name to guide me into modern times. As it turned out, thirty-five years later, I was elected chief in 1968 and served the Stoney-Nakoda People for more than a quarter of a century—twenty-eight years—as one of the Chiefs of the Stoney Tribal Council.

When I was an older boy, Jonas and his wife, Mary, explained to me why I received my name *Intebeja Mani*, Walking Seal, according to our tradition. He said that the seal is a unique creature, a versatile animal. The seal lives west and north of here—we don't see the animal in these parts. Then they both took turns in explaining and interpreting the importance of my name to me. Mary was always proud of my name and got excited when talking to me about it. The old couple were real elders, loving and caring, real human beings who cared for our families and our people. They would say, the seal walks on land and it glides over sand, snow, ice, and water with ease. The seal can survive in all kinds of weather on land or at sea. The seal is an animal with great determination to live. It adapts to changing seasons as they progress from spring to summer, and autumn to winter, always adjusting to these changes according to the Creator's plan. I, too, who carry this name, would also adjust to the changes and challenges of modern times. "Carry your name well and your name will carry you well." He told me to always honour our traditions and to bring honour to our people. I am proud of the Nakoda name given to me by one of my great-grandfathers.

My parents accepted my Native name and always called me by it. I was known as *Intebeja* (Seal) for short by my siblings, family, extended family, and tribal members before I was sent to attend the residential school at the Morley townsite. When I entered the residential school, they gave me a haircut, and I was known as John Snow, an English name given to me by my father, who had lost his older brother, named John Snow, in an automobile accident in 1929 at the crossing at Bow Fort Creek. So I carry my uncle's name in the English language today.

So this is my true history as an indigenous person born on this Great Island. This is how I received my Indian name of Walking Seal, given to me by one of my great-grandfathers according to our traditional ways when I entered this world. Just as the seal learns to walk, glide, dive, and swim over the sand, water, ice, and snow with ease, I, too, was guided through life by our heritage. The teachings I have learned over the years from our elders are still with me today. I was taught that we are part of this beautiful land and this beautiful land is part of us. We are all related. We are one with nature. We are one with the cosmos. This might be called mythic history by non-Native historians, but it is my history. I have experienced it, I have lived it, and I treasure it today. I will treasure it more and more as I experience and understand the deeper meanings and truths about our traditions as I continue life's journey.

Introduction

In the literature of Alberta's First Nations leaders, in its understanding of the history of Treaty Seven, and as a contribution to the history of the Stoney Nakoda people, Chief John Snow's book *These Mountains Are Our Sacred Places: The Story of the Stoney People* is an exceptional accomplishment. His book stands beside those of other Native leaders such as Harold Cardinal, George Manuel, John Tootoosis, Dan Kennedy, Max Gros-Louis, and Billy Diamond.[1] It is both an autobiography, infused with Chief Snow's personal viewpoints, philosophy, political analysis, and vision for his people, and the most comprehensive history of the Stoney people available. Arising from his traditional name, Walking Seal, Chief Snow eloquently explains how he has come to follow in the footsteps of the chiefs of days gone by.

When Chief Snow first conceived *These Mountains Are Our Sacred Places* in the early 1970s, he had a number of goals for the book, including the documentation and analysis of treaty rights and land claims issues. His active involvement in the documentation process started with his appointment in 1971 as the first director of the Indian Association of Alberta's Treaty and Aboriginal Rights Research (TARR) program.[2] As part of that mandate, he initiated land claims and treaty rights research on behalf of Alberta's forty-four First Nations.

As part of his Tribal Council responsibilities for the Stoney Nakoda Nation, Chief Snow was asked to take the leadership role in preparing its land claims and protecting its Aboriginal title and treaty rights. Subsequently, in April 1972, the Stoney land claim report, "The Kootenay Plains and the Big Horn Wesley Stoney Band–An Oral and Documentary Historical Report, 1800–1970," was presented to the minister of Indian Affairs, the first documented land claim to be received by the federal government from an Indian band. It was a proud day for the Stoney chiefs and councillors, elders, and research staff who, guided by Chief Snow, had laboured long and hard to record the oral history of the Stoney Nakoda people. This collection of interviews with Stoney Nakoda elders was recorded in the Nakoda Siouan language to preserve their stories for future generations.

The Stoney land claim was initially rejected by the Department of Indian Affairs, which argued that the Stoneys were not entitled to additional reserve land under the terms of Treaty Seven. In response,

Chief Snow asked Dr. Lloyd Barber, the first Indian Claims Commissioner (1969–77), to intervene. After conducting a detailed review, Commissioner Barber concluded that the government had at least a "moral obligation" to settle the claim, even if it continued to reject it as a "lawful obligation."

The main legal precedent for Aboriginal title at that time was the Supreme Court of Canada's decision in the Calder case, also known as the N'ishga case, rendered on 31 January 1973. The landmark dissenting view of three of the justices, which suggested that the N'ishga still held title to their land based on occupancy, contributed to the Liberal government's August 1973 acknowledgement of its "continuing responsibility" for fulfilling the treaties and for the administration of "lands reserved for Indians." This was the first time that the federal government had agreed to consider claims involving Aboriginal title, and it prompted additional federal funding for specific land claims research.

In the spring of 1974, Jean Chrétien, the minister of Indian Affairs, agreed to increase the existing Bighorn Reserve 144A from 5,000 acres to a maximum of 18,000 acres under the terms of the 1930 Natural Resources Transfer Act (now the Constitution Act, 1930). The Stoney communities and their leaders rejoiced when they learned that their long-standing land claim would be among the first settlements to be reached under the new federal land claims policy announced in 1973. Their joy was short-lived, however. Because natural resources are provincially owned, the Conservative government of Alberta, led by Peter Lougheed, had to agree to the federal settlement with the Stoney Nation before additional reserve land could be designated to the Bighorn people. Instead, the province announced that before it would agree, it wanted a judicial review of its ". . . legal obligation to transfer any lands to the Federal Government for the Big Horn Stoneys" under the terms of the 1930 Constitution Act.[3] The matter is still unresolved.

In 1977, three months after the centennial commemoration of Treaty Seven, the Stoney Nakoda Nation filed a Statement of Claim in the Federal Court of Canada, alleging that both Crown governments were in breach of their fiduciary trust and treaty obligations. Since then, although preliminary legal proceedings were started, there has been no trial and the matter has remained in abeyance. In 2000, new legal counsel advised the Stoneys to redraft their land claim as a Treaty Land Entitlement (TLE) in accordance with the federal government's 1998 amended policy regarding TLE claims. The

Stoney Tribal Council plans to submit its research findings to the Specific Claims branch of the federal Office of Native Claims in 2005. Judging from the Office's current track record, it will take another decade of analysis and negotiation to reach a final settlement of this specific claim, which was first presented to the federal government in 1972.

The political activism of Chief Snow on behalf of his people during the 1970s was reflected in and enhanced by the growing political power of provincial Native organizations across Canada. He helped the National Indian Brotherhood and Indian associations across Canada to defeat the Liberal government's "White Paper" proposal to amend and eliminate the Indian Act, in 1969–70. Provincially and nationally, he played an influential role in First Nations' politics. He envisioned and implemented a model of empowerment and self-determination that combined traditional Nakoda values with the modern concept of local governance, in effect, a fusion of band custom with some of the administrative provisions of the Indian Act. His philosophy was to select the best of both worlds to create a balance between traditional tribal practices and modern democratic principles of fairness and justice and to articulate the advantages of living in a bicultural (Nakoda-Canadian) and bilingual (Nakoda-English) world.

During these years, he also worked on community development and education for the Stoney people. His initiatives included the establishment of an Oral History Program, which recorded the stories of the Stoney Nakoda elders; support for the Stoney Language Program, which resulted in the adoption of a phonetically based written Nakoda language using a modified English alphabet; and sponsorship of the Stoney Cultural Education Program (SCEP), which operated with federal funds from 1972 to 1975 to promote training for young adults. The SCEP project brought university classes to the Morley Reserve, and the four community members who graduated with teaching degrees continue to serve the Morley Community School. A printing department operated by the program produced locally developed curriculum materials in both English and Nakoda. SCEP also trained secretarial staff, provided interpreters and translators for research projects, and encouraged the leadership and management aspirations of some staff. Many alumni still refer to their SCEP days as a highlight of their personal and professional development.

In 1977, Chief Snow decided to focus his energies on writing his autobiography, motivated in part by the coming centennial commemoration of Treaty Seven in September of that year. John Snow's philosophy was to share the elders' teachings found within the Stoney land claim report with the wider non-Stoney community. He used the research done for the report as the documentary source for the history of the Stoney Nakoda people found in his book and as a solid starting point for the story of his own life. On 22 September 1977, a special leather-bound copy of *These Mountains Are Our Sacred Places* was presented to Prince Charles during the re-enactment ceremonies of the signing of Treaty Number Seven at Blackfoot Crossing, situated on the Siksika Nation Reserve east of Calgary. The initial one thousand paperback copies of Chief Snow's book sold quickly. Hardcover editions for libraries and collectors were offered, as was another softcover version. In some respects, the volume helped to launch Chief Snow into the national spotlight, with a growing reputation as a speaker, a spokesperson on political issues, and a spiritual leader and adviser. At the same time, he continued to lead his people as chief of the Wesley First Nation.

While in print, Chief Snow's book was required reading for many Native studies and history courses in colleges and universities. Passages and extracts from his book have appeared in anthologies of Native American writers, in conference brochures, and even in a children's magazine,[4] as well as in numerous theses and documentary reports, Native newspapers, and occasionally the Alberta legislature or Canadian Parliament. His book is acclaimed for its insight into treaty rights, Native spirituality, Indian education, cultural education, economic development, Native self-determination, and Indian law. Commentators have described it as "a remarkable combination . . . to introduce today's Indian culture, history, and family life with footnotes" and "touching as well as scholarly." A recent article, "Mountains Made Alive: Native American Relationships With Sacred Land," reiterated Chief Snow's essential argument that if Mother Earth is desecrated then all life will suffer and the "spirit" of the Earth will leave that area.

Although Chief Snow has not authored another book, he has continued to be a prolific writer on treaty and Aboriginal rights, and is often asked to present at prestigious conferences.[5]

Others have written about the Stoney Nakoda people. Peter Jonker's book about Frank Kaquitts focused on vignettes from his career rather than the historical background of the Chiniki people. (The Chiniki First Nation is one of the three Stoney First Nations in southern Alberta, along with the Wesley First Nation and the

Bearspaw First Nation.) Grant MacEwan's study of a Bearspaw leader, *Tatanga Mani: Walking Buffalo of the Stoneys*,[6] provided very little documentation of the Stoney people, although MacEwan did provide some context for several major developments, such as the construction of three Calgary Power dams on the Bow River that required land surrenders from the Stoney people—the Seebe dams in the early 1900s and the Ghost Lake dam in 1929.

Stoney elders have been featured in more recent publications. In the early 1980s, Calgary entrepreneur Sebastian Chumak produced a limited edition anthology of interviews with Stoney elders, called *The Wisdom of the Stonies* [sic] *of Canada*.[7] When Chumak was refused permission to conduct interviews with elders on the Morley Reserve, due to the Stoney Council's concerns about intellectual property rights, his researchers collected elders' stories from the more isolated Eden Valley Reserve in the foothills west of Longview. Another writer to interview Stoney elders was *Windspeaker* journalist Dianne Meili. Relying on Chief Snow's book for Nakoda historical and cultural background, she provided profiles of Stoney elders Killian Wildman (from the Bighorn Reserve) and Jenny Slater (from the Morley Reserve) in her informative and culturally sensitive book *Those Who Know: Profiles of Alberta's Native Elders*.[8] The most recent, and most comprehensive, Stoney oral history was produced by the Treaty Seven Tribal Council treaty review process, headed by Dorothy First Rider from 1991 to 1996. Based on interviews with elders from the Treaty Seven First Nations of southern Alberta—the Bloods (Kainai), Peigan (Pekuni), Blackfoot (Siksika), Stoney Nakoda, and Tsuu T'ina (Sarcee)—the resulting publication offered a unique insight into the elders' understanding of the Crown promises, recorded through the oral history of each Nation.[9]

None of the several academic theses and research studies that have focused on the Stoney people and the Morley community since 1970 have attempted to chronicle the numerous local developments or to provide socio-political insight into past events and their impact on current social, economic, political, and cultural developments within the Stoney Nakoda communities at the Morley, Bighorn, and Eden Valley Reserves.[10]

The print media's coverage of Stoney Nakoda issues and of Chief Snow has been controversial. Chief Snow was quoted frequently until the mid-1980s, when, unexpectedly, a large urban newspaper undertook an extensive "investigative report" that was critical of the social and economic conditions on the Morley Reserve. This report polarized many family factions within the Stoney community. Ten years later, the national news media cited a judicial report that criticized Chief Snow for apparently not solving the many social, economic, and educational problems on the Stoney Reserve, although the same issues continue to overwhelm many Native communities across Canada. To his credit, Chief Snow has been the subject of many favourable reviews, as well.[11] The Stoney Nakoda communities at Morley, Bighorn, and Eden Valley Reserves are also often featured in articles in newspapers from neighbouring communities. Typically, their coverage remains brief and incomplete, and their commentary on the complex issues facing Native people is one-sided and biased.

Since its publication in 1977, *These Mountains Are Our Sacred Places* has been the essential source for providing a culturally appropriate context for understanding both the historical and contemporary life of the Stoney people. John Snow's account remains the only comprehensive history of the Stoney Nakoda people from a Native perspective. His inclusion of traditional wisdom, his commentary on contemporary Native issues, his defence of treaty rights, his involvement in constitutional issues, and his historical account of the Stoney Nakoda Nation make his book a unique and invaluable contribution to this Western Canadian Classics reprint series.

Ian Getty has been the Stoney Tribal Administration Research Director since 1980 and has been an active participant-observer in many of the events and challenges faced by Chief Snow, alongside other First Nation leaders across Canada.

Notes

1. Please see: Harold Cardinal, *The Unjust Society*. (Edmonton: Hurtig, 1969); Harold Cardinal, *The Rebirth of Canada's Indians*. (Edmonton: Hurtig, 1977); George Manuel and Michael Posluns, *The Fourth World: An Indian Reality*. (Toronto, 1974); Peter McFarlane, *Brotherhood to Nationhood: George Manuel and the Making of the Modern Indian Movement*. (Toronto, 1993); *John Tootoosis: A Biography of a Cree Leader*, as told to Norma Sluman and Jean Goodwill. (Ottawa: Golden Dog Press, 1982); Dan Kennedy (Ochankugahe), *Recollections of an Assiniboine Chief*. (Toronto: McClelland & Stewart, 1972); Max Gros-Louis, *Grand Chief of the Huron-Wendat Nation*. (Quebec); Roy MacGregor, *Chief: The Fearless Vision of Billy Diamond*. (Viking, 1989).

2. Similar TARR centres have since been established in most provinces across Canada, particularly in BC, Saskatchewan, Manitoba, Ontario, and Nova Scotia. The recent trend elsewhere is to have tribal associations and individual First Nations conduct their own research into specific claims and breach of trust legal actions.

3. Other Alberta First Nations, such as the Lubicon Cree people, were pressing similar outstanding treaty land claims.

4. *TWIGS Magazine*, 1978.

5. "Identification and Definition of Our Treaty and Aboriginal Rights," in Menno Boldt and J. Anthony Long, eds., *The Quest for Justice: Aboriginal Peoples and Aboriginal Rights*. (Toronto: University of Toronto Press, 1985) 41–46.

   "Recent Decisions of the Supreme Court of Canada Affecting Aboriginal Peoples," National Aboriginal Law Section, Canadian Bar Association Conference, 25–26 April 1997. (Speech presented to the Conference Opening at the University of Calgary in relation to the G8 Summit, June 2002)

   A Glance Back: Relations Since 1877. (Mod-Nu Set, 1977) 72–76.

6. Hurtig, 1969.

7. The Alberta Foundation, 1983. Subtitled: "An Illustrated Heritage of Genesis, Myths, Legends, Folklore, and Wisdom of Yahey Wichastabi [sic], the People-who-cook-with-hot-stones."

8. NeWest Press, 1991.

9. Treaty Seven Elders and Tribal Council, *The True Spirit and Original Intent of Treaty 7* (Montreal: McGill-Queen's University Press, 1996).

10. During these years, the Stoney population grew from 1,662 in 1970, to 2,224 in 1980, to 2,968 in 1990, to 4,119 in 2003.

11. Please see: "The Stoney Perspective," Alister Thomas in *Calgary Commerce* magazine. (vol. 18, no. 5, June/July: 1986); and "Chief John Snow: A Native Writer Unearthed," Ken Bregenser in *Skylines Magazine* (Calgary: Mount Royal College, April 1989).

A Note on Stoney Social Structure

The terminology of Indian society—band, tribe, chief, and so on—is frequently confusing to whitemen. One reason is that our social structure is very different from that of the Europeans. It is not so compartmentalized; lines of authority are not so rigid; we use a different approach to decision making. These differences have led to many misunderstandings.

The nineteenth-century missionaries and government officials who first encountered us did not bother to learn much about our culture since they saw their mission as one of imposing their culture on us. What they did see of our social structure they interpreted in their own terms. Modern anthropologists have sometimes compounded the misunderstandings. They have indeed tried to study our arrangements, but sometimes they have relied on insufficient data and sometimes they have misinterpreted the data because they were unable to escape their own cultural assumptions.

This book is not an anthropological text and therefore is not the place to deal with our social structures in any detail. But a brief sketch of these structures, in both their traditional and their modern forms, may help white readers to understand our story a little better. Such a sketch is naturally incomplete, but it may at least clarify terminology and give some idea of our attitudes and values in the area of social organization.

In traditional times, Stoney society was based primarily on an *extended family system*. It was patrilineal and men held most positions of obvious leadership, but women's opinions on many topics were heard carefully.

Leading a simple, nomadic life, one or several extended families could go their own way much of the time without the need for extensive organization. Among the adult members of a family some individuals were sure to have skills at least in the two areas most needed for survival: hunting and medicine. A group oriented to sharing and to survival recognized and made use of such talents in whomever they appeared, without worrying too much about job titles or the accidents of birth.

Leadership, coordination, and additional knowledge for the extended family could be provided quite informally by the *elders*— the senior member or members of the family group. They had lived long, full lives; they had learned the ways of Mother Earth: they had survived. They were listened to with respect, and their advice was usually good so it was usually taken, although it was not imposed and carried only psychological authority.

On winter camping grounds, on large-scale hunts, and on other occasions, a number of these extended family groups came together into a *band*. This many people living and working together called for more formal organization. Leadership of the band was provided by a *Chief*. The position was at least semi-hereditary, but a Chief whose leadership was not wise or generally accepted would not last long. Neither was his leadership autocratic. He was aided by *Councillors*, who, with him, formed the *Band Council*. The Chief selected the Councillors himself, but always with a view to making sure each family of the band would be well represented in the decision-making process.

Decision making was conducted not by *fiat* or by majority vote; rather the aim in the band council, as in the extended family, was reaching consensus. Coming to agreements that are generally acceptable to all concerned is never an easy task, but within a society conditioned by thousands of years of co-operation, working together, and sharing for survival, it usually was possible—a fact the whiteman has often had difficulty in grasping. And if consensus could not be reached, within such a nomadic society a dissenting family could simply leave—temporarily or permanently. A band chief had no authority to hold them under his leadership against their will. Indeed the chieftainship is best understood not as a position of authority but of stewardship, of caring for the people who looked to it for leadership and guidance but not control.

Certain situations, of course, did not lend themselves to decision by consensus, which is a time-consuming process. For example, the running of large-scale hunts or inter-tribal skirmishes demanded quick decisions by a single, accepted leader. So for such occasions, temporary special leaders (and assistants) were appointed, usually on the basis of talent. They were given special titles: *hunting chief, war* (or *fighting*) *chief*. Their authority was extensive and strict, but, as their titles imply, it lasted only during the specific, limited situation.

Also outside the structure of the band chief and his council were two important leadership groups—the *elders* and the *medicine men* and *women*. Both illustrate our traditional, almost automatic recognition and acceptance of wisdom and skill wherever they may appear. In theory, all older men and women were elders and their experience was regarded as a great resource on which the group could draw. In practice, the wiser the advice offered by an older person—be he a former chief, the senior member of a family, or simply an individual who showed a talent for understanding—the more he was listened to.

As explained in the text of this book, medicine men and women were not appointed nor did they actively seek the honour. Rather it would become clear to the individual and to those he lived with in such an intimate society that the Great Spirit had given him special talents of healing or of control over the manifestations of nature.

The band, based on a grouping of several extended families under one accepted leader, was the most important unit of traditional organized society. But for some purposes—religious and other ceremonial occasions, all-out war, the division of hunting territory, and so forth—a larger unit was needed. This was the *tribe*, the coming together of several bands who all spoke the same language. Each band remained under its own Chief; these Chiefs (and their Councillors) formed a *Tribal Council*, which, it is important to understand, was a meeting of equals. If a Chief had superior native talents or if he led a larger, stronger band, he might gain a psychological superiority over his peers, but this was never formalized. In the tribal council, as in the band council and the extended family, decision making was by consensus. Because the tribe was quite an informal structure, a chief who was unhappy with a decision could easily lead his band away from the large group.

Today, one hundred years of being confined to the reserve have done little to change the basic attitudes ingrained by this social system and attitude toward authority. The coming of self-government has, however, meant some amalgamation with the whiteman's ways. The most important is probably election to office on the basis of one man, one vote; another is the principle of representation in Council partially by place of residence rather than by family.

Under self-government, each Stoney band at the reserve at Morley elects a Chief and three Councillors; in addition, the Eden Valley Reserve elects two Councillors and the Bighorn Reserve one. The franchise is open to all men and women over twenty-one years of age. Anyone can run for these positions, but traditional considerations of family play a large part in who gets elected.

The fifteen men and women are elected for two-year terms; together they form the *Tribal Council*, which regulates the affairs of the entire tribe. This includes the administration of all land owned by the tribe and all funds derived from the land and other tribal assets.

But although the Tribal Council has far-ranging authority (within the limits imposed by the Department of Indian Affairs and the Indian Act), the Stoneys still operate very much within tribal custom and tradition. *Elders* who do not happen to hold Council seats are often consulted. Decisions are usually made by consensus rather than by forcing a question to a majority vote. Emphasis is placed on the Council's responsibility to use resources wisely in a way that everyone can share; although we are sometimes called upon to administer large amounts of money, it is never used simply to make more money but rather to care for the community—now or in the future.

The very structure of the Council itself is typical in its respect for tradition. The Chiefs of the three bands continue to meet there as equals. We have adopted the European way of selecting a chairman—one man who can speak with authority for the entire tribe—but the chairmanship changes each month, with the three bands rotating in turn.

One final warning to the reader about terminology. In an effort to achieve clarity, I have attempted throughout this book to distinguish consistently between band and tribe, band council and tribal council, and so forth. In practice (as is evident from several of the quotations), this is rarely done. Partly because we still regard the band as our basic unit, partly because of the terminology used by the Department of Indian Affairs, the Council that administers the entire tribe is often referred to as the *Band Council*, and the moneys at its disposal are nearly always called the *Band Fund*.

Part I
The Old Path

The Oral History of the Stoneys

L ong ago my ancestors used to go to the mountaintops to pray.
They were a deeply religious, sincere, and tradition-oriented
people who followed, observed, and upheld the teachings, customs,
and beliefs of our forefathers, respected the creations of the Great
Spirit, and lived in harmony with nature. They were Stoneys—members
of the Great Sioux Nation who spoke a dialect of the Nakoda
branch of the Siouan language family. Today we, their descendants,
speak the same tongue.

The word Sioux conjures up the whole of the rich history and
culture of the Plains—Sitting Bull, the Custer battle, great buffalo
hunts, magnificent eagle-plume headdresses, and beautiful quill-
decorated buckskin clothing. This is the heritage we share with the
Dakota and the Assiniboine and the Oglala through our language-
family connections. Our other neighbours were the Algonkian-
speaking people—the Ojibway, the Cree, and the Blackfoot—with
whom blood feuds were a continual fact. Nearby, too, were smaller
groups, such as the Athapascan-speaking Sarcee. To the west our
contacts were with the people of the mountains, the Kootenay, the
Shuswap, and occasionally the Flathead; our relations with these
were somewhat more cordial, but not always peaceful.

Indian traditions and oral history say that my people were always
present in this part of the Great Island (the native name for the
North American continent), roaming along the foothills out onto the
prairies to the east and deep into the Rocky Mountain country to the
west. Our traditional hunting territory seems to have extended
north to the Brazeau River-Jasper area, south a little past what is

now the international border, east beyond the present-day city of Calgary, and west into the Rockies beyond what would become the British Columbia border.

In order to understand the vital importance the mountains had—and still have—to my people, it is necessary to know something of our way of life before the coming of the whiteman. It is not enough to say the mountains were the Stoneys' traditional place of prayer because our life was not a fragmented one with a compartment for religion. Rather, our life was one in which religion (and reverence for nature, which revealed religious truth) was woven throughout all parts of the social structure and observed in conjunction with every activity. Our forefathers were a proud people because they knew they had been selected by the Creator to receive a precious gift of special understanding and they have handed that gift down to us as a sacred trust.

In the days prior to the coming of the whiteman, we lived a nomadic way of life, hunting, fishing, and gathering from the abundance of this good land. There were literally millions of buffalo roaming on the western prairies, along the foothills, and even into the Rocky Mountains themselves. There were game animals of all kinds—moose, elk, deer, wild sheep, and goats—readily available for us to hunt and to enjoy. The land was vast, beautiful, and rich in abundant resources. Our Mother Earth called us from the forests, the prairies, the valleys, the mountainous areas, the lakes, rivers, and springs. "Come, my children, anyone who is hungry, come and eat from the fruits and gather from the abundance of this land. Come, everyone who thirsts, come and drink pure spring waters that are especially provided for you." Everywhere the spirits of all living things were alive.

We talked to the rocks, the streams, the trees, the plants, the herbs, and all nature's creations. We called the animals our brothers. They understood our language; we, too, understood theirs. Sometimes they talked to us in dreams and visions. At times they revealed important events or visited us on our vision quests to the mountaintops. Truly, we were part of and related to the universe, and these animals were a very special part of the Great Spirit's creation.

Our livelihood, our very culture were based on the necessity for hunting animals, but the hunt was never for the sake of killing them. We did not hunt for head trophies and kill off the game in the process. When we were in need of meat, when we were hungry, the medicine man of the tribe performed sacred ceremonies before the

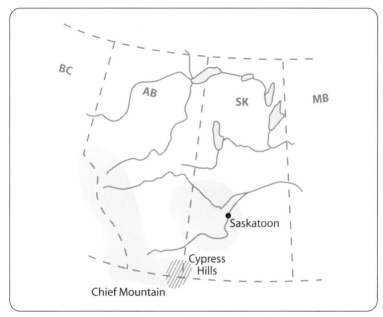

Stoney country prior to the 1800s, along the eastern slopes and foothills of the Rocky Mountains, ranging from north of the Athabasca River to Chief Mountain, and east into central Saskatchewan and the Cypress Hills.

hunters went out. When the game was killed, the hunters observed a Stoney ritual of eating certain parts of the animal and thanking the Creator for providing us with food. We even shared some of the game with our brothers, the wild animals of the forest and the prairies. We would leave a special part of the animal for the birds of the air and other small animals. After the meat was brought back to the encampment, the medicine man held a special ceremony and made a humble offering of incense, sweet grass, and a special part of the meat to thank the Creator for His providence.

We made use of the whole animal for our livelihood. The buffalo's head was (and is) sacred to us; we used its skull in the sacred Sun Dance. From the game animals we received ribs and other bones for making knives, needles, and other needed tools. From the hides we made clothing, moccasins, teepees, and robes for bedding in the cold winter months.

The eagle held a very sacred place in our society. Ceremonies, prayers, and fasting took place and visions had to appear before an eagle was killed. The hunters were taught that the eagle is a sacred messenger created by the Great Spirit. Therefore, no Indian hunter was to kill the eagle unless the feathers were required for a ceremonial occasion. So even the feathers of the birds were used in our way of life.

Truly, our people respected the Creator's beings, and as a result, in our long history of dominance on this continent, none of the animals we hunted ever became extinct.

Later summer and fall were the main hunting seasons in this harsh climate. But except during the winter we spent most of our time migrating along the foothills in search of food, preparing for the cold months ahead.

The tribe did not travel as a unit, but lived in several bands, usually breaking off into smaller, extended-family groups as we moved about. The elderly and sick were left at a base camp, with a few men to provide daily food. The rest of the band or family group moved for

We use eagle feathers for only the most sacred and ceremonial uses, such as the making of headdresses like this one worn by Ben Kaquitts.

several days or weeks along the foothills or into the mountains. If the hunt was good, we might stay in one place for some time, preparing the meat for storage. If the hunt was less successful, we kept moving.

There was one band of Stoneys, divided into two main groups, who usually travelled north of what is now Morley. These groups migrated along the foothills north to the Brazeau River area. Another band of two groups roamed around the Morley area and west past what is now the British Columbia border. A third band of three groups migrated south of Morley in the Chief Mountain area and on beyond the present international border.

During the hunting season there might be several or no returns to the base camp depending on the distance travelled. During the winter the band came together in protected winter camp grounds. For ceremonial and other occasions the entire tribe gathered.

Such a migratory people required many types of shelter. Some of them were seasonal and portable; others were permanent.

Our seasonal dwellings, generally used during the summer, were spruce-bark teepees. The spruce bark was taken usually in the month of June when the bark was easiest to peel off. The spruce trees were not cut down, and only the bark at the bottom of the tree was taken. The sap is rich at that time, so it was a good time to take it. Also, we made shelters from poles and fir, pine, or spruce branches. In the hot summer, such shelters were made from poplar branches with their leaves left on to make shades and arbours. There were also portable dwellings, used as my people travelled from place to place. These were, of course, teepees made from the tanned hides of buffalo, moose, and elk.

The permanent shelters were pole-and-moss dwellings of two kinds. One was a teepee, about ten feet across at the base, constructed with poles twelve to sixteen feet high. The poles were set in a circular teepee style, all very close together. Then green moss was stuffed between the poles. Another layer of poles was set around them, and additional moss put over them, making a double layer of poles and moss. A fire was made in the centre to heat the dwelling.

The other type of pole-and-moss dwelling was larger and resembled a roofed modern-day house. It was about fourteen feet high, twelve feet wide, and eighteen to twenty feet long. Again a double layer of poles and moss and clay or mud was used to build it. The fire was made at one end.

These pole-and-moss dwellings, cool in summer and warm in winter, served somewhat as communal tourist lodges. Their locations were known to all tribal families—they were the property of no one, yet belonged to everybody, and were available for those travelling light and staying in the locality but briefly. Like everything we possessed, they were designed to meet a need—and they did, for we were a migratory people.

But a migratory people are not necessarily a people who lack civilization, not if "civilization" is taken in the sense of a law-abiding and caring society. My people were a proud and noble race, a great prehistoric society. We did not have written laws—we did not have a written language. Neither did we have one type of home for the rich and another for the poor in those days—there were no rich families and no poor families. If one member of a band went hungry, everyone went hungry. If one family had meat cooked on the campfire, everyone had meat. The whole tribe shared and lived as one big family. We had no old people's homes where we placed the aged to die "out of sight, out of mind." Old people were a very important part of the tribal society. They were the wise elders with a lifetime of rich experience that was valued by all. They taught our children, tutored our youth, advised younger adults and Tribal Councils. We did not have mental institutions. We did not have jails. Locks and keys were unnecessary in our communities because we were taught honesty and integrity, and we respected the creations of the Great Spirit. We were taught to respect other people's belongings, just as we were taught to respect their religions and traditions.

Human kindness was imprinted in our hearts, and the law of the Great Spirit, the Creator, was the only law that we observed. Our society was built around the concept that the Creator is the Supreme Being, the Great Mystery; recognizing Him as the One who provides all things was the very first step and beginning of our tribal society. The recognition of the Creator in all of life was essential for our survival here on earth and in the hereafter.

In this society there was no need to convince anyone that there was a Creator who made all things. In our long history there was never a story of a Stoney atheist. The theory of atheism was foreign and unknown in our society. (I am sure that this was generally true of all tribal societies on this Great Island before the coming of the whiteman.) When a child began to talk and understand things, one of the very first lessons he or she received was about the Great Spirit. A child would grow up learning about nature and the importance of respecting all things in creation.

There was no formal education as such, but education was interwoven into the life of the tribal society. A very important responsibility of the tribal members was to pass on valuable information to the next generation by the spoken word. Parents, grandparents, and elders told and retold stories and legends to the children by the campfires, in the teepees, on the hillsides, in the forest, and at special gatherings during the day and at night. It was an ongoing educational process about religion, life, hunting, and so on. Other topics were bravery, courage, kindness, sharing, survival, and foot tracks of animals, so it was a very extensive study of many things.

With such an education based on religion, the child was established in Stoney tribal society. He or she was one of the Great Spirit's people.

A very special religious education was in Indian medicine. This was usually taught by experienced medicine men and women, although knowledge was sometimes received in dreams and visions.

I cannot discuss my people's medicine in detail here because it is sacred to us. But I can describe our general approach to healing, although it may be difficult for the modern reader to understand it.

Our philosophy of life sees the Great Spirit's creation as a whole piece. If something in the environment harms man, it is reasonable that the Creator has provided a specific herb to cure the sickness or has given some person the wisdom to heal it. Man is a complex being of body, mind, and spirit. We have always known that a sick mind or spirit can cause the body to show symptoms of physical sickness. (Western medicine today partially recognizes this interrelationship and speaks of psychosomatic illness.)

In the traditional times, we were basically a healthy people. Our diet was mainly meat and fish, supplemented by wild vegetables and fruit. Because of this, we were lean and hard. We were outdoor people and developed high tolerance to cold. Our lifestyle was probably responsible for a low incidence of heart disease and other diseases of the main organs. The diet assisted in good dental health. Herbal remedies (by which I include mineral and animal remedies) were available for all the common ailments.

Some of these herbal remedies were known to all, but many were known only to one person and regarded as closely guarded secrets. As in any society, a person's reputation in herbal medicine grew as cures were made and talked about. Among the Stoney people, both men and women became respected practitioners in herbal medicine.

The collecting and preserving of herbs was an important activity of these medicine people during the warm months of the year.

The sacred waters of the mountains—the mineral hot springs—were also important to maintaining our health and curing illness. A person would journey to the sacred waters at the direction of a medicine man or woman and use them with suitable preparation and prayer.

Prayer was the essential part of all medicine; it put the person troubled by illness into a proper relationship with the Great Spirit and His creation. The medicine man who understood the relationship of the body, the mind, and the spirit of man to the Great Spirit could be a great healer. The counselling skills of the modern psychiatrist were well known in our culture. Combining these with a full awareness of unity of the Great Spirit's creation, gained through fasting and prayer, the medicine men and women were able to heal the whole person.

Such wisdom was acquired through a lifetime of study, experience, and prayer. The candidate for such knowledge had to be touched by the Great Spirit Himself. He learned of his selection by a sign which could not be misunderstood or denied. With this vision came much understanding, a direction for the future, and a change in the individual's personality, which made it clear to all that this individual had been touched by the Creator's hand. None recognized the new candidate better than the old men of wisdom. He then began his studies at their feet.

The medical skills of my people reinforced our belief that the Creator's teachings and lessons could be learned by observing the universe around us. So we studied the laws of nature and we lived by them. The creations of the Great Spirit have revealed many mysteries to us.

For example, there was no fear of death in our society because there was no concept of "Hell." Death was part of life. The elders interpreted it as entering another life beyond in the beautiful land of the spirits, the Happy Hunting Grounds. This was not difficult to understand when we watched the sunset. Each sunset was unique and glorious, foretelling of a land beyond. But the land that awaited us was far more beautiful than all the sunsets.

Again, the little crocus reminded us that there was a second life after death. Along the Rocky Mountain foothills the crocus is one of the first wildflowers to blossom in the spring. It blooms beautifully for a while, then fades away. But in the autumn, usually in a good year when all the spring and summer flowers have bloomed and gone, the little crocus comes out again. It appears twice in the same year and fades once more, as though to say: "So long for this summer, but I'll be the first one to return next spring." The appearance of the crocus twice in one calendar year revealed to us that there is more than one life.

So, too, from nature did my people garner much symbolism, which they used in formulating their principles, theories, philosophies, and religion. For instance, the number four is a complete number in our tribal society, like the four winds of the earth and the four seasons that complete a year's cycle. A circle was interpreted in theory as a whole or something complete. The sun comes to a complete circle in a year. The moon is round like a circle. Therefore, the religion of the Great Spirit is based on a circle. There is no beginning and end to the creation and creating powers of the Great Spirit. All things in creation are related to His huge circle and all have a part to play in the universe. We held our Tribal Council and conducted our meetings sitting in a circle. Indian teepees are set in a circular formation, and there is the closely knit family circle. So using this symbolism of a circle, religion could be seen as the heart and the centre of Stoney tribal society.

Being members of such a complete society, the Stoneys were always a proud people. I will try to explain what I mean by being a proud people. I am not thinking of a foolish man's arrogance. The pride that I am thinking of is a native pride in being part of this Great Island. It is something the Creator instilled in every member of His Creation.

The bald eagle soars to great heights and takes pride in the strength of his wings. He does not pretend to be something else. He takes pride in the realization that the Creator has allowed him to share the bird kingdom's unique ability to fly. The mountain lion is also proud of what he is. He will climb the tallest mountain, not to show off foolishly but to proclaim his pride in being one of the Great Spirit's unique creations.

Likewise, we, the Stoney Indians, are a proud people. We walk in beauty and in dignity. Whenever we stand to speak or to dance in a pow-wow, we do it with pride and dignity. This is a pride we must never lose because it was a gift the Great Spirit instilled in our being at the time of Creation. Each of us must stand erect and tall and say: "I am an Indian. I am proud to know who I am and where I originated. I am proud to be a unique creation of the Great Spirit. We were the

The Stoney drum-beater is particularly important to the music of the dance.

first human beings on the Great Island. We are part of Mother Earth."

Pride and bravery were the marks of the great warriors of our tribe. To be brave was to be a true Stoney warrior. It was the bravest warriors and the most successful hunters who became the tribal leaders.

Our world was not without perils for our people, so bravery was a survival factor for the individual, the family, and the tribe. Food might be in short supply for long periods. The freezing temperatures of winter were a constant threat. Blizzards and avalanches killed in those days as surely as they kill today. Many animals—bears, mountain lions, and others—might kill the unwary hunter. Warriors from other tribes, particularly the Blackfoot and Cree, were a day-to-day danger. Occasionally tribal wars were fought over hunting areas or in retaliation for the killing of a chief's son by another tribe. The Stoney warriors were not called *Wapamâthe* (throat-cutters) for nothing. The *Wapamâthe* won more than their share of the battles.

Since bravery was a treasured quality in our society, every warrior instructed his son in it, even at a very early age. He would say: "My son, when you go to war, be brave, be like a true Stoney-Sioux warrior, and never turn back in defeat from your enemies. You must never run away from the enemy, because the survival of your tribe rests with you as you go to war. If you are defeated, that means we are all defeated as a tribe. If you are victorious, then we as Stoneys are victors and will retain our hunting territories. My son, perhaps some day you might be killed in battle, and if your wound was in the back I, your brave warrior father, would be embarrassed and sad because it would look as if you had been running away from the enemy. But if the arrow mark or wound was on your chest or on the front, then I would be proud of you, my son, for it would show that you were facing your enemy bravely when you were killed. I would know that you died as a true warrior because you were protecting your people and defending your beautiful country with its animals of all kinds, birds of all colours, its beautiful lakes, rivers, and streams."

Having been so instructed from boyhood, warriors faced their enemies courageously, and many tales are told about the deeds of bravery performed by our forefathers. Indeed, much of what we know of the past is preserved for us in the Indian oral tradition. Much of the wisdom acquired by our people throughout the ages is passed on to us by our elders through the legends that tell of Stoney courage, history, and religious life. These legends are like parables; they convey social teachings and religious truths.

There are many Stoney legends of warriors, braves, and medicine men and women, who, when in difficult situations, changed into animals and birds. Such stories usually praise some virtue while reflecting our concept of the unity of nature.

George Ear, a present-day Stoney elder, tells a favourite legend about a Stoney warrior named Wolf-Come-Into-View. His father was a great warrior named Ear; he had been loved as a champion of justice and feared as a fighter, but he was killed by cowardly enemies who did not have the courage to face him in open battle.

During his own life, Wolf-Come-Into-View was approached by a spirit of wolf guise, who imparted a gift to him. Wolf-Come-Into-View often relied on this gift to help him out of difficult situations, as was the case one time at Cochrane Hill, east of Morley.

Legends can be seen as well as told. In this teepee decoration, the significant circle combines with the picture of the camp and the hunt. *(Glenbow Archives NA-7-149)*

On that day he was hunting buffalo and he climbed Cochrane Hill in order to look over the valleys below. Upon reaching the summit, he spotted enemy warriors; they, too, were viewing the land below for buffalo herds and saw him before he could duck out of sight. They immediately gave a loud whoop and came after him, but Wolf-Come-Into-View ducked into the nearby bushes and called upon his guardian wolf-spirit to deliver him.

The enemy warriors scoured the bushes attempting to find him, but to no avail. Finally one of them pointed northward toward the next hill and said, "Look over there." The others looked and saw a wolf loping away. The enemy leader said, "Do not bother. That man has turned into a wolf. He must be spiritually gifted. He must be a great warrior." From that time on, Wolf-Come-Into-View was respected by all enemy warriors.

This was only one of many feats that he performed in his lifetime.

When the missionaries first came to this part of the country, Wolf-Come-Into-View and all his brothers were given the surname of Ear. But Wolf-Come-Into-View himself elected to change his name to Mark because it was more appealing to him. Today all who go by the surname of Mark are his descendants. They have every reason to be proud of him because he was a brave man in every true sense of the word.

Some of the most exciting and unusual legends and stories in the history of the Stoneys concern Iktûmnî, a great medicine man, a wise teacher, a prophet.

When I speak to whitemen of Iktûmnî I find I run into one of the great problems of dealing with another social group: language. Different cultures produce different value systems, which in turn produce diverse vocabularies. Sometimes I find it almost impossible to translate certain Stoney words into English and keep the true meaning or give the correct connotation.

The name *Iktûmnî* offers such a problem. Literally, the word in the Stoney language means one who is out of his mind or crazy; but this English translation doesn't really convey the proper meaning. However, Iktûmnî had two names, and when both interpretations are combined they may better describe his character in English. This other name was *Thichâ-Yuski*, meaning one who outwits others or a person with deep understanding and extraordinary wisdom.

Iktûmnî had deep understanding of the ways of the animal world. There was a legend told of a race between Iktûmnî and a fox. One day Iktûmnî was walking along a lake when he found several duck eggs. He gathered the eggs very carefully, made a fire, and cooked them. Before he ate the eggs he continued his walk and met a fox. Iktûmnî challenged the fox to a race around the lake. Iktûmnî told the fox that he had cooked some eggs at the other end of the lake and whoever got there first could eat the eggs.

The fox was limping and said he could not run. So Iktûmnî said, "In order to make a fair race, I'll tie a rawhide around my ankle and drag a big stone while I run. That would make the race more fair to you since obviously you are lame."

Along one side of the lake were trees; the other side was flat and open. The fox said, "I will run along the side where there are trees."

The race started. The fox limped until he was out of sight in the trees. Then he ran like the wind. He was not lame at all. Iktûmnî ran dragging the big stone behind him. All the forest could hear the big stone thumping as he ran.

When the fox got to Iktûmnî's fire, he ate all the eggs, then put the shells back together so they looked as if they were not eaten, and then left. Iktûmnî came to the fire at last. He sat down beside the fire and said to himself, "Poor old lame fox." He started to open the eggs and found that they had all been eaten.

He was very angry when he found out the fox had tricked him. He said to himself "Wait till I see that fox again."

The animals took similar advantage of Iktûmnî on many occasions but as he got to know them and learned their ways, he eventually came out as the hero.

Iktûmnî was wise because he was able to talk and commune with both the natural and the spiritual world. He was able to interpret the animal world in human terms and understanding to the tribal members. The animals and the birds were his brothers and he lived with them, so he was able to talk with them in their own language. The rocks and trees were also his brothers, so he communed with them and learned the secrets and ways of nature. He communicated and talked with the spirits of the mountains, who revealed ancient truth, philosophies, and prophecies to him. In turn, he taught these things to the Stoney people.

We believe that Iktûmnî was sent to us by the Great Spirit to teach us the laws of the Creator—laws about medicine, about religion, and about life. To this day during the medicine ceremonial songs, prayers, and dances, Iktûmnî's name is mentioned as the keeper of medicine. When the medicine bundles are opened, Iktûmnî's name is mentioned in a respectful way as the one who taught the secrets of various healing herbs and medicine to our tribe.

Iktûmnî was perhaps the most famous of all the Stoneys in finding truth in nature, but he was by no means the only such seeker or even the only successful one. Indeed all the Stoney people were continually searching for the truth by observing the universe around them.

The most sacred search was a special religious journey into the rugged mountains, seeking wisdom and divine guidance. This was known as the vision quest, a tradition handed down through the centuries and practised by us as a means of approaching the Great Spirit. If the seekers were favoured, the Great Spirit would deliver a revelation and thus give direction and guidance to our tribe.

Sacred ceremonies and rituals were observed by these seekers of truth before they journeyed into the rugged mountainous country. In this preparation they were guided and aided by many members of the tribe who spent much time fasting and praying in the sweat lodge.

The sacred lodge was erected by a chosen few who were appointed by the elders; its construction was vigilantly and prayerfully observed by everyone. The lodge's frame was usually made from willow wood and branches shaped into a dome-roofed, circular building about eight or ten feet across and about five feet high;

An old picture shows the building of the sacred lodge in a ceremony.

this was usually covered over with animal skins and hides, although sometimes spruce bark and branches and poplar leaves were used. A man or men were appointed by the medicine men to make the lodge ready for the ceremony. One of their chief tasks was to gather choice rocks to be heated in the sacred fire.

When the sacred lodge was completed, one of the medicine men would, in traditional style, rub two sticks together to create the spark that would start the sacred fire. The old wise men or elders, the medicine men or holy men, the ceremonial leaders, and the brave warriors would take part in this religious ceremony. Upon this sacred fire they would burn sweet grass, cedar branch needles and boughs, and other incense that ascended to the Great Spirit, the Creator. (Similar fires were used during various other ceremonial observances.)

The sacred pipe was brought in next. The peace pipe and its rituals were handed down to us by our forefathers for use in religious ceremonies and prayers. The holy men would offer the pipe of peace to the Sun, Mother Earth, the four winds, and the spirits that the Creator appointed to be our guardians here on earth. One of the leaders would offer a prayer using the sacred pipe and offer it in a circular manner beginning from the east (from where the sun rises), then to the south, then to the west, and concluding by holding the stem of the pipe toward the north.

After the purification ceremonies were prayerfully observed in the sacred lodge, the seeker of truth and insight into religious thought would be prepared to set off on the vision quest. There in the mountainous wilderness he would be alone; he would live close to nature and perchance he would receive a special revelation. It might come through a dream or a vision, through the voice of nature, or by an unusual sign. It might be that the wild animals or birds would convey the message of his calling to him.

Many a brave has sojourned to these sacred mountains of ours in search of his calling—the purpose for which he was born. He searched in hope that the Great Spirit would make known to him his future task so that he could take his place in the tribal society, and help his people.

Even if no specific vision was granted the seeker, the Great Spirit's presence was never doubted. In times past He appeared and revealed Himself in various ways. He appeared in dreams, visions, and sometimes He spoke to us through the wild animals, the birds, the winds, the thunder, or the changing seasons. The Great Spirit was always present in the Stoney Indian history—He was everywhere.

In our migrations, as in our vision quests, my people continued to observe the animals, plants, rocks, trees, streams, winds, sun, moon, stars, and all things. Our teaching has always been that everything was created for a purpose by the Great Spirit. We must, therefore, respect all things of creation and learn as much as we can. There are lessons hidden in creation that we must learn in order to live a good life and walk the straight path. Behind these lessons and teachings is the Creator. These things can only be understood through the Great Spirit.

Century after century the rugged Rocky Mountains sat there in majesty, and nature seemed to say:"Your thoughts must be as firm as these mountains, if you are to walk the straight path. Your patience and kindness must be as solid as these mountains, if you are to acquire understanding and wisdom."

The old Stoney medicine man had said:"You must continue to go to the sacred mountains. You must fast and pray for many days and nights, and perchance you will see a vision upon the mountains." Before he went to the beautiful land of the spirits beyond the sunset, the old man with a century of experience spoke these words: "You must search and search and you will find ancient truths and wisdom that shall guide you in the future." He continued:"My grandfathers told me these things when I was just a little boy and in my youth it was told to me over and over again by the campfire and in the tribal encampment, so it has been imprinted in my heart ever since that time."

And the medicine man stated further: "My grandchildren, you must search and continue to search in order to find them. When a revelation is open to you, you will become a special person to our tribe. It may be that you will gain courage and bravery and become a hero in many battles. It may be that you will be given understanding and wisdom and become a Chief amongst Chiefs. It may be that you will become a great hunter, knowing the paths and circling of the four winds, knowing where the animals roam and birds migrate at the seasons appointed for them by the Creator. It may be that you will be given the gift of prophecy, see into the future, and will advise and guide your people along the straight path."

Upon these lofty heights, the Great Spirit revealed many things to us. Some of my people received powers to heal. They could heal the physical body with herbs, roots, leaves, plants, and mineral spring waters. They could also heal the broken and weary soul with unseen spiritual powers. Others received powers over the weather. These gifted religious men and women could call for a great storm or calm the weather; they could call on the winds, rain, hail, snow, or sleet, and they would come. From these mountaintop experiences my fellow tribesmen and -women were given unique tasks to perform to help the tribe prepare for things to come.

Therefore the Rocky Mountains are precious and sacred to us. We knew every trail and mountain pass in this area. We had special ceremonial and religious areas in the mountains. In the olden days some of the neighbouring tribes called us the "People of the Shining Mountains." These mountains are our temples, our sanctuaries, and our resting places. They are a place of hope, a place of vision, a place of refuge, a very special and holy place where the Great Spirit speaks with us. *Therefore, these mountains are our sacred places.*

Part II
The Crossroads

The Two Cultures Meet

There is a common saying among Indians today: "Before the whiteman came we had the land, they had the Bible. Now, we Indians have the Bible, they have the land."

Sometimes I think the entire history of Indian-non-Indian relations on this continent is summed up in that statement. When the Europeans first came to the eastern shores of this Great Island, we—members of the huge intertribal society that occupied this land—welcomed them and helped them survive. We taught them what we knew and eased their period of adjustment to this Great Island considerably. This was the general response of the native North Americans when the Europeans first came over.

My people were hospitable and generous and shared what we had with the newcomers. We were quite prepared to share the land as well. But the newcomers were not satisfied with just sharing it. Despite the fact that many of them arrived preaching the Christian virtues of brotherhood and understanding and Christian emphasis on spiritual things over material things, their actions proved that what they wanted was to own and control the land and to control the minds and actions of my people as well. At least this is the way we Indians have experienced the history of the last centuries.

For my people, the Stoney Tribe, contact with the whiteman has been, of course, considerably shorter than it has been for our brothers on the eastern seaboard and in Central and South America. The whitemen were well established in the eastern parts of the Great Island before we Indians of the western plains and mountains encountered them.

But the westward push of the newcomers was relentless. Long before the land-hungry settlers began to look toward the plains at the foot of the Rocky Mountains, word of the whiteman and perhaps even some of his artifacts filtered to us through the long "moccasin trail" of intertribal meetings, rumours, and encounters. Then came the explorers and, more important, the trappers. The latter were Europeans or Métis, usually guided by Indians. The Stoneys greeted their brother hunters with hospitality. In return they received news of a new and congenial means of livelihood—trapping for trade—and trade goods, some of which were very useful to us. They also received liquor, "firewater," which proved one of the greatest curses the whiteman introduced into our society. It is possible that the trappers who brought it actually thought they were doing us a favour (while lining their pockets and those of their employers with the proceeds from our land's beautiful fur-bearing animals).

In fact, a deadly curse fell upon my people with the whiteman's firewater. The peaceful and cooperating tribal society was never quite the same. It was worse than the smallpox epidemic or any other disease of the whiteman. My people really needed a new law and order after the whisky traders invaded our country because we had had no previous experience with the whiteman's firewater and the dealings of unscrupulous traders. We had known only honest people and honest deals prior to the advent of the whisky trader. To this day we still have alcohol-related problems among the Indian population of Canada.

Not far behind the trappers and traders came the missionaries, determined to Christianize the "heathen savages" of this "new" land. They, too, were received with hospitality—and a great deal of interest.

If one understands the native religion of my people, it is not difficult to understand why so many of us embraced the gospel of Christianity. There was simply not that much difference between what we already believed and what the missionaries preached to us. What differences there were did not seem very important.

The Christian concept of sharing was nothing new to us. In fact, it was the way of life in the Stoney tribal society. Our community was a sharing community—that is one of the reasons why we survived for so many centuries. We shared our food and clothing and held our land in common. The hunting grounds, the ceremonial grounds, the sacred mountainous area—all were held in common for the tribe.

The concept of God as Creator was nothing new to us. The only thing that was different was the terminology. We call our God *Wakâ Tâga*, the Great Spirit. The doctrine of the Trinity—the Three in One God: Father, Son, and Holy Spirit—was new but this was something that could be accepted in time.

The other difference was the concept of the hereafter: the Happy Hunting Grounds or Heaven. There was a contrast between getting to the Happy Hunting Grounds and getting to Heaven. Are the Happy Hunting Grounds and Heaven the same place? But why worry about trying to convince each other if we both know how to get there? The concept of Hell in the hereafter was something entirely new to my people. There was no such word in our language. We had to invent a new word: *Wanâri Dââsi Ti* (the Bad Spirit's House).

So there were questions regarding the new religion, but it sounded good and its basic teachings were not unfamiliar. Besides, we did not have disputes regarding religion. There were some disputes over hunting grounds and fishing areas, but not religion! We were aware of the diversity of forms of worship among the various tribes, but the Supreme Being was the Great Spirit. We had been taught not to question various forms or ways of worshipping the Creator. Who were we to question? It was up to the Great Spirit and the tribe or the individual who was given a vision on the mountaintop or other sacred ground. We were not there when the religious experience happened to the individual or group. Therefore, we felt we were not qualified to question or dispute.

Another theory among us is that in creating so much diversity in nature the Great Spirit revealed his love for diversity: the diversity of peoples, cultures, and languages, of animals large and small, birds of all colours, fish of all sizes, plant life so numerous, rocks as huge as the mountains and as small as the sands of the seas. Surely such a Creator would accept more than just one religion. Would he listen to prayers of only one conventional form of worship? Surely not. Besides, these questions must be too deep for finite beings—here but for one short season—to comprehend.

And so we listened to the missionaries and many converts were made. It is important to realize, however, that the period of discovering the Christian religion, like the entire process of meeting the whiteman and adopting some of his artifacts and ways, was a very gradual one for us.

Throughout the first three-quarters of the nineteenth century, my people, the Stoneys, lived as we always had, little influenced by the

The view that greeted the settlers as they reached our land.

whiteman. We roamed, hunting, in the foothills and on the plains from the headwaters of the North Saskatchewan to the United States border. We hunted and lived in family groups, coming together in larger bands for special occasions and ceremonial purposes, and for wintering at Morleyville, the Kootenay Plains, or the Highwood River area. There were frequent skirmishes with neighbouring tribes, especially the Blackfoot, whose tribal areas adjoined ours, but no large-scale warfare.

It is difficult to estimate the total population of the tribe at this time. A missionary made a count of 284 for one group of Bearspaw's Band in April 1873.[1] We know that the three bands incorporated seven such smaller groups. So, rounding the missionary's figure to allow for individuals absent at the time and assuming seven groups of equal size, we can assume 2,000 could be a reasonable estimate of the Nakota-speaking population in the foothills of Alberta in the mid-1800s.

By the 1850s, Stoney life had altered in some details. The horse had completely replaced the dog for transportation; firearms had replaced the bow and arrow; trade goods were common in our camps. Trading had changed our way of life a little because of the need to trap fur-bearing animals for barter, over and above what was needed for daily use. But trade with the whiteman never became the basis of our economy as it did for some tribes. We continued to support ourselves by our own hunting, trading only when we wanted some useful goods.

It is difficult to assess whether living standards had improved over traditional ones. Steel axes and knives, as well as firearms, reduced the pressure to make our own tools and weapons. Thread and beads were easier for our women to work with than the traditional porcupine quills; woven cloth also entered our lives, although we also continued to use the skins produced by the hunt. Intertribal skirmishes declined, especially in the 1860s and 1870s, when the stories of encroaching settlement drew the tribes together in a way they had not considered before.

But by and large life continued unchanged. We were still dependent on hunting for our food. The freedom of the woods and the plains and the mountains was still ours and still the most important part of our lives. The land-hungry settlers were still unknown to us. Even the white traders and missionaries, whom most of us saw only occasionally, were still a curiosity.

One of the very first missionaries to visit the Stoneys came in 1840. He was the Reverend Robert Rundle. When he was travelling through this area, he was warmly welcomed and made to feel at home. Others followed at scattered intervals, but it was not until the early 1870s that a permanent mission was established here. This was

1907. Two children on a travois, the traditional means of family transport.
(Glenbow Archives NA-2313-27)

done by the Methodist father and son, George and John McDougall, who were to play a large role in the fate of my people.

George and John McDougall had apparently encountered our tribe in the course of working with the mission that was established in the late 1860s in what is now Edmonton. Father and son decided to push on into the wilderness with their Christian calling.

The place the McDougalls chose for their permanent mission was in the Bow Valley, at what is now the townsite of Morley, one of my people's traditional winter camping grounds. Every year the warm chinooks melted the snow in the valley, and it was a good place to spend the winter.

In a modern book entitled *Mission Among the Buffalo*, the Reverend Ernest Nix describes the arrival of the McDougalls at the mission site.

In the early days, however, the southern part of the Canadian prairies was virtually unknown to white men. The country had been opened for the exploitation of the fur-trade, and naturally travellers followed the waterways of the wooden north. Moreover, the reputation of the Blackfeet in war made the open plains seem dangerous to the white man. Upon the advent of the Yankee traders, however, the Methodists immediately saw the urgency of establishing a mission in the south. It was determined that in the interests of safety this mission should be located in the foothills, where the friendly Mountain Stoneys would give some protection.

On April 29, 1873, the elder McDougall started for the Bow River to meet his son and together locate what would be the new Morleyville mission. The country through which they passed was totally unsettled, and after the first one hundred and fifty miles it was unknown even to the McDougalls despite their ten years' residence in the country. Reaching the Bow River, the party followed its beautiful valley upstream until they were within some fifteen miles of the mountains. Here they met a mountain Stoney, the first human they had seen on the trip. This man took them at once to his camp where the elder McDougall records, they found "42 tents, 73 men, 82 women, 58 boys, 71 girls, 199 horses and 24 colts and 169 dogs." The faithful Stoneys were overjoyed to see their old missionary friends, whom they entertained royally in Chief Bear's Paw's tent at a supper of white swan's flesh.[2]

In less than two years the missionaries had opened a school at Morley with Dr. George Vexey as teacher. He was replaced later in 1875 by Andrew Sibbald, who stayed for some time. The school was usually referred to as "The Orphanage," though the reason for the name is not clear; my people's extended family system made the use of European-style orphanages unnecessary and records suggest that many children in this institution certainly had parents who were willing and able to care for them. (One reason may have been that the McDougalls raised money through the Church for the construction of an "orphanage" to serve all the tribes of the area. Another reason was almost certainly the desire to indoctrinate into Christianity any children the missionaries could find an excuse to take into their care.)

"Christianize" was the key word. Even before putting up a school, the first thing the McDougalls wanted was to build a "House of Prayer." The first church in what is now southern Alberta was built in Morleyville, in 1875. The missionaries and my people worked together in cutting logs, hauling them down to the proposed church site, and constructing the building. Services of worship were held every Sunday and most of my people were in attendance.

Even those of my people who did not accept Christianity had no objections to allowing the missionaries to build the church and later the school on the Tribe's land. They thought, at the time, that because it was their church and their school it was all right to locate it on their land.

What my people did not understand was the non-Indian's point of view, the point of view of their new "friends." There is every indication that the Europeans believed that the "new regime" brought by the whiteman was truly ordained by God and that the whiteman was predestined to come to North America to bring "law and order" and the Gospel. They thought they were called on to bring Christianity and "civilization" to a wild and dark continent of savages who roamed aimlessly, without God, without a written law or language, and without money. Poor souls, they thought of my people.

They did not consider that we had lived here for thousands of years, even ten thousands of years, without money and without a written law. The law of the Creator was written in our hearts. We lived and observed a religious life in the freedom of the winds. We were well versed in the law and order of another age, in another language, and in the ways of an unspoiled world. We followed the law of the human heart. Because we studied nature, we respected it, and we lived in harmony with it. We did not try to remake or destroy our environment. We did not have any money; therefore, money was not our God. Instead the Great Spirit was and is our God.

As more and more whitemen followed the trappers and missionaries into the North West (the territory that is now known as central and southern Alberta and Saskatchewan), this lack of understanding became more and more obvious to us. Once the whiteman's government took over control of the territory, it became quite clear that the missionaries were simply "advance men" for the new way of life.

Indeed, the stated goals of the government's Indian Administration, in the most simple terms, was to "*educate, Christianize,* and *civilize*" us. The government was to educate and civilize the savage. The Church was to Christianize the savage. These three words, *educate, civilize,* and *Christianize,* were used synonymously by both state and Church. Sometimes it was difficult for my people to recognize whether they were talking to government representatives or Church personnel because it was almost impossible to distinguish between the two.

The whitemen had another goal beyond their stated one, a goal which was to them more urgent—gaining control of the land. Gradually, pioneer settlers were beginning to move west, and plans were developed in the east to have them followed by more and more, until the migrant trickle turned into a veritable flood.

But even the government realized that if plans for large-scale development were to become a reality, then some agreement would have to be reached with us. We were there first and, although we had no concept of "owning" land individually, although we believed everyone had a right to use it to survive and sustain life, we might object if our way of life was disturbed sufficiently.

It had happened elsewhere, and, at that time, numbers were on our side. If the various tribes of the Western plains and the Rocky Mountain region had confederated at this point in history, they would have had enough strength and more than enough warriors to wipe out all the white settlers then in the area.

So the government sought to move in, making a show of concern for our welfare, and then to sign treaties with us. In this effort, the government requested and received complete support from the pioneer missionaries. For example, in 1874 the Methodist missionary at Morley, George McDougall, was requested:

. . . to impress on the Indians that it is the aim of the Queen and Her servants to deal fairly and justly by them, as she and they have always done in Her Territories, wherever situate, and that their welfare is as dear to Her, and them, as that of her white subjects. I have requested the Chief Commissioner of the Hudson's Bay Company to place at your disposal presents of the value of $1500 for distribution amongst the Indians you may visit.[3]

This was not an isolated instance of Church-state cooperation for the McDougalls. As the Reverend Ernest Nix recounts so vividly:

But even without government support, the McDougalls made on their own initiative many journeys amongst the Indians with the object of keeping them loyal and persuading them that the government would, in time, deal justly and fairly with them. On numerous later occasions, in 1871, 1874, 1875 and 1885, the McDougalls conducted official visitations amongst the Indians at the request of the Dominion government. These visitations had much to do with the peaceful entry of the North West Mounted Police into the country in the fall of 1874. Their coming had been announced to the Indians by John McDougall in the summer of 1874 at the request of the government. John explained "the full purpose" of their coming, and he thus became, as he said, the "John the Baptist" of the new regime they inaugurated.[4]

Left: The Rev. George McDougall *(Glenbow Archives NA-659-44)*

Below: The Methodist church, built in 1875, as it appeared in about 1900. *(Glenbow Archives NA-1913-2)*

It should be noted that the arrival of the North West Mounted Police was one action of the whiteman's government which my people really did appreciate. They thought at the time that it was the whiteman's firewater that brought murder, stealing, and countless other problems and that it might be possible to use the whiteman's law and order to correct one of the worst conditions and situations in our entire history. (In all fairness, the missionaries also attempted to help us to alleviate the problems of alcohol and the whisky trade.)

Meanwhile the government was reorganizing in preparation for its takeover of the North West. In 1870 "ownership" of the North West Territories (Rupert's Land) was transferred from the Hudson's Bay Company to the Dominion of Canada. The government assumed responsibility for the administration and the settlement of the Western prairies. Perhaps the Queen of England recognized the absurdity of accepting land from the Hudson's Bay Company, instead of dealing with my people, the real owners of the land. At any rate, she instructed her representatives to negotiate and make treaties with us. The new Dominion government was given responsibility for formal negotiations under the terms of the British North America Act of 1867. The federal government was, therefore legally committed to deal with us or to compensate us for our country when Rupert's Land officially became part of Canada.

A government body, headed by the Lieutenant-Governor in Winnipeg, was established to bring political order to the North West Territories. In December 1872, Alexander Morris succeeded Adam G. Archibald as Lieutenant-Governor of Manitoba and the North West Territories. The Territories were under the general supervision of the federal government until Saskatchewan and Alberta received provincial status in 1905. However, the area was given its own Lieutenant-Governor under the North West Territories Act of 1875. That was the basis of territorial administration during the time of treaty making with my people in what are now the provinces of Saskatchewan and Alberta. In 1873 a Department of the Interior was created, with both an Indian Branch and the North West Mounted Police under it. This federal bureaucracy handled most administrative contact with my people—and still does insofar as we remain under direct federal control.

The purpose of these administrative changes and appointments was to lay the foundation for the settlement and the administration of our land. The territorial government was concerned primarily with enacting legislation concerning taxation, property rights, the judicial system, public roads, and other local problems. Only incidentally was it concerned with making a treaty with us regarding land, and then only because of the government's concern for controlling Indian land. In other words, it is now clear to my people that the contemporary government saw the treaties as an expedient way of resolving the question of our aboriginal rights to this continent.

It is important to remember that at this time the Queen's chief representative was simultaneously the Lieutenant-Governor of the North West Territories and the Indian Commissioner. For example, Alexander Morris held both positions when the North West Territories were established as a separate jurisdiction, and David Laird, who replaced him in the fall of 1876, did the same. Holding two government offices simultaneously was an accepted practice during this period of Canada's political growth. Owing to the shortage of administrative personnel in the Territories, the government was willing to ignore the fact that there might be a conflict of interest when its officers served in two or more positions.

These high officials were, however, far away from our land. It was the North West Mounted Police, after their arrival in 1874, who were the visible legal representatives of the Queen's government. Their primary objective was to bring the whiteman's law and order to the prairies because by now settlers and squatters were coming into contact with many Western Indian tribes. As already noted, the functions and duties of the mounted police had been carefully explained to my people by the McDougalls and others, and we welcomed them to our land. The influence of these mounted police was given instant credence by the enthusiastic acceptance of their role of peacemakers by the Indians, and this friendly relationship in turn prepared us for the peace treaties of 1876 and 1877.

As these organizational developments were carried out in the North West, so were the plans for land "development." The situation was one of uncertainty and potential conflict. Thousands of Indian people, representing various tribes, were hunting on the vast prairies, roaming freely in the North West. Many white settlers were eager to come and take Indian land to start cattle ranches, agricultural enterprises, and other enterprises. It is a well-known fact that the railway was planned by the government in 1872 to help these people settle on our land.

The westward movement of the whitemen was much encouraged

by some of their brothers whom we had taken to be our friends. For example, the missionary to the Stoneys, George McDougall, used his influence to promote the west and told his own people about the abundant rich soil, water, pasturage, and coal along the foothills. (Today the descendants of Reverend McDougall still have the rich soil and best agricultural land just east of Morley, and my people, the Stoneys, have the reserve, which is on rocky ground unsuitable for farming.) The missionary wrote:

> No government policy or patronage can settle intermediate plans between here and Red River until the Eastern Slopes of the Rocky Mountains are filled up.[5]

He advised the government that the most pressing needs were to have the police enforce law and order, to negotiate treaties with the Indians, and to pass legislation to secure the land claims of new white settlers.

His son, John, was equally enthusiastic in his efforts to promote the whiteman's settlement of the West and our acceptance of the new regime. Historian Ernest Nix writes:

> To promote the west and its settlement was such a ruling passion with John McDougall that he appended an epilogue "Manitoba and the North West" to his earliest published book (1888); the biography of his father setting forth his evaluation of the west's resources under the headings: size, climate, soil, pasture, water, minerals, timber, appearance, and his belief "in the capability of this part of our great Dominion for the maintenance of a large population." His published memoirs in five volumes, two novels and a large number of occasional articles in magazines and newspapers all extolled the west. His intimate knowledge of its geography and people were recognized when he was appointed Commissioner to the Doukhobors and Special Commissioner to the Indians by the Dominion Government. In this capacity he visited hundreds of reserves throughout the west, listening to tribal councils and individual Indians, and relaying their grievances and requests to the government. John McDougall was much in demand as a public speaker, and travelled from coast to coast with but one subject, said John Maclean, "The Gospel of Jesus Christ and the great North-West."[6]

In other words, all this time we thought the missionaries were making the best possible deal for us, but in fact they were working to secure land for white settlers.

But as George McDougall had suggested and as the terms of the British North America Act required, whitemen's land claims were not going to be accepted before the government made apparently legal and fair agreements with the Indians by treaty. Ottawa was conscious of the bloodshed that had characterized "settlement" in the United States, and its own precarious position was brought home by the Riel hostilities of 1870.

In addition, public opinion in some quarters had progressed to a point where it was politically advantageous to deal with aboriginal peoples in a way that seemed legal, right, and just. To persons in countries outside Canada—and perhaps to some whitemen inside it—treaties appeared to be such a way. This might even have proved true if the treaty agreements and promises had been understood by both parties and if North American Indian law and European (British) law had been binding, carried out, and fulfilled accordingly.

And so, between August 3, 1871 and September 22, 1877, seven treaties were concluded with the majority of the Indian tribes of the North West Territories. The Lieutenant-Governor of the Territories, along with specially appointed treaty commissioners, was delegated to carry out the government's obligations of extinguishing or taking away our title to the land.

This was something that was difficult, if not impossible, for Indians to understand because we had no concept of individual land "ownership" in the European sense. In those days, we did not "own" the land by receiving title or patent from a tribal authority. My people had always believed that the land was created for its indigenous inhabitants—animal, bird, and man. Our philosophy of life is to live in harmony with nature and in accordance with the creation of the Great Spirit. Anyone wanting to live by those principles is more than welcome, and, if he wants to, he may participate in our traditional ways, religion, and culture. He does not have to make a treaty with us to do this. Certainly only a greedy person would make a treaty with us and then break it to destroy our land and our way of life.

Now we realize that the treaties were the vehicle through which the government achieved its objective of opening the North West Territories to settlement and commercial exploitation. In its haste, it did not live up to the spirit of the treaties nor even honour some of the specific promises made by the treaty commissioners.

But at the time of the treaty making, we had no idea that the government would not honour the spirit or the letter of its promises. We were not, however, ignorant of what was going on. For many years our medicine men, chiefs, and elders had heard by moccasin telegram of the Europeans arriving continuously on the eastern shores of the continent. When the time came to negotiate Treaty Seven, we were well aware of the many white people in the eastern part of the continent. There were so many of them and more and more were arriving. They were described as ants on an ant hill because there were so many of them coming from Europe.

We knew that if the various tribes of this area joined together, it would be possible to wipe out the white settlers on the western prairies at that time. But we also knew it was possible that more and more would come and ultimately the battle might be lost.

By the time of Treaty Seven, too, we knew that Treaties One through Six had been signed with most of the other Indians of the North West—the Saulteaux, the Cree, and our relatives, the Plains Assiniboine, who occupied the prairies and parklands to the east of us and along the North Saskatchewan River.

Two experiences with whitemen also had much to do with our decision to sign the whiteman's treaty. One was our contact with the missionaries, George and John McDougall, whom we believed to be generous and sincere men. On their own and (unknown to the Indians) at the request of the government, they had urged cooperation from the beginning. Now, as the treaty making approached, they increased their efforts. Reverend Ernest Nix gives this account:

> In the summer of 1875, reaching Winnipeg on his way back to the Saskatchewan after his year's furlough, he [George McDougall] was requested by the Hon. Alexander Morris, Lieutenant-Governor of Manitoba and the North-West, to visit as many Indian camps as possible in the interests of the government. The Minister of the Interior, the Hon. David Mills, in his report for the year 1876, thus alluded to Mr. McDougall's services:
>
> "The Rev. George McDougall, who had been resident as a missionary amongst these Indians for upwards of fourteen years, and who possessed great influence over them, was selected by his Honour to convey this intelligence to the Indians, a task which he performed with great fidelity and success. Being able to report on his return that although he found

the feeling of discontent had been very general among the Indian tribes, he had been enabled entirely to remove it by his assurance of the proposed negotiations during the coming year."

According to a letter he wrote to Richard Hardisty from Rat Creek on the 11th of August 1875; it was George McDougall who arranged for Treaty No. 6 to be signed by Alexander Morris with the Indians at Fort Carlton on August 18, 1876, and later at Fort Pitt. When the Blackfeet signed Treaty No. 7 in 1877 at Blackfoot Crossing on the Bow River, John McDougall was one of the signatories and advisers to the Indians.[7]

In short, the McDougalls were key people as witnesses, signatories, advisers, and interpreters during Treaty Six in 1876 and Treaty Seven in 1877.

The role of the missionaries cannot be overestimated in understanding why we signed the treaty. Their gifts and persuasions were not of primary importance. What was important was that they were believed to be both important leaders and men of God. The two roles were often combined in traditional Stoney culture. And under that culture a good leader, a good medicine man, has the full trust of the people—what he says is true. Hence, to our minds, the equation was simple. The McDougalls were men of God and counsellors or advisers to the Great Queen's representatives. Therefore, what they said about the importance and the promises of the treaties must be true.

The other factor in establishing a degree of trust in the whiteman had been our contact with the North West Mounted Police, who had won the confidence of the tribe. Our leaders agreed with the words of the Blackfoot Chief Crowfoot, "The Police have protected us as the feathers of the bird protect it from the frosts of winter."[8]

And so, although our warriors and braves were prepared to fight for our land and our freedom if war was what was required, at the time it was decided that negotiations would produce better results and offer a better future for our people. It was agreed our chiefs would sign the peace treaty at Blackfoot Crossing.

All the North West Treaties were similar in their goals. First and foremost the treaties were a legal manoeuvre to wipe out our claim to the land. But the underlying motive was to bring "law and order" to the North West Territories in order that settlers and developers might exploit the land. To that end the treaties all aimed at locating my people on reserves in order that we might be collected into easily controllable communities. Only there could we supposedly become self-supporting through agriculture, only there could schools be constructed for our children to teach them "industrial pursuits," to develop "moral improvements," and to learn "social grace."

The lack of understanding—or caring about—our ancient society is suggested by these goals. It is made even more explicit in a contemporary report explaining the federal government's Indian policy:

A persevering effort had for a number of years been made to prevail with each head of an Indian family to establish a homestead to be transmitted to those who succeed him as its head. The plan is now finding increased acceptance among those people. Its tendency is to elevate them in the social scale. Each has or can have the boundary of what thereby became his property defined by lines of survey. He acquires what he had not before a species of freehold and learns to attach to his possessions a respect which it [sic] had not previously, *and thus an important step is taken towards assimilating the conditions of the Indian people to that of those of other origins* [italics added].

The transactions for acquiring the Indian title to lands in Manitoba and the North West were molded on those which preceded them in the late Province of Upper Canada and thus the inconvenience and danger of attempting to pass over the Territorial rights of the numerous bands who might (had justice been withheld from them) have become formidable has been avoided. Thanks to the missionary Societies the work of the Education had already been initiated, and the assurances given in the traeties [sic] that the work of education would be sustained by the Government has been to the required extent veryfied [sic].

With reference to agriculture among the Indians of that part of the Dominion the supplies of ploughs, harrows, spades, hoes, scythes, and axes and farming stock delivered [sic] to such as were prepared to take proper care of them, and will enable them from the produce of the soil, to support their families.[9]

It is revealing in the above statement that the Deputy Superintendent of Indian Affairs was trying to teach us something that we knew more about than he and his staff did. He was trying to teach the Indian how "to attach to his possessions a respect which it [sic] had not previously." He was trying to teach my ancestors how to respect the land by surveying it so that a piece would be owned by an individual and so that no one else would be allowed on another's piece. The survey was a ploy used by the government to confine the Indian to a small plot of land and to take the vast estate away from him. And yet, the government officials used the ridiculous argument that they were teaching the Indian how to respect his possessions and land!

All the North West treaties were also similar in structure, although they differed in certain details because of additional demands made by the various tribes as our leaders became more aware of the government's anxiety to make a settlement with us. In 1875 several "outside promises" (verbal agreements not included in the written document) were even formally added to Treaties One and Two. (Perhaps the government felt pressured by the need to achieve settlement; perhaps this was one time it actually fulfilled what it had already agreed to but failed to incorporate in the original treaty.)

Treaties Three to Five were all very similar in content. Our people received reserve allotments based on population number; presents were offered to win our confidence; our hunting and fishing rights were not to be taken away; and an annuity was to be paid each year.

These annuity payments were raised from those in the earlier treaties, and the proportional basis for determining the size of the reserves was increased from 160 acres to 640 acres per family of five. The government said that it wanted everyone to become agriculturists. (This provision was included despite that fact that we had been given a guarantee that the treaty would not interfere with our traditional way of life or our hunting and fishing rights.) In return, we supposedly ceded all rights to land in a stipulated geographical area outlined in the treaties, and we promised to be loyal subjects of the Queen.

Treaties Six and Seven, in addition to the above promises, contained several significant differences from the other treaty agreements. The differences in terms of the treaty had important ramifications for all our brothers and not just us, the Stoney tribe. I will outline them in the next chapter.

Treaty-Making Days on the Prairies, 1876–1877

T reaty Six and Treaty Seven reflect much of the uncertainty and confusion that characterized treaty making. Variations among treaties, the long list of adhesions (agreements by bands within a treaty territory to sign the treaty later than the date of original signing), the conflicting reports between the published reports of the Dominion government[1] and the personal correspondence of Lieutenant-Governors Adam G. Archibald and Alexander Morris[2] amply document the uncertainty and misunderstanding that characterized the treaty negotiations.

The treaty commissioners performed their assigned tasks oftentimes unaware of the full meaning of aboriginal law and title, without knowledge of our language, and without the benefit of the most elementary background as to our history, culture, and way of life. Many of our present-day problems derive from the consequent confusion, misunderstanding, and apprehensions which surrounded the signing of the treaties.

The cultural misunderstandings surrounding the treaties were very deep and very serious indeed. During the treaty making, two parties, representing two significantly different cultures, attested the signatures. One was my people, who had an oral tradition and history. Under North American Indian law, whatever words were spoken and oral promises given, during formal negotiations, were remembered and were legally binding. The other party was the federal government, representing the Queen of England. Under their system, only the written word, in black and white, was the law.

Common justice and common sense suggest that both North

American Indian law and British law should have been binding in the treaties. Yet I am sure that the government representatives at the negotiations were well aware that in the future only the written statements contained in the documents would be honoured and upheld in the courts if there were any disputes. (This is now true. Only a narrow and literal interpretation of the treaties, in most cases, is upheld in court today.) But my people, who had an oral tradition and had honoured verbal agreements in the past, thought that the government would also honour what was spoken during the treaty making.

This basic cultural difference was heightened by problems with that symbol and result of culture—language. Usually everything that was said during the treaty negotiations had to be translated, sometimes through two or three stages. For example, during the Treaty Seven negotiations, three languages often had to be used to communicate between the government and our tribe. Our chief spoke in Stoney, which was translated into Cree to an interpreter who understood both Cree and English, who communicated with the government representatives. Imagine the confusion! The alternative to this two-stage process was translation by the missionary John McDougall, whom we now know had a vested interest in the outcome. Sometimes, too, because of cultural differences, there were considerable difficulties in translating from one language into another.

The result of these linguistic problems was that our understanding of the treaty agreements was very different from what was contained in the parchment written in a foreign language.

Another basic misunderstanding at the negotiations concerned the purpose of the treaties. The federal government wanted legal title to the entire North West Territories so they could be "developed" by the whitemen, and the treaties were a natural outgrowth of federal policy. We, on the other hand, understood them to be strictly peace treaties. Given the difficulties in translation and the different cultural attitudes toward the use and ownership of land, our forefathers did not realize that they were ceding land to the whiteman for all time. The question of restricted land and number of acres per family never came up until the coming of surveyors and railways, with the subsequent flood of ranchers and settlers.

That we understood Treaty Seven in such fashion was recently given vivid explanation by Peter Wesley, an old Stoney whose Cree-speaking mother was present at the negotiations. He said:

On the morrow the Chief asked him [the Lieutenant-Governor] what was the real meaning of this proposal? The answer was, "To make peace between us. We will have friendship when and where ever we meet. I am asking you to put your rifle down in exchange for a peace treaty. The money I am just about to give you is for this purpose. Not to kill each other. And further more I am not going to take over your land, but I am willing to pay you money if you put down your rifle and make peace with me, this is what I mean." This was the answer given by the Lieutenant Governor. So that was how peace was made and that is the way it was. Nothing besides peace-making was talked about. The chief had been told that he could still use his land in the same manner as before and there would be no interruption either, these were the final words put forth by the Governor through the interpreter. My mother talked and understood Cree very well. That was why my mother understood all the conversations held between the Governor and the Chiefs.[3]

It seems that some of this misunderstanding was intentionally allowed by the government because it was to its advantage to extinguish title to Indian land as quickly as possible. By creating a "legal" situation in which it could soon send out surveyors and make legislation stating that there must be legal land descriptions and titles to the land, the government set its own stage for control of our land and resources. The government kept these papers in its office and therefore controlled the land; my people had very little say, if any at all, about the land after the treaties were signed.

If my forefathers had known what all this would mean to our people: the disappearance of the buffalo and diminishing of other game, the restrictive game laws, the plowing and fencing off of all the lands, more whiteman's diseases, attacks on our religion, culture, and way of life, the continual eroding of our other treaty rights; if they could have foreseen the creation of provincial parks, natural areas, wilderness areas, the building of dams, and the flooding of our traditional hunting areas, they would never have signed Treaty Seven. But they relied on the missionaries, who said, "The Queen's government will honour the promises in the treaties."

However, in the mid-1870s all this was in the future. Between 1870 and 1875 Treaties One through Five had been signed. The government treaty makers, spurred by the demands of white settlers and entrepreneurs, then turned their attention to the Cree people of Saskatchewan and southern Alberta. Their territory was a vast one which attracted the envious eyes of the Government of Canada and European settlers. But the Cree had turned back members of the geological survey and interrupted the construction of the transcontinental telegraph.[4] Nervous government leaders in Ottawa immediately entered into treaty negotiations with them.

Treaty Six was signed in 1876, mostly by the Cree people of what is now Saskatchewan and central Alberta. The written agreement contained the usual terms of land surrender, and the promise of reserve lands and annuity payments. However, to the dismay of the federal government, the treaty commissioners, Lieutenant-Governor Morris, James McKay, and W. J. Christie, had incorporated additional promises into the treaty to induce the Indian spokesman to sign the agreement: the promise of agricultural implements and seed grain, and the promise of providing rations to the Indians in the event of famine. (This latter clause was to be of great importance to them when the buffalo were exterminated several years later.) Minister of the Interior David Mills felt these terms were "more onerous than those of former treaties" and especially objected to the promise of rations in case of need because it would "predispose them to idleness."[5]

Stoneys signed the treaty as equals. The Canadian experience was different from the American. The Indians of the prairies were not a vanquished people, and they came to the treaty signing in a spirit of co-operation, not forced to sign after years of bloodshed.

It is interesting to note that David Mills made no objection at Treaty Six to the now famous promise of the medicine chest for each band. This was a promise that the agent would keep whiteman's medicines at each reserve and use them for any of our people who fell sick. The promise that the government would provide for our sick was, of course, another not-too-subtle demonstration of immigrant superiority: Indian peoples had well-developed medical skills, but the Church and the government wanted to do away with all "heathen and uncivilized" practices by the Indian medicine men. (One of the methods used by the whiteman to "civilize" my people was condemning the practice or the use of Indian medicine and its medicine men. As a result, much of our knowledge of Indian medicine has been lost. We were forced to abandon many of the Great Spirit's gifts—the knowledge we acquired of healing herbs and plants, and psychological knowledge of healing both body and soul, which was revealed to my people in Nature. No human being can impart these gifts of healing and understanding to the coming generations. I am sure that they will be revealed again, in due time, by the Great Spirit to my people.)

Throughout the Treaty Six negotiations, the relationship between Minister of the Interior Mills and Lieutenant-Governor Morris was strained. At one point, Morris wrote in exasperation, "I protest against your ignoring the responsibilities of the Minister of the Interior and placing it on me."[6] Morris defended the inclusion of additional articles in the treaty because of the Indians' apparent willingness to adopt an agricultural life. And in the end, despite David Mills' expressed fears that Treaty Six's favourable terms might raise dissatisfaction among the Indians who had already signed previous treaties, and despite his other objections, the government reluctantly agreed to it, "believing that the mischief which might result from a refusal to do so might produce discontent and dissatisfaction, which would ultimately prove more detrimental to the country than the ratification of the treaty."[7]

After coming to terms with the Cree, the next step for the government was to sign a treaty with the powerful Blackfoot Confederacy of southern Alberta. Ottawa started arrangements for it during the summer of 1876 and spring of 1877.

Then events moved quickly as the need for this peace treaty was dramatized by the deteriorating situation in the United States. In the summer of 1877, the United States Bureau of Indian Affairs decided to remove the Nez Perce of Idaho, under Chief Joseph, to a reservation after trouble had arisen between the Nez Perce and encroaching white settlers and gold miners. Historian Peter Farb has described the course of events as follows:

Chief Joseph of the Nez Perce in Idaho rebelled in 1877. Before he was trapped only thirty miles short of refuge in Canada, he had consistently outwitted and outfought a superior United States Army across a thousand miles of Rocky Mountain terrain. It was also one of the most honorable of the Indian wars, at least on Chief Joseph's side; for, although he forbade his warriors to scalp or to torture, the Whites massacred his women and children. Finally, with most of his warriors dead, his people starving, freezing, and maimed, Chief Joseph walked toward the White generals, handed down his rifle to them, and said: "I am tired of fighting. My people ask me for food, and I have none to give. It is cold, and we have no blankets, no wood. My people are starving to death. Where is my little daughter? I do not know. Hear me, my chiefs. I have fought, but from where the sun now stands, Joseph will fight no more forever."[8]

Before Chief Joseph surrendered, it had been rumoured that he was headed to join forces with the Sioux Tribe under Chief Sitting Bull, who was already camped in southern Saskatchewan near Fort Walsh. This speculation caused anxiety in Ottawa because, were the United States tribes to unite with the Indians of the Canadian North West, the entire settler population would be at their mercy. The Canadian government was, therefore, anxious to win the confidence of my people on its side of the border by concluding a treaty and reassuring them of its peaceful intentions.

At this same time, Minister of the Interior Mills was worried about the prospects of an Indian-settler war in British Columbia. The critical nature of the situation in British Columbia was clearly outlined to Mills by the federal government's commissioners, G. M. Sproat and A. M. Anderson:

Indian situation very grave from Kamloops to American frontier. Outbreak possible, Indians attempting to confederate. American Indians representative present at meeting. Magistracy, clergy and white people full of alarm and entreat us to communicate. Very prudent action necessary to prevent immediate bloodshed. We decided after deliberation and consultation that at least 100 Mounted Police should be secretly sent to Kamloops.[9]

To move one hundred Mounted Police to British Columbia would seriously weaken the divisions stationed in the North West Territories.

So the government was understandably anxious to conclude a treaty with the remaining Indian tribes in southern Alberta, and it had little time to prepare for the treaty negotiations.

The government's anxiety may not have been unjustified. It is certain that in the year immediately prior to the signing of Treaty Seven, our leaders were alarmed by the increasing number of whitemen entering our hunting grounds. Lieutenant-Governor Alexander Morris recorded:

Official reports of the Mounted Police Force, and from other parties, showed that a feeling of discontent and uneasiness prevailed very generally amongst the Assiniboines [i.e. Stoneys] and Crees lying in the unceded territory between the Saskatchewan and the Rocky Mountains. This state of feeling, which had prevailed amongst these Indians for some years past, had been increased by the presence, last summer, in their territory of the parties engaged in the construction of the telegraph line, and in the survey of the Pacific Railway line, and also a party belonging to the Geological Survey.[10]

John McDougall was asked by Lieutenant-Governor Morris to allay the fears of our people.

As noted in the previous chapter, the missionary fulfilled his assignment very well. Many of our tribe, as well as numbers of the Blackfoot Nation, assembled at Blackfoot Crossing to negotiate Treaty Seven.

The government commissioners at Treaty Seven were the Honourable David Laird, who had replaced Alexander Morris as Lieutenant-Governor of the North West Territories, and Lieutenant Colonel James F. Macleod, Commissioner of the North West Mounted Police stationed at Fort Macleod.

These commissioners were directed to negotiate a treaty in the unsurrendered southwest angle of the Territories: north of the international boundary, east of the Rocky Mountains, south of the Red

Deer River (Treaty Six limit), and west of Cypress Hills (Treaty Four limit). This portion of the North West was occupied by the Blackfoot, Blood, and Sarcee and Piegan Indians, "some of the most warlike and intelligent but intractable bands of the North West."[11]

(As we shall see, the territory described in the commissioners' directives did not cover all Stoney territory, nor did the directive specify obtaining a signature from us. The confusion that was to result from having us sign Treaty Seven—rather than an adhesion to Treaty Six, which might have been more appropriate—was considerable and long-lasting.)

For the signing of Treaty Seven, in September 1877, the Blackfoot bands came in great numbers; their prominent figure and head Chief was Chief Crowfoot. Many of our bands also travelled from various points along the foothills of the Rocky Mountains, and from the Highwood River, Morley, and Kootenay Plains areas to Blackfoot Crossing to sign the "peace treaty."

Our head Chiefs and spokesmen for the three main bands—the Bearspaw, the Chiniquay, and Jacob's—were Chief Bearspaw, Chief Chiniquay and Chief Kichipwot (also known as Chief Goodstoney) respectively. (Note that the Chiniquay people have since changed the spelling of "Chiniquay" to "Chiniki.") John McDougall acted as interpreter and adviser to my people.

The provisions of Treaty Seven were more or less similar to those of Treaty Six. There was no specific promise of a medicine chest, but the Stoney negotiators were given verbal promises that all benefits in Treaty Six would be understood to be included in Treaty Seven. There was a written, if reluctant, promise to provide the seed and the equipment necessary for an agricultural economy. The request for this provision is recorded as having been made by our tribe. It was probably done under the influence of McDougall since, in order for his mission at Morley to succeed, my people would have to change from their nomadic, hunting way of life to that of agriculturists. (However, as we shall note later, hunting proved to be the only reliable way for our livelihood. Attempts made by the Indian Affairs Branch during the 1880s and 1890s to establish an agricultural community at Morley proved to be a fiasco.) Certainly we requested, and understood that we had been promised, the continuation of our traditional life of hunting, trapping, fishing, and gathering berries, plants, and herbs in our traditional hunting grounds. We had no idea we would be forced to settle on a small piece of land and become agriculturists.

This sort of misunderstanding was common to nearly all the

Indian signators to the treaties. In addition, there were confusions about Treaty Seven and the Stoneys that were particular to my people and have caused many problems during the past hundred years. Chief among these were why we were asked to sign it at all (rather than one of the other treaties), whether it covered all the tribe, and exactly what territory was involved.

The question as to why we, the Stoneys, were included in Treaty Seven may never be answered. The mission at Morleyville lay within the land specified in Treaty Seven, but our Bighorn–Kootenay Plains territory did not. Neither were we part of the nation for whom that treaty was intended.

In all the government correspondence, official reports, and Orders-in-Council that preceded the Treaty Seven negotiations, there is no mention of the fact that our tribe was to be included in it. The Privy Council order, which appointed Lieutenant-Governor Laird and Colonel Macleod as treaty commissioners, stated:"That the Territory to be included in the proposed treaty is occupied by Blackfeet, Crees, Sarcees, and Piegans and may be estimated approximately at about 35,000 square miles in area." Primarily the treaty was to be with the Blackfoot Nation.

One of the earliest government reports which mentions the Stoney people clearly indicated that we were viewed as being entirely distinct from the Blackfoot Nation. W. J. Christie, in outlining his views on the urgent need to conclude treaties with the native people in the Saskatchewan district (at Fort Pitt, Prince Albert, Carlton House, Victoria, and Edmonton House), noted that:

> Treaties made with the Indians frequenting the above Posts would cover the whole country in the valley of the North Saskatchewan to the Rocky Mountains, with exception of the country south of the Red Deer River, and along the base of the Rocky Mountains to the Boundary line, which is the hunting grounds of the Blackfeet, Pagans [sic] and Circee [sic] Indians.[12]

Christie intimated that there was no immediate need to negotiate a treaty with us, the Stoneys. In addition to the above statement he pointed out:

> There is a band of Rocky Mountain Stoney Indians who hunt in the Valleys of the Rocky Mountains, and about Bow River,

trading at the Rocky Mountain House, they are good quiet peaceable Indians, and have had Wesleyan Missionarys [sic] among them.[13]

Although Christie did state in this report that the Blackfoot and our tribe occupied the same hunting area "in the valley of the North Saskatchewan," it is evident that he was careful to draw a clear distinction between the tribes. His concern was with the supposedly more hostile Blackfoot tribe since the Wesleyan missionaries had achieved such a large measure of influence among our people.

The McDougalls certainly knew that we were a separate tribe and, in their familiarity with the government's workings, thought that we should fall under the terms of Treaty Six. Indeed, in 1876, when John McDougall was asked by the Dominion Government to report on the date and location most convenient to negotiate a treaty with us, his reply indicated that he was under the assumption that our tribe came under the purview of Treaty Six, which had already been signed, and that we should simply make an adhesion to it:

> Whereas the Assinaboines [sic] or Stone [sic] Indians *are included within the limits of Treaty No. 6*, I would recommend the following dates and places as the most convenient for the meeting of these Indians with the Commissioner who may be sent *to secure their adhesion* to the Treaty next summer. [italics added].[14]

But when Lieutenant-Governor Laird arrived at Blackfoot Crossing to conclude Treaty Seven with the Blackfoot, it appears that he simply assumed that we were present to participate in the new treaty, not to sign an adhesion to an earlier one. Laird did, however, understand that we were a separate tribe since he wrote in his report on Treaty Seven:

> The Stonies [sic] are the only Indians adhering to this treaty who desired agricultural implements and seed; these things may be understood as merely applicable to that tribe.[15]

According to official records, John McDougall, despite his previous advice, never questioned why those of our leaders who were from the Bighorn-Kootenay Plains area, the major part of our traditional territory that was not included within the geographical limits of Treaty Seven, did not sign an adhesion to Treaty Six. One explanation could be that the treaty commissioners assumed, from what the Wesleyan missionary said, that all our people lived at Morleyville, and that John McDougall found that false assumption very convenient.

Whatever the reason for the misunderstanding, all three major bands of our tribe present at Blackfoot Crossing did sign Treaty Seven rather than Treaty Six, although it would have been proper to have the Bighorn-Kootenay Plains group sign an adhesion to Treaty Six (or even Treaty Eight, which was signed much later). It is doubtful that the commissioners, from the evidence at their disposal, were able to conceptualize the far-ranging territory which my ancestors traditionally regarded as their hunting, camping, and ceremonial grounds. But since the northern boundary of Treaty Seven was roughly the Red Deer River, Laird probably assumed that his mandate gave him authority to include the three Stoney Bands, even though we had not been specifically mentioned in either the terms of reference outlined by Minister of the Interior Mills or in the Order-in-Council appointing him commissioner. It seems that the government negotiators were not even aware that some of our people resided north of the Red Deer River.

The question of which treaty we should have signed is not an empty legalism since it touches a problem that plagues us to this day—the problem of what land we were going to get. Although the Stoneys did not realize it, Treaty Seven meant that we would receive only one reserve, which was to be located at Morleyville. But at the time of signing, Chief Goodstoney expected to receive a similar reserve in the Bighorn-Kootenay Plains area for his people who lived there before the treaty was signed, and Chief Bearspaw expected to receive land for his band south of Morley. This was done for the different Blackfoot bands, who received reserve land at Gleichen, Cardston, and Brocket; our Chiefs expected the same consideration for the three bands of our tribe.

We now know and realize that John McDougall had a personal interest in having one large reserve established at Morleyville; the church was there, his home and farm buildings were there, the hay fields were nearby, and a small area was under cultivation. It was apparently his feeling that the Church could not continue effectively Christianizing my people if we did not all settle on one reserve.

Another question that has plagued us since Treaty Seven is

whether our Chiefs and Councillors who attended fully represented the entire Stoney Tribe. There is every indication they did not. Even the government records show it was a confusing situation. Colonel Macleod estimated that thirty Chiefs and Headmen would be present at Blackfoot Crossing, but he candidly admitted:

> It was very difficult on account of the changes which are continually taking place amongst the Indians, and more especially now when they are not obliged to hold together under recognized heads for the purpose of protection to ascertain exactly who are the Chiefs as distinguished from headmen or Councilors, but thirty, I am informed will conclude the whole.[16]

Most important was the misconception that the Chiefs present at Blackfoot Crossing truly represented all the various, widely dispersed bands of the tribes that signed Treaty Seven. Two anthropologists conducted interviews with members of the Blackfoot tribe in 1939 and 1941; they have recorded that the dominant figure in that tribe's treaty negotiations was Chief Crowfoot.[17] Through their research they have concluded that Crowfoot was actually elevated to his status of head chief by the government authorities and that "the Blackfoot [people] never considered him a leader authorized to make decisions on their behalf and be responsible for tribal conduct."[18]

Whether the anthropologists' findings are true or not for the Blackfoot, could something similar have happened with the Stoney

Tribe? Could it be that a false assumption was made regarding the authority of the Stoney representatives attending the treaty meetings? Chief Chiniquay, Chief Jacob Goodstoney, and Chief Bearspaw were treated by the commissioners as the Head Chiefs for the entire Stoney Tribe. There is some doubt as to whether this was correct. At the time

Chief Crowfoot, of the Blackfoot. At treaty, when told the government would feed us in times of famine, he replied, "I don't think you can, for you will run out of breath." *(Glenbow Archives NA-4216-32)*

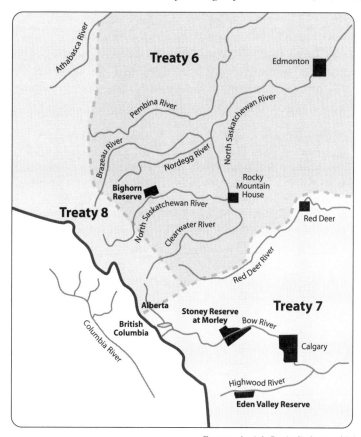

The areas taken in by Treaties Six, Seven, and Eight.

several groups of Stoneys were in British Columbia hunting, while others were camping in the mountains north of the Red Deer River. (This further helps to explain why the group from the Jacob's Band living on the Kootenay Plains still believe that they were overlooked when the time came to select their reserve lands.)

In his Treaty Seven report to the government, Lieutenant-Governor Laird spoke of the presence of the Stoneys, but he mentioned only those from the upper part of Bow River.[19] There is substantial documentation to prove that a significant number of our people resided permanently on the north branch of the Saskatchewan River (on the Kootenay Plains) and that others lived along the foothills south of Morley (Eden Valley group). It is unclear from the official records whether Chief Jacob Goodstoney was empowered to speak on behalf of those absent.

There was also a serious geographical oversight. If one looks closely at the boundary description of the land areas covered by Treaties Six and Seven, it can be seen that the Kootenay Plains region was omitted from consideration in both treaty documents. Treaty Six sets down the following boundary limits:

> Commencing at a point on the international boundary due south of the western extremity of the Cypress Hills; thence west along the said boundary to the central range of the Rocky Mountains, or to the boundary of the Province of British Columbia; then north-westerly along the said boundary to *a point due west of the sources of the main branch of the Red Deer River* [italics added]: thence south-westerly and southerly following on the boundaries of the tracts ceded by the Treaties Numbered Six and Four to the place of commencement; and also all their rights, titles and privileges whatsoever, to all other lands wherever situated in the North-West Territories, or in any other portion of the Dominion of Canada.[20]

Comparing this description with that of the boundaries of Treaty Seven, it is clear that the traditional hunting and camping grounds of the members of Jacob's Band on the Kootenay Plains were not incorporated as a part of either Treaty Six or Treaty Seven. The omission was discovered by the time Treaty Eight was signed in 1899, on which occasion the narrow strip of land bordering the Great Divide and the Red Deer River was incorporated in the text:

> Commencing at the source of the main branch of the Red Deer River in Alberta, thence due west of the central range of the Rocky Mountains, thence north-westerly along the said range to the point where it intersects the 60th parallel of north latitude; [the description then covers the northern and eastern limits] thence including said lake [Cree Lake] south-westerly along the height of land between the Athabasca and Churchill Rivers to where it intersects the northern boundary of Treaty Six, and along the said boundary easterly, northerly, and south-westerly, to the place of commencement.[21]

But the Stoneys of the Bighorn-Kootenay Plains area were not invited to participate in the Treaty Eight settlement, nor have they ever been permitted to sign an adhesion to any treaty. The question still remains outstanding, despite our repeated petitions to Ottawa.

Over the years the government has been inconsistent in the arbitrary distinctions it has employed to cover those of our people who were overlooked at Treaties Six and Seven. One year after Treaty Seven a Stoney band west of Edmonton signed an adhesion to Treaty Six. Similarly, two other tribal groups were each given reserves northwest of Rocky Mountain House: the Sunchild Band signed an adhesion to Treaty Six on May 25, 1944, and the O'Chiese Band received a reserve on May 12, 1950. Yet our band members living on the Kootenay Plains (which is only forty-five miles west of the O'Chiese Reserve) have never been able to sign any agreement for their land.

Why? Perhaps the answer is not so different now than it was in 1877. We were not a large tribe, and our Kootenay Plains group was

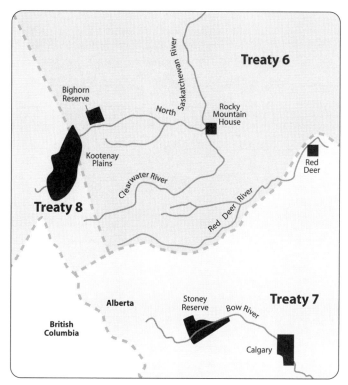

The location of the claimed area on the Kootenay Plains and the Bighorn Reserve, established in 1948, 100 miles north of the Morley Stoney Reserve created by Treaty Seven.

quite small. The commissioners were so intent upon reaching an agreement with particular groups of Indians and were so interested in Indian land that the more isolated, smaller bands were overlooked.

Certainly this desire for haste and concentration on large groups regarded as potential troublemakers seem to explain why the Treaty Seven commissioners lacked sufficient background information to draft a fair and equitable treaty with the three bands of our tribe.

The Treaty, the Survey, and the Aftermath, 1877–1890

Treaty Seven, as has already been suggested, was signed with several misunderstandings on both sides. My tribe understood that the commissioners had made us oral, *binding* promises that the treaty would not interfere with our traditional way of life. We understood that we were free to go wherever we wanted to in our traditional hunting territory. We had the right to trap fur-bearing animals. We had the right to hunt game in any season for livelihood, food, and clothing, and also to fish at any time of year in all streams, rivers, and lakes. (At that time we all expected that the buffalo would be present in large numbers as usual for many years to come.)

But from the government's viewpoint, Treaty Seven was based on the premise that my people would adopt agriculture as their main livelihood. (We have already noted that Commissioner David Laird had promised the necessary agricultural implements and seeds in order to fulfill the missionaries' goal of establishing a sedentary community adjacent to the Morleyville church.)

It is true that the McDougalls had converted a segment of my tribe to an agrarian lifestyle. However, the treaty commissioners made the erroneous assumption that an agricultural settlement situated on one large reserve would make the ideal economic and social setting for the entire Stoney Tribe. They also assumed that we would be able to establish a self-sufficient agricultural economy there practically overnight. The first assumption was not consistent with our heritage of a hunting culture and a nomadic way of life.

And the second, given the nature of the reserve lands alloted us and the paucity of materials actually received, was probably impossible to fulfill even if every Stoney had been willing to abandon his or her traditional life for that of an agriculturist.

Given the government's viewpoint, it was natural that it should proceed as quickly as possible to mark out those lands promised us by treaty to which it intended to confine us. In 1879, A. P. Patrick, District Land Surveyor, arrived at Morleyville to survey our reserve. His hasty work was influenced by two further misunderstandings— where our reserves were to be located and who had the right to speak for the tribe. The results of these related misunderstandings plague us to this day.

All three Stoney Chiefs who had signed Treaty Seven had been promised by the commissioners that, when the time came to select their reserve lands, they could choose the location in their familiar hunting and camping grounds. But when Patrick came to survey the Stoney Reserve, he surveyed only land surrounding the Methodist mission on the Bow River.

In comparison, the Blackfoot, Blood, Piegan, and Sarcee Chiefs who signed Treaty Seven were all given the option of selecting their reserve lands. Perhaps our leaders were not given a similar choice because of the over-riding influence of John McDougall at the treaty negotiations. And, as already noted, he had a stake in having the largest possible amount of reserve land located near his mission.

An additional problem was that only Chief Chiniquay was present at Morley when the reserve was surveyed. With the aid of John McDougall as translator, he seems to have acted as the spokesman for all the Stoneys, although his authority was only over the Chiniquay Band. Chief Bearspaw, who was the head of the Bearspaw Band, was in the south with his Band, and Chief Goodstoney, of Jacob's Band, was in the north, hunting. Why didn't the Indian agent and the surveyor (not to mention John McDougall) wait for the other two Chiefs before the survey was made or make some arrangements for consulting with the leaders of the other bands? A quorum of the Stoney Chiefs or a quorum of the Tribal Council was not present when the Stoney Reserve was surveyed. Chief Chiniquay was under the impression that he was receiving land only for his band,[1] whereas it is obvious that Surveyor Patrick believed that the Chief was representing the entire tribe.

This mistaken assumption continued for some time, as is clearly borne out in a later report by John C. Nelson, chief surveyor in charge of Indian reserve surveys,[2] after he revisited the Morley reserve in November 1887:

> Before leaving Morley, Chinniky [sic] *on behalf of all the other Indians*, urgently requested, through the Rev. Mr. McDougall, to have the boundaries of the reserves re-established, as the old marks, owing to heavy brush fires, are now nearly all destroyed, and it is difficult for them to know when trespass is committed [italics added].[3]

John McDougall and Chief Chiniquay apparently enjoyed a close working relationship, but most important of all, the surveyor misunderstood them. John Nelson assumed that they spoke for "all the other Indians," as A. P. Patrick had eight years earlier.

Two deductions can be considered regarding Chief Chiniquay and John McDougall. First, Chief Chiniquay may have purposely intimated that he was the Head Chief of the Stoneys, perhaps for the prestige and favour it won him with government representatives.

His representations at the surveys are not the only actions that suggest this. Whenever a dispute arose on the reserve, Chief Chiniquay invariably aligned himself with the government. W. Graham, a farm instructor on the Stoney Reserve, later recorded one of his speeches at a meeting concerning the use of reserve land by the three bands:

> I am not Chief today only. I was Chief at the Treaty and my appointment was confirmed by the Government. I chose my Councillors. We must follow what our Government say. The Government and Police are with me.[4]

The Europeans would have accepted such an attitude on Chief Chiniquay's part since they assumed that an Indian tribe would have one spokesman (in spite of the fact that the Chiefs of the three Stoney bands were recognized as representing three distinct groups by the commissioners at Treaty Seven).

Chief Chiniquay in 1887,
in a classroom at Morley.
(Glenbow Archives NA-662-2)

Wherever possible, the government preferred to deal with just one Chief; for them it simplified the decision making. Apparently the white community falsely gave the mantle of leadership to Chief Chiniquay, even though he had the smallest band of the three. It was an unfortunate mistake which gave rise to misunderstanding and ill feelings with my own band, Jacob's Band (later renamed Wesley's Band), who later sent numerous petitions to the Indian Affairs Branch asking when our reserve was to be surveyed.

Another (not contradictory) explanation may be that, in view of his eagerness to have the reserve surveyed at Morleyville, John McDougall accepted the opportunity of having this accomplished even though the other two Chiefs were away in their traditional hunting areas along the foothills. Since he had a good working relationship with one of the Chiefs, it is possible that he influenced him to get the survey over with.

In his first annual report, Indian Commissioner Edgar Dewdney erroneously reported that the Morley Reserve was surveyed "to the satisfaction of the Indians."[5] But when the boundary was resurveyed in 1883, John Nelson wrote:

> I am of the opinion that this reserve, surveyed by Mr. Patrick and myself four years ago (in 1879), is not in a suitable locality. Its proximity to the Rocky Mountains exposes the crops to the detrimental influence of summer frosts as attested by experience during the last four years. *When the survey was made many of these Indians wished to have the reserve at the Dog Pound or Red Deer River* [italics added].[6]

Surveyor Nelson was not empowered to relocate the reserve in another locale without special enabling legislation. But it is significant that from the beginning of the reserve system some tribal members did not want to establish their reserve near Morleyville. We members of Jacob's Band maintained—as we do to this day—that we were promised "land at the head of the Saskatchewan River in the mountains" during the negotiations at Blackfoot Crossing in 1877.[7]

Very shortly after the days of treaty making on the prairies, most of the Indians of the Western plains faced the second great crisis that was caused by the whiteman. The first had been the introduction of smallpox and alcohol. Now the buffalo, on which most tribes depended for their livelihood, disappeared.

The virtual extinction of the great animal of the plains was very sudden. In 1870 the herds roamed as they had for hundreds, thousands of years. By 1877, the year Treaty Seven was signed, they were diminishing but still plentiful. By 1880 they had nearly vanished from the Canadian prairies.[8] Although the unusually harsh winter of 1879 was a contributing factor, their slaughter in previous years by whitemen in the United States was a significant cause. Some of this slaughter was a deliberate attempt to weaken the Indian's position. Historian Peter Farb has noted:

General William Tecumseh Sherman attributed the final victory of the United States Army to the railroads, which were able to transport his troops as far in one day as they had been formerly to march in a month.

General Phil Sheridan, on the other hand, had urged the destruction of the bison herds, correctly predicting that when they disappeared, the Indians would disappear along with them; by 1885 the bison were virtually extinct, and the Indians were starving to death on the plains.[9]

For those tribes whose entire economy was based on hunting the buffalo, the vanishing of the herds did indeed mean disaster. With their traditional means of support gone, they had little choice: starve or move onto the reserves and depend on the ration houses. The government had promised under treaty to feed them in time of need. And it did make some attempt to do so when the disappearance of the buffalo caused famine, although there was great confusion. The funding was limited, the distance across the prairies was long, and inevitably, amidst the chaos and panic arising from the situation, miscalculations were made in carrying out the treaty promises. Famine was not always averted. This had been foretold by Blackfoot Chief Crowfoot who, when the treaty commissioners promised to manage our country and feed us in time of famine, replied: "I don't think you can, for you will run out of breath." The government, very early, seemed to run out of breath in trying to keep its treaty promises.

Even some of the government's own people were disgusted with its failure to provide as it had promised. One of the first employees stationed at Morley, R. W. Gowan, expressed his disappointment with the ad hoc nature of the government's policy:

I find that there are somethings that are not satisfactory with the Indians and from what I can see before me in all matters connected with the agency, I cannot carry out the instructions laid down to me.[10]

In this letter of resignation, Gowan concluded with the sad comment: "Indians verry [sic] much disatisfied [sic] with rrations [sic] Chiefs will not return anymore."[11]

For many tribes, rations were very scarce indeed. But the government, quick to turn the disaster to its advantage, required the hungry Indians to move onto the reserves before issuing any rations at all. With scant food and a restricted life, the few years following the disappearance of the buffalo broke the lives and spirits of many once proud people.

My own tribe was not so unfortunate. Although we had hunted buffalo, our way of life had also depended on many other animals. So, although the disappearance of the buffalo caused us some inconvenience and some changes in the way we did things, our economy was not broken. We could—and did—continue to live by hunting moose, elk, deer, sheep, and goats, although it required a more extensive and more far-ranging hunt to sustain ourselves.

Nevertheless, the early 1880s saw the moving of many Stoneys onto the Morley Reserve. The ration house was not so necessary to us as it was to many of our brothers, but it was a convenient way to provide for the sick and elderly who could not go out on the hunt. In former days they had been left at base camps under the care of a few stronger band members. Now, as the hunt grew longer and more difficult, every strong member was needed to provide for a family. Besides, the government rations were a treaty right—why not make use of them?

In most cases the move to the reserve seemed quite natural. The land at Morley was both a traditional camp ground and ours by treaty. Therefore it made a convenient base camp. From it we could go out on far-ranging hunting trips. In that early decade there was no move to stop our hunting; indeed, faced with filling so many ration houses on which other tribes had become completely dependent, the government was only too glad to see us provide our own livelihood, to feed only those unable to hunt—and even those only partly because the bands always brought back some provisions for those left behind.

A pattern emerged in which most of our tribe wintered at

Morleyville or other traditional sites. In the summer the bands applied to the Indian agent at the reserve for the annual treaty payments—$25 for each Head Chief, $15 for each Councillor, and $5 for each band member—and then returned to their respective hunting grounds to carry on their traditional lifestyle. The Indian agent's monthly reports show that most of the tribal members hunted every summer and fall, leaving behind only the "old, sick, and crippled" to be cared for by the agent.[12]

Within a few years of the survey the majority of the Stoney people had agreed to use Morley as a base camp while continuing to hunt on traditional grounds along the foothills and into the mountains. However, several families continued to live on the Kootenay Plains, and others lived to the south. During the 1880s, the boundaries of the Morley Reserve were resurveyed to mark them with permanent posts. By then the government had simply decided to survey one reserve for all three bands, despite our requests for the survey of a reserve at Kootenay Plains.

On the Morley Reserve we lived in cabins that were built shortly after treaty. They were small log structures, with roofs of logs and an outer covering of sod. Each had a mud fireplace and most had mud floors. Originally, many lacked window sashes but had parflech (translucent rawhide) stretched over the openings. (Over many decades some improvements were made. Plank and shingle roofs replaced the sod, window frames were added along with plank flooring, and proper plaster replaced the mud used to seal the chinks between the logs. At first the furniture was rough and homemade, but gradually our people made improvements according to our limited means—for example, wood-burning stoves replaced the mud fireplaces for heating and cooking.) Most families used the cabins only in winter and moved into teepees or tents in summer—even when remaining on the reserve.

Although the gathering-in of families and bands to the reserve was the whiteman's first disruption of our social life, this was not apparent at this time because we could continue our hunting way of life.

The fact that some hunting remained for my people was truly an intervention of the Great Spirit, for the attempts to turn us into an agricultural society at Morley proved relatively useless. With the assistance of John McDougall, some of my people at Morley did raise cattle and plant crops. Nevertheless, the majority of my people retained their traditional way of life. As early as 1880, when much of the territory was still in the grip of the famine caused by the extinction of the buffalo, Indian Commissioner Dewdney observed, "These bands of Indians are good hunters and trappers, and spend a good deal of their time in the Rocky Mountains, between the Boundary Line and Jasper House."[13]

Some of the band members, even those who would not or could not accept becoming agriculturists, did earn some income, doing such seasonal work as working as ranch hands or cutting wood for fire logs and mine supports. But the majority continued to hunt, trap, guide, and roam through the foothills. While the Blackfoot and Sarcee came to depend almost entirely upon government rations of beef and flour after the disappearance of the buffalo, my people continued to live by trapping and hunting. We were, according to Hayter Reed, Assistant Indian Commissioner, "good hunters and live in a part of the country where game is still plentiful."[14]

For a period of time, government policy, influenced by lack of funds, adapted to our persistence in our old ways. We were not confined to our reserve, as the Blackfoot were, because the government wanted to save money by not issuing us rations. Reed outlined the de facto policy in 1886:

> The intention of the Department is that all the able bodied members of the band should, as far as possible, be self-supporting, and that rations should, excepting in the event of the hunt being a failure and of the Indians being unable to otherwise obtain their own subsistence, be given only to widows, orphans, and aged or sick Indians, who should be carefully looked after.[15]

During the 1880s the reports of the Indian agents describing our progress frequently commented that we were making a good living from hunting in the foothills. The necessity of the hunt for survival was as important as it had been traditionally because the government and the Church failed to establish a viable agricultural economy at Morleyville. The Superintendent General of Indian Affairs reported in 1885:

> The soil [on the Stoney Reserve] is totally unadapted for raising either grain or root crops. After a trial of several years, it was at length concluded last spring to give up the attempt to cultivate land here and to withdraw the farming instructor.[16]

The following year the superintendent noted that, although a few residents of my tribe cut timber on the reserve, the majority "depend upon hunting fur-bearing animals and game for a subsistence. They are excellent hunters, and this stands them in good stead, as the soil on their reserve is not adapted to agriculture."[17] (The annual report of the Indian Agency Inspector in 1883 also recorded that the river valleys north of Morley along the Red Deer and North Saskatchewan Rivers were the traditional hunting and trapping grounds of Chief Jacob Goodstoney and his Wesley Band members.[18] The

Despite the efforts of the government to confine us to the reserve, we continued to hunt in the mountains.

government might have saved my people—and perhaps even itself—a lot of trouble and misery if it had studied its reserve land policy in light of this comment.)

In short, even the government was coming to realize that there was little hope for an agricultural economy at Morley Reserve. Such an economy had been a clear hope of the whitemen who negotiated Treaty Seven. Several of its provisions suggested this and, on the whole, these were kept. It had promised that families of five persons wishing to settle would be given two cows, with an increase to a maximum of four cows for families of over ten persons. Each Chief was to receive one bull. Agricultural implements and seed were to be provided for every three families wishing to settle and use them. (Each family requesting such agricultural aids was to receive one cow less.) However, as the government report itself suggests, it did not matter what agricultural help was provided; much of this assistance was of little or no value to most Stoney families—only the cattle and garden seed were really useful, considering the local climate and rocky soil conditions.

After 1885, our life became more uneasy and disputed. Our attempts to grow crops failed, and, more important to my proud, nomadic people, both fur-bearing and big game animals began to diminish. The primary cause was the completion of the Canadian Pacific Railway in that year. In its wake the Alberta plains witnessed a rapid influx of European farmers and ranchers. At the same time, coal, copper, timber, and other natural resources along the railway line were being extracted by private entrepreneurs. "Visiting sportsmen" came, too, decimating the animals we depended on for food. Forest fires ravaged the animals' natural habitat. Breeding sanctuaries along the foothills were destroyed by the inroads of "civilization." Other Indian tribes, who had once mainly hunted the buffalo, were now driven to hunt other animals in the mountain foothills of what had always been considered my tribe's territory. The Indian Affairs report for 1886 graphically records the impact that the railroad had upon the Stoneys:

> The hunt of these Indians for fur-bearing animals and game has not been attended with the same success since the railway was built. The latter had the effect of driving the animals to much more distant parts than they were formerly wont to frequent, and to these points, when the Indians have followed them and game in sufficient quantity to sustain life was not found, relief has had at times to be sent by the Department to the hunters, to enable them to return to their reserve.[19]

Under the direction of Agent W. C. de Balinhard, (1885–1887), full rations were distributed to the entire Stoney Tribe, not just the "old and sick" as the government regulations had stipulated. But when this practice came to the attention of the commissioner's office, Assistant Commissioner Hayter Reed mailed a reminder to the agent:

> You must remember that while we have the Indians to care for and do all we can for their comfort and benefit, we have a duty to perform to the public, whose means we are using, and it is for us, while dealing liberally with the Indians, to exercise all the economy possible in the expenditure of the people's money.[20]

By 1888, our hunters were complaining of the difficulty of obtaining enough food for their families. The monthly diary kept by the farm instructor, W. Graham, contained numerous comments on the dejection felt by the hunters. In his 1889 report he noted that "Indians who have returned from the summer hunt say that game is hard to get, in nearly every case they came in hungry."[21] The problem was becoming more urgent now that Rocky Mountain Park (Banff National) had been created two years previously, restricting the area open to hunting.

From 1885 onward, my people's economic plight was compounded, as we shall see in the next chapter, by government measures, caused in part by intense public pressure, to keep us on the reserves and away from our hunting grounds. Incredibly, one reason that was often given for this pressure was that we were especially to blame for the scarcity of wildlife. We were accused of destroying young trees for campfires, of killing young, defenceless animals, and of removing "every duck egg" from the nesting grounds.[22] The cries from the Calgary, Lethbridge, and Fort Macleod newspapers became more vitriolic during the late 1880s and 1890s. They demanded that the Indians be strictly confined to their reserves and that the government revise the game regulations and employ wardens to enforce the law.[23] Surely some government employees must have at least noticed the irony since my people had often spoken against the damage the loss of hunting areas and mineral and other natural resources was doing to the environment. We knew the damage because food was becoming more and more scarce. Nobody, however, listened to our protests.

Other events also made it more difficult for us to support ourselves by hunting. Our traditional territory extended well below what had become the Alberta–Montana border. The Stoneys defended their right to hunt in the United States, claiming that "they had always done so, and would continue to do it, as the United States Indians they met were old friends, who did not object to them visiting and hunting amongst them."[24] But the whitemen's law recognized boundaries different from ours, and as the West became more "civilized," it became more and more difficult to cross their border.

Stoney hunters also made frequent excursions into British Columbia. These trips brought them into conflict with the Kootenays and Shuswaps. The Kootenays resented the invasion of their hunting grounds, and their agent asked the government in 1892 to take

Cassie Abraham at the Kootenay Plains. Her great-grandson, Jim Wildman, resides on the Bighorn Reserve today.

remedial action.[25] In response, the Stoney agent promised that "on the return of Chief Chiniquay's Band from British Columbia, I will endeavor to prevent them from returning to that country to hunt,"[26] but his efforts were to no avail. The authorities finally arranged a meeting between the two tribes at Golden, British Columbia, in the fall of 1893.[27] Chief Chiniquay represented the Stoneys (because it was mostly members of his band who hunted in the headwaters of the Bow River); he was accompanied by John McDougall, P. L. Grasse, and an official from the Indian Commissioner's office.[28] We eventually agreed to accept the Great Divide as the demarcation between our respective hunting grounds.

This agreement left us with a smaller game territory for our use, but our elders had always taught us that we must respect other tribes and that if there were conflicts over hunting territories, they should be settled without the shedding of much blood.

To supplement their diet, the Indian leaders petitioned the government, in May 1892, to grant exclusive fishing rights to the Spray Lakes. This request was rejected. Although the agent was then issued several sets of fish nets, he was instructed to maintain close control over their use:

> You will distribute these [nets] to the best advantage and only when they are prepared to leave for the lake. In that purpose to go North—which probably refers to the North Saskatchewan Valley and the Kootenay Plains, thereby—on any pretext, must not get nets. This may help you conciliate the soreheads.[29]

The wide expanse of territory traditionally travelled by the Stoneys in hunting and camping was gradually being whittled down. There was little game at the Morley Reserve, but the government increased efforts to keep us on it. Yet this pressure, the greater difficulty in finding game, the government and Church's attempts to establish an economy based on agriculture, the prejudiced outcries from the newspapers and the public—none of these deterred us from our attempts to hold to our traditional life pattern. The Indian agents in charge of the Morley Reserve submitted essentially the same report each year:

> The Stonies [sic], of Morley, although much further advanced in civilization, do not take to farming so well. They all leave early in the spring for the mountains, and do not return till

near treaty time, unless the hunting is a failure. They leave scarcely any able-bodied men behind, consequently their crop has to be looked after by the old men and women, who are unable to go out with them.[30]

The official reports would record the increased acreage planted, the larger herds of cattle, the erection of a slaughterhouse, the new school buildings and houses, or the income from cutting timber; but all these were a meaningless gauge to measure "progress" because the same reports always included one compromising statement: "Immediately after the [treaty] payments the Stoneys departed for their hunting grounds,"[31] or "The Stoneys went their old routes, north, south, and west, in the mountains."[32]

It is difficult for the non-Indian to understand this determined effort to cling to our nomadic hunting life. But imagine a deer or a mountain goat who has roamed freely in the forests or mountainous areas. Such an animal would find it almost impossible to adjust overnight to life in a cage. The animal would lose, to a large extent, its former keen perspective, instinct, and sense of direction that had guided him in the wilds. The cage, therefore, would deprive the animal of its natural heritage. Perhaps the animal might reluctantly live a lifestyle that was contrary to the life of freedom that it had enjoyed; as a result, it would become dependent on others. This would not be the wish or dream of the animal, but it had been forced into the cage. Eventually, the animal would give up all hope of ever being free again, and of living its independent life in the forests and mountainous areas.

That is what the small reserves, the ration houses, the welfare have done to some of my people. It is like being locked up in a small cage and given a different kind of food. The environment offers very little, if any, real challenge or opportunity. And yet the government thought that if we were collected onto a small piece of land, we would be independent, progressive, and part of "civilization."

This misconception was borne out by the fact that the majority of our tribe continued to roam the foothills in search of game long after our reserve was surveyed. Even today, hunting, fishing, trapping, gathering, and camping in forest woodlands are an integral part of our cultural values, religious beliefs, and economic base.

Part III
The Long Rocky Trail

The Erosion of Indian Rights, 1885–1895

In the aftermath of the Riel insurrection of 1885 there was a great deal of criticism of the government's Indian policy, or as some critics contended, nonpolicy.

A great outcry arose against all Indian people. This was truly ironical because the majority of contemporary Indian leaders in Canada were opposed to the armed violence. Certainly the outbreak by the Métis and their few allied bands of Plains Cree and Assiniboines was a traumatic shock for the Treaty Seven tribes.

News of the outbreak reached the Stoney Tribe through the moccasin telegraph and the raging rumours that spread about the killing.[1] Even though we had many grievances against the government, we were a peaceful tribe. We had smoked the sacred peace pipe with the Queen's representatives only eight years before. We had trust and faith in the government, and our leaders believed that in time the promises of the treaty would be honoured. It was too early to judge the North West Mounted Police, the missionaries, and the Indian agent; our people would not break that sacred promise regardless of our disappointments. Our leaders reaffirmed their allegiance to the Queen in a telegram to the Indian Commissioner at Regina:

> We the Undersigned Chiefs of the Mountain Stonies desire at this time to say to the Government through you that as heretofore our trust is in the two Great Powers [.] First Almighty God as revealed to us in Christ [.] Second British justice as represented to us by the Canadian Government.
>
> Signed: Jacob Bearspaw
>   Jacob Bigstoney
>   John Cheneka[2]

Despite such peaceful demonstrations by the Treaty Seven tribes, the Canadian public reacted with near hysteria, and further restrictions were placed on the movements of the various tribes in this area. Only a handful of the native population had been involved in the rebellion, yet, when the shooting was over, and the leaders tried, the general public sought revenge and "protection" from all Indians.

Editorials in the Calgary and Fort Macleod newspapers demanded that we "savages" be forced to remain on our reserves. My people were accused of killing range cattle, and we were viewed as a burden upon society and a hindrance to advancing civilization.

One editorial in the *Calgary Herald* callously observed:

> The plain fact is that the Indian knows as well as we do that his position in this country is simply that of a minority in hopeless opposition. They know very well that they can never be anything more than the pariahs of the civilization which has surrounded them, [and] in spite of pow-wows and promises and treaties they are not in the least convinced that they have received anything like a fair equivalent for the land which that civilization has taken from them.[3]

The inferences to be drawn from this passage (and many similar ones) are interesting. My people's requests for additional reserve land had not gone unnoticed, but in the typically condescending and racist attitude of the nineteenth century, the writer considered the imperatives of his "civilization" more urgent than our needs and assumed what little compensation we had received was "fair." There was no recognition that we were not requesting that someone's land be given to us, but that the land that was ours in the first place be recognized as ours. As the newspapers reflected, the white immigrants wanted us "simple and careless children of the prairies"[4] forced onto some large, remote reserve where we would be fed, clothed, and educated, "civilized," and trained as agriculturists by the government and the Church.

The memoirs of a contemporary North West Mounted Police officer give an even more illuminating account of the public's attitudes toward my people. Sir Cecil Denny, who helped build Fort Macleod and was later appointed Indian Agent at Fort Walsh, wrote frankly:

> The white settler coming into the country to raise cattle or farm cared little what became of the poor Indian. If a cow was

killed or a horse stolen, the Indians were to blame. Their land
was looked upon with covetous eyes and they were regarded
as a nuisance and expense. The right of the native red man was
not for a moment considered or acknowledged, though more
from ignorance than actual hard-heartedness. He was an inferior being to the lordly white man and doomed to pass before
advancing civilization.[5]

It must have been very difficult for the government to keep up
with such public pressure and at the same time try to fulfill the
treaty agreements and promises. In an attempt to reconcile these
conflicting demands, the Indian Affairs Branch took a more militant
approach toward "civilizing" my people. The Commissioner's office
examined its organizational structure and discovered that it was
decidedly inadequate for the more remote reserves. (How this decision was arrived at and who was involved in the decision making is
unclear, but there is every indication it was a unilateral decision
made by the great white father in Ottawa.) Simultaneously, the very
government that had created and legislated the treaties began to
reinterpret them: their promises were recognized less and less year
by year by the non-Indian society.

During the early 1880s, the Indian Affairs Branch had administered the Stoney and Sarcee Reserves from its office at Blackfoot
Crossing, about one hundred miles away from Morley. In 1885,
because of the great distance to Gleichen, an agent was stationed at
Sarcee to administer both that reserve and the Stoney Reserve. A
central location would benefit Indian Affairs "both as regards cost of
management, and advancement of the Indians."[6] The agent could
supervise the people in their work, assist them "in their endeavors
to improve their condition," and care for the old and destitute.[7]

On August 1, 1885, the farm instructor at Sarcee Reserve, Major
W. C. de Balinhard, was promoted to Indian agent in charge of the
Sarcee-Stoney Agency. He was instructed to devote "a regular pro-
portion" of his time to the Stoneys.

In giving de Balinhard his instructions, Indian Commissioner
Dewdney was not optimistic about the economic future of our
reserve at Morley. He directed our farm instructor:

It would be well to inaugurate a thorough system for the pros-
ecution of work, both as to the cultivation of Roots, etc., and
stock raising. This latter will I am afraid require to be looked to

in future as the main means of subsistence for these Indians as long as they are satisfied to remain in that Section of country.[8]

In other words, the Indian Affairs Branch, despite its policy of attempting to keep Indians on the reserves, still condoned the Stoneys' hunting to save money on rations. It was beginning to accept the reality that an agricultural economy was impossible for us because of the rocky soil which characterized most of our reserve land. But it now believed we would eventually be converted to a ranching life, something Treaty Seven suggested in its provision of cattle for each family.

Commissioner Dewdney recognized that no "cast iron rules" could be applied to all Indians, but the agents were instructed:

> In case without precedent or instructions how to act, you will be required to use your own judgement in dealing with them which I have no doubt *will always be exercised in the interest of the Government.*[9]

The agents were encouraged to "become more thoroughly acquainted with them, as to their mode of life, character, etc.," but the purpose of that interest was to promote "greater progress" in order that

> your Indians will be the first to develop themselves in matters (such as farming, ranching, education, and personal hygiene) conductive to their advancement in life.[10]

In bureaucratic fashion, all this was to be achieved with as little expenditure as possible. At the same time an agent was assigned to the Sarcee and Stoney Reserves, the services of the clerk at Morley were dispensed with, and the agent was directed to see that "the expenditure [was] kept down as much as possible."[11] The government gave more attention to less "civilized" Blackfoot tribes, relying on the Methodist Church to continue its work of educating, Christianizing, and training the people at Morley. (I often wonder how the government measured "civilizing the Indian" in those days. Was he more civilized when he could speak the English language? When he grew crops? When he stopped feeding his family by not going out hunting in his traditional areas?)

The new combined agent for the Stoneys and Sarcee was stationed on the latter's reserve, but he was to visit Morley once a week. Even this proved to be impractical. The two reserves were thirty miles apart, a hard distance to travel frequently, especially in bad weather. Agent de Balinhard bitterly complained that "I am not only Agent and clerk, but farm instructor to both reserves."[12] Although a farm instructor was stationed at Morley within a few years, all the administrative chores, such as treaty payments, issuing of rations, purchase of seeds and farm equipment, were performed by the Indian agent living at Sarcee. This fact alone reflects the little attention the government paid to our needs on the Stoney Reserve.

After the hysteria following the insurrection of 1885, the Indian Affairs Branch also began to enforce a pass system in an attempt to control the movements of all Indian groups. Any Indian person found off the reserve without a pass was treated as a vagrant and summoned to court. (Many non-Indians were also wandering the land without passes, but they were not considered vagrants!) A treaty Indian was ordered back to his reserve; a non-treaty Indian was asked to decide which band he wanted to settle with. The alternative was jail.

The pass system did not prevent us from continuing to hunt for our livelihood, although it was another pressure on us to remain on the reserve as agriculturists. Indeed, although there was no public writing on the subject, there is much material in the files that suggests Indian Affairs remained quite happy to have as many of my people as possible depend on the hunt rather than on the expensive ration houses. (This contradictory, unspoken policy lasted many years.) Of course, as far as my people were concerned, going off reserve to hunt on unoccupied Crown lands was doubly a treaty right: we had been promised we could continue our traditional way of life, and the land we roamed was part of our traditional territory.

The pass system did work hardship on my people in another way. It was the common practice of tribal members to travel to neighbouring reserves to attend pow-wows, Sun Dances, and other special events. Now the farmer in charge of the rations at Morley was reprimanded for issuing flour and beef to "straggling Indians"—our fellow tribesmen from other reserves. "Such a practice only tends to encourage these Indians to rove from their reserves, where they should be engaged."[13]

The law continued to be tightened. In 1889 a directive ordered that no rations be issued visitors to Morley even though they held passes because "it tends to frustrate our efforts to prevent wandering about. In future, when issuing passes to your Indians, you will inform them that they need not expect rations, while on pass, from other agents."[14] The commissioner's office began to scrutinize carefully all returns from the Agencies to see that agents were complying with directives.

In 1890, "large reductions" were made in the Indian Affairs' budget estimates. All field staff were informed that it had been found necessary "to cut down in every direction."[15] Furthermore, that spring, the issuer of rations at the Sarcee Reserve, J. J. English, resigned his office following a dispute with Agent F. C. Cornish.[16] Apparent irregularities were found in the treaty paylists and in ration sheets, which resulted in the transfer of Agent Cornish to the Manitoba district. (It was the general practice and unwritten policy of the Indian Affairs Branch for years that if an agent or other employee didn't do well on one reserve, he would be transferred to another reserve instead of being fired.)

In an effort to reduce travel expense in the Sarcee Agency, the new acting agent was directed not to visit Morley unless otherwise instructed by the Commissioner's office.[17] There was also an order to cut down on the number of visits by doctors to the two reserves because of the expense. Since the government and the Church had condemned Indian medicine and medicine men, this was a real blow, and the ones who suffered were, again, our people.

These economy measures of 1890, probably prompted by the deteriorating national economic situation, were the beginning of a series of cutbacks that affected us seriously.

In 1891, the government ordered a new food supply program for Treaty Seven tribes "to curtail as much as possible their issue of beef." If rations could not be cut back each week, the directive suggested, then "it might be done every second week, or in any other way" which would save money. In particular, Commissioner Hayter Reed asked the Sarcee agent why the Stoneys received more rations than the Sarcees:

> These Indians certainly should not get nearly as much as the Sarcee, being hunting Indians, in fact not more than half.
>
> Again, the Sarcees are receiving .35 lbs. of flour, and the Stonies .46 lbs., which is greater. Something is wrong here, and you should endeavour to rectify it, and creane [sic] the saving desired.[18]

In looking at the population of the two tribes, the Stoneys were a larger tribe, almost three times more numerous than the Sarcees, and yet we were to receive half as much. When complaints were registered about the cutback in rations among the Stoneys in Treaty Seven, Indian Affairs called the allegations "almost foundationless." The government vaguely attributed the problem to "the machinations of interested parties, who have a direct interest in any increase in expenditure which might be procured through such agitation."[19]

One consequence of the restrictions placed on the issue of rations was a corresponding rise in cattle rustling. Ranchers vehemently protested the killing of range cattle allegedly by marauding groups of Indians. Some cattle associations had for several years permitted the Indian people to retrieve the hides of dead cattle; now they accused them of killing cattle and disturbing stock in the spring, which resulted in cows losing their calves.[20] In support of the ranchers' accusations, the *Calgary Herald* observed that agents permitted the Indians to go hunting in order to keep the ration sheets "clean." The paper argued that since big game was scarce, the Natives must be killing cattle, as evidenced by the tanned hides in the teepees. The goal of raising "self-supporting" reserves was a noble one, but the gerrymandering of ration returns and blue book figures would not affect that end. The *Herald* argued that "hunting" meant "cattle killing," and called upon the government to abolish its program of clean ration books.[21]

To counteract this adverse publicity, the agents were directed to "exert themselves to disprove all contentions that the Indians are kept so short of rations as to be compelled to commit depredations."[22]

Despite this goal of good publicity, when the agents were directed to submit their budget estimates for the year 1894, they were reminded that "only a small sum of money is at the Department's command" for seeding crops. Therefore, "*you should ask for nothing that the Indians can, in any way provide for themselves*, from their own crops, by the sale of cattle, or from their earnings." The fiscal budget could not be exceeded "under any circumstances," and if the requisitions were considered excessive, they would be reduced at head office.[23]

The government was determined to reduce its flour and beef rations. At the same time, it was directing its officers to limit the amount of seed for crops. It was a confusing situation whereby the government was determined to attain contradictory goals while maintaining a good public image.

Understandably these moves to save money by reducing essential services, in defiance of treaty obligations, aroused the ire of the Indian leaders. The loudest criticism concerned the reduction in rations. The buffalo were gone; the crops on the rocky soil failed; the restrictive game regulations, the creation of National Parks, and the influx of Europeans into the area had diminished our hunting territory and made game hard to come by. Therefore, our people asked, where is the promise that the government made when it stated, "I will provide food for you in time of famine" and again, "I will manage your country well"?

During this period there was no cutback at all in one area—the effort to "civilize" my people. Indeed, during the 1890s, increased pressure was placed upon the Indians to adopt the details of the European way of life. The department wanted to get all families off "the assisted list" in order that they would be "self-supporting." It was noted that a few of the women did knitting but such examples should be the "rule and not the exception of the home life." The agent was expected not only to teach but also to inculcate "thoroughness in the performance of domestic duties, such as the sweeping out of corners and under the beds, as well as the centre of the room, the keeping of clean dishes, and the practicing of habits of cleanliness and tidiness." All department employees were to devise "new methods whereby the spare time of their Indians, more especially during the many hours of the winter days spent indoors, shall be profitably occupied." For example, some economies could be affected by the erection of mud ovens to promote bread making. Of course, as usual, special attention was to be given to agriculture and stock raising to ensure that the crops and animals were properly attended.[24]

The Sarcee-Stoney agent was specifically directed to hold special classes during the winter months to teach the people proper agricultural techniques:

> It is highly necessary that Indians learn to handle their working oxen properly: that is, instead of dragging them by a rope attached to the head, to guide and turn them with a whip, a stick or driving lines as a white man does.[25]

As a special incentive, two prizes of two dollars each were to be presented to the "best all-round drivers of their oxen."

The Sarcee-Stoney agent was also ordered to inculcate European

Teachers and children at the Morleyville "orphanage"—school—in 1890. Left to right, *front row*: I. M. Butler, principal; Rev. John McDougall; Mrs. I. M. Butler; *second row*: Becky Beaver, two unidentified children, unidentified teacher, another teacher, a Wesley family child, Sarah Wesley; *third row*: Jake Twoyoungmen, unidentified, Moses Wesley, unidentified, Morley Beaver, four unidentified children; *fourth row*: John Bearspaw, Abraham (?), unidentified, a Wesley family child, Philip Beaucette, Jonas Ear, two unidentified children, Tim Beaver, David Bigstoney; *back row*: Jessie Rider, Mrs. Moses Jimmy John, Libby House, Eliza Hunter, unidentified, Sarah Fox, unidentified, Gussie House, Flora Twoyoungmen. *(Glenbow Archives NA-1677-1)*

busy-ness. In an 1891 directive, the commissioner "regretted that nothing has been done by the Indians in the way of employing their idle hours in the manufacture of ox collars, fork handles and so forth."[26] The government had formulated its Indian policy and it was the agent's responsibility to ensure that the people attained these unrealistic and unchallenging goals set down by the Commissioner's office.

The government was blind to the fact that our people not only had no interest in constructing ox collars, but also that few families had "idle hours" to spare—the hunting of scarce game, the cutting of logs and the building of lodges and cabins, the drying of meat and the tanning of hides were time-consuming tasks. The government was oblivious to the real needs of the family life of the people on the reserve.

Rather, the insistence on even the trappings of the European lifestyle continued. To promote a better image of its work, the department asked its agents to include in their monthly reports:

such matters as the condition of the houses, progress in the manufacturing of agricultural implements, and articles of domestic utility, and the advance made by women in matters of domestic economy and household management. It is in such matters that the influences of civilization most readily make themselves felt.[27]

No consideration was given to preserving any part of the culture, beliefs, heritage, and the values essential to the Indian way of life. It was assumed that the people would aspire to the "superior" level of European civilization. The farm instructor's reports for the reserve were generally optimistic: "the Stonies [sic] are improving in health and are getting the idea that the[y] will have to conform to the white man's way of living."[28] Considerable attention was given to statistics tabulating the increase in the number of acres under cultivation and noting the progress of the cattle herds. The agents were requested to provide "a short, concise report" on such topics as "the attention given by the Indians to the care of their garden and root crops, particularly the weeding and thinning out of turnips."[29] The program entirely disregarded the local rocky ground and was meaningless for my tribe, whose only wish was to be left alone to follow our traditional way of life, hunting and worshipping as our forefathers had done. Every new change the government introduced further alienated my people.

Granted, the government was trying to improve the conditions on the reserves, but at as little cost as possible and with no recognition of, much less respect for, our heritage. No attempt was made to suit goals to specific local needs and conditions. A blanket policy was devised regardless of the differences among reserves. This policy, for example, paid no regard to such questions as: Do we want to grow crops? Can we tolerate foreign-tasting foods? (On the latter point it was reported that the Stoneys "disliked the taste and odor of beef and some of them to this day make the statement that the odor from white people is unpleasant to them because it reminds them of the disagreeable smell of beef and milk."[30] The Indian people were accustomed to living on wild meat and natural root plants and wild berries, yet it was expected that they would automatically accept whatever advice and assistance the government offered to them, without regard for their tastes.)

The government's entire policy was rooted in the nineteenth-century whiteman's assumption that his own civilization was far superior to any other lifestyle. The prevalent attitude toward our culture was clearly demonstrated in the Indian Commissioner's own biased observations and correspondence regarding the Stoneys. For example:

It is reported that the Indians appear to be lazy, too fond of travelling about, still wear the blanket and in fact show less sign of progression than any others visited.[31]

This public (and governmental) view of the people as lazy, ignorant "savages" was all-pervasive. For example, when an "offensive epithet" was apparently applied to the commissioner by an Indian, Assistant Indian Commissioner A. E. Forget reprimanded the agent on the scene for repeating the statement but excused the accuser because "great allowance has to be made for the ignorance of Indians and what would be intolerable if coming from white men, may be passed over in silence when emanating from savages."[32]

In 1893 public attitudes and government goals combined to lead to the first outright, straightforward breaking of the treaty: the

A coat made from a Hudson's Bay blanket. The blankets were traded for furs
when the whiteman first came.

Indian Affairs Branch firmly and specifically committed itself to a policy of restricting the hunting of game. Agents were informed:

> By virtue of section 133 added to the Indian Act, by section 10 of Vic. 53, Chapter 29, the laws respecting game, in force in the Northwest Territories will, on and after the first of January, 1894, be made applicable to the Indians within your agency.[33]

The penalties for breaking the law were to be fully explained to the Indians:

> . . . but this should be done in a manner to secure their sympathy; by reasoning with them patiently, and showing them that the preservation of the game is fully more in their own interests, than in those of the white population.[34]

All regional offices were issued a copy of the new Game Ordinance passed by the North West Territorial Government and the agent was to "carefully preserve" his copy "for reference."[35]

The following spring the Sarcee agent was again reminded:

> to inform your Indians that no Indians are to be allowed to hunt or trap within the limits of the Rocky Mountain Park. The Police have been asked to see that this prohibition is enforced.[36]

The agent was to notify the nearest police detachment of any absentees from the reserve, and he was to patrol the reserve to see that stray cattle from neighbouring ranches were not slaughtered.

My people found these pronouncements from head office unbelievable because they were violations of our treaty rights. Moreover, the simultaneous cutback in rations posed a real threat to our very survival. There was a saying amongst us, voiced by our medicine man: "The day will come when you will starve knocking on the white man's door." Perhaps some of the Indian people thought this prophecy was coming to pass.

To meet Indian needs and to achieve its own economic goals, the government embarked on yet another program of self-support. In the past, local agents had purchased beef for the bands either from neighbouring ranches or from successful Indian cattlemen. Now the government proposed to slaughter cattle it was holding in trust for the tribe and credit the amount of beef to the use of the needy families. To the Indian people this was a negation of another treaty right, and there was a great outcry against the injustice of the government's policy.

In 1894 agents were requested to investigate quietly a rumour of a general Indian uprising in southern Alberta.

> A rumour has been conveyed to the Department that the Southern Indians, those of Treaty No. 7 have, in view of dissatisfaction with the treatment at present accorded them by the Government, decided to send messengers to all the Indians in the Territories, inviting joint action on their part, and to the effect that some twenty-five emissaries had already been sent to the tribes south of the boundary-line, asking their cooperation.[37]

Indian Affairs gave no credence to the report, but, nevertheless, agents were to "keep a close watch upon affairs in your agency, and the movements of your Indians." The arrival of any strange Indians or anything unusual was to be promptly brought to the attention of head office. The Indian people were unquestionably agitated, and although the Commissioner's office didn't believe the various tribes would take any overt action (as indeed they did not), it was sufficiently concerned to increase rations and to make preparations for restricting the movements of any large tribal group.

As so often happened, the government was very sensitive to public opinion and rumours of trouble. It was determined to implement its economic, educational, and social programs. But it had already found that before it could hope to do so, it was necessary to win over the leaders of the Indian bands. The Indian Affairs Branch maintained tight control over all aspects of administration through its agents and the Band Councils. To this end, even the democratic right of the Indians to elect freely their own Chiefs and Councillors was curtailed. Before the government would approve the election of a Chief or Councillor, the agent was to be sure that "the man's character is good, and he is competent to fill the position."[38]

In the Indian tradition, "Chief" was a meaningful, prestigious, and honourable title; it had always been held only by those with unique talents, skills, courage, and wisdom. Now it was denigrated, made fun of, and abused by government officials who wanted to put in "progressive" leaders who agreed with the policy of assimilating the Indian people into European society. The farmer in charge of the

Stoney Reserve was set straight on this matter when the Indian Affairs Branch informed him:

> The policy of the Department is to reduce, rather than increase the number of Chiefs and Head Men, and when vacancies occur they should not be filled unless the Department is compelled by Treaty stipulations to consent to the same being done, as past experience has taught the Department, that the Indians get along much better without Chiefs or Head Men and there is less difficulty in dealing with the Indians when there are no Chiefs or Head Men to raise objections and place obstacles in the way of the Department and its officers.[39]

In the past, the Indian Chiefs had cooperated with the missionaries and the Mounted Police, and after the signing of the treaty they had continued to work closely with the reserve farm instructor and the Indian agent; nevertheless, the government now viewed them as purposely obstructing its program designed to educate and "raise up" my people. The only use it had for them or for our traditional Tribal and Band Councils was to fulfill legal formalities under its supervision and control.

In some ways my people actually cooperated in allowing this to come to pass. Indians did not have a good understanding of European society, and what little we knew about it was that it demonstrated a very selfish and greedy way of life. Therefore, we did not really care to be educated in their strange ways. So out of necessity we had to rely on the advice of the trusted white associates when dealing with the Europeans. The European says something, but he writes it down on paper differently. Later he says, "I didn't say that," and "I wrote it that way and what is written is the truth." This was very strange to us.

Gradually, under the growing domination of the Indian agent, the Tribal Council's main function evolved into that of a rubber-stamp group which merely made an X-mark on documents requiring their signature and ratification. All tribal business and correspondence was conducted through or by the agent. The Indian leaders were often away hunting and, besides, they understood very little of the parliamentary rules of procedure and other legal niceties. They signed legal documents because they thought this was the expected way to do things and the agent told them they should.

For example, when the Canadian Pacific Railway began negotiations with the Indian Affairs Branch in 1889 to compensate the Stoneys for getting a right-of-way through the reserve at Morley, all correspondence with the company was conducted by Indian Affairs officials in Regina and Ottawa. The Canadian Pacific Railway offered $1.00 per acre, but Indian Affairs maintained that $2.50 be paid, since this was the regulation price. After a great deal of argument, a compromise was reached in 1893, and the Canadian Pacific Railway agreed to pay $1.25 per acre.[40] (This was the lowest rate the railroad paid for a right-of-way through any Treaty Seven reserve land.)

The terms of the easement were likely explained to the Stoneys' Tribal Council before it gave its endorsement, but at no time during the four years of negotiations is it recorded that my people were called upon for their views as to what they considered adequate compensation. Indeed, my father used to tell me that he had been told by our elders that when the railway came through the reserve, the Indian agent said that it was something the people would have to accept and live with because it was a government order. Undoubtedly, the agent tried to avoid the point for fear that the people might raise embarrassing questions.

Another area in which the authority of the tribe was gradually controlled was that of complaints against the Indian Affairs Branch. When complaints were registered against an agent or any employee, the Inspector of Agencies would conduct an investigation. In the majority of cases the charges were not proven to Indian Affairs' satisfaction or witnesses declined to give evidence. To prevent undue inconvenience and expense, a new directive was issued in 1892:

> It is now been determined to pay no attention to any demands made by individual Indians into the conduct of an officer of the Department, unless such charges are confirmed by a Resolution of the Indian Council of the Band which considers itself aggrieved, and in every case the memorial and the resolution requesting investigation must be accompanied by a list of the witnesses who are prepared to furnish evidence, and the date must be stated upon which they will be present at the investigation.[41]

It was the agent who was to read the circular to the Council, and, if any investigation was judged too "frivolous or groundless," the cost was to be charged to band funds. Additionally, in many cases the Council was dominated by the Indian agent, and any investigation would likely be held during the summer and fall months when prospective witnesses would be away hunting. The procedure served to streamline the system for redress of grievances, but writing complaints against the agents by the Indians also put a damper on criticism of department officers. Such criticisms may be valid in a democratic country, but the bureaucrats found them otherwise.

This structuring of local administration only served to alienate us further, and we were becoming more and more suspicious. Year by year our suspicions proved to be well founded. By 1895 the situation had deteriorated to its lowest ebb since the Riel insurrection of 1885. We were angered not only by the reduction of the rations during the winter months, but also by the scarcity of game, the new hunting regulations and other instances of treaty breaking, and the pass system and other efforts to tie us to the reservation. Then came the depletion of root crops and food reserves through the 1894 drought. Furthermore, in the same year, the department instituted new regulations to make school attendance compulsory.[42] Any event might spark trouble with feelings running so high.

The calm exterior was suddenly shattered by the murder of Frank Skynner, the ration issuer at the Blackfoot South Camp Reserve. A former North West Mounted Police officer, Skynner was apparently very unpopular—and rightly so. On April 3, 1895 he was shot to death in his home on the reserve by Scraping Hide, who was himself killed two days later as he fled the Mounted Police. Contemporary evidence on the incident is colourful but conflicting. Some newspaper accounts suggested extenuating circumstances: the rumour was that Skynner had refused food to Scraping Hide's dying son. Testimony at the inquest and evidence in the Indian Affairs files, however, suggest that the unfortunate man had, in the words of the Indian agent on the scene, "brooded over [his son's death] . . . till he became partly insane and thought better to get killed than to commit suicide on the grave."[43]

The incident was widely covered in the local papers and, although it did not prove to ignite much more Indian-whiteman trouble in the area, it is indicative of the desperation of my brothers at the time.

Feeling among the Stoneys was perhaps a little less desperate since we were not as dependent on the ration houses as the Blackfoot, but there is no question that we suffered from the pressure to restrict us to the reserve. The apparent choices left us were resisting this growing pressure violently, trying to eke a living hunting in the Morleyville area where game was so scarce, or giving in and attempting agriculture in the reserve's poor soil.

But several Morley families from Jacob's Band decided to accept none of these options. Instead they decided the best solution was to defy government regulations and move back to their traditional hunting grounds on the Kootenay Plains along the banks of the North Saskatchewan River.

The leader of my people who decided to move back north to the Kootenay Plains was Peter Wesley.[44]

Peter Wesley grew up with a group of Stoneys known as the "Buck Lake People," who hunted and camped by a lake of that name in the Kootenay Plains area. According to Agency records consulted by teacher John Laurie, he was frequently registered absent from the Morley Reserve on hunting trips. Although the records indicate that Wesley did supply beef to the ration house, his first love was the traditional Stoney way of life and, in recognition of his attributes and skills as a great hunter, he was given a second Indian name as an adult, a great honour among my people. This name was *Ta-otha*, Moosekiller. (A more accurate translation of the sense of the Indian word might be "the one who provides.")

Wesley settled for awhile at Morley with Jacob's Band under

Peter Wesley, who led about one hundred members of Jacob's Band up to the Kootenay Plains, as he was in the 1930s. The Wesley Band, which had been named the Jacob's Band, later, in 1905, took its name from him. *(Glenbow Archives NA-714-11)*

Chief Jacob Goodstoney, but the increasing number of restrictions imposed upon the Stoneys led to his discontent. The restrictive game laws, the gradual encirclement by white settlers, the government regulations, the confinement to the reserve, and the reduction in rations caused growing resentment. This was finally climaxed by a dispute with government officials.

Today no one is quite sure what this dispute was about. Wesley's grandson, Moses Wesley, says that the event which precipitated his grandfather's moving back to the Kootenay Plains was the result of cattle being killed at Morley by hungry families. As Moses Wesley tells it:

> He left Morley because of the Indian Department cattle problem [rations?]. There was a man named John Abraham who killed his cow to eat. At that time they didn't allow them to kill or sell these cattle, unless you got a permit from the Indian Agent. But this man killed the cow without the Indian Agent, knowing it. They arrested John Abraham and put him in jail for two nights before Peter Wesley got him out when he heard this happened because Peter Wesley was out hunting at the time. The court was on the next day. Peter Wesley told the judge, "why don't you let me know before you arrest my people. I have a right to govern my people here on my reserve, you have nothing to do with it, besides you have taken all my vast land away from me."[45]

Some of researcher John Laurie's information suggests that Peter Wesley was also disappointed with the leadership of Chief Goodstoney.

Whatever the reason for the break, Peter Wesley's decision to return north to his ancestral grounds is not recorded in either the official records or the letterbooks of the Indian agent.

It has been estimated that approximately one hundred members of Jacob's Band (about one-third) joined Wesley in his return to his ancestral territory; some of the prominent families were the Abrahams, the Beavers, the Houses, the Hunters, and the Wildmans, all of whom had long resided on the Kootenay Plains.

Although there is no written record of the event, Peter Wesley's decision has lived on in the tribal memory. John Laurie's informants have recreated what might have been Moosekiller's words to the agent when he left the Morley Reserve:

My children are hungry; they cry in the night. My young men have empty stomachs and there is no meat in my camp. So I and mine go back to the Kootenay Plains. There we shall have meat and the children shall grow fat and happy. Grass grows there for our horses and no snow lies there in the winter.[46]

Peter Wesley's action was not without its counterpart in other tribes. Within the last decade, Chief Robert Smallboy, leader of the Ermineskin Band of Hobbema, took a similar trek into the wilderness because of the many problems on his reserve caused by the Department of Indian Affairs, and because he and his people were denied the opportunity to continue their traditional ways of life. Chief Smallboy has specifically stated some of these problems:

When the white man first negotiated with the Indian long ago, it wasn't intended for the Indian agent to control the Indian. Rather the white agent's position as I understand, was to be an agent or assistant to the Indian people when they needed him. But, what happened is that we have relied on these white agents to control our office. We let them set up our various programs and meetings, and this is why they are slowly taking full control of our lands and making decisions for us. The councillors and chiefs are not able to reach their people any longer, because of the nature of their association with the white government's agents.[47]

Peter Wesley's decision to reject the supervision and culture of the whiteman increased his stature among the Stoneys. When Jonas Goodstoney, son of Chief Jacob Goodstoney, resigned from the chieftainship of Jacob's Band, Moosekiller was elected as his successor and the band was renamed Wesley's Band, the name it keeps today. His courageous action was a joyous and happy occasion for my people; with him they returned to their traditional life of freedom: to hunt, to fish, to roam, and to worship the Great Spirit. The mountains again presented the challenge to any young man who wanted to go to their tops for a vision quest and for fasting.

Many a Moccasin Wore Out, 1898–1910

The long journey of the Wesley Band to the Kootenay Plains area by no means solved all the problems of that group, much less the problems of the majority of the tribe who remained based at the Morley Reserve. From the time of the first survey of the reserve, in 1879, there had been basic problems about land—its insufficiency, its poor quality, and its placement in terms of the treaty promises. The battle to solve these problems, even by following the whiteman's law and methods, began as soon as my people began to feel confined; it continues to this day.

In the first years after the treaty and the reserve survey, the government did not greatly interfere with our traditional way of life. Some tribal members did settle around the Morleyville mission and attempt to take up agriculture. But most continued a nomadic, hunting life. Our hunting grounds were not limited by the arbitrary limits of the reserve; there was no recognizable problem over land nor a need for a larger reserve territory because few restrictions were placed on our movements outside the reserve boundaries. The Stoneys thought that the government was recognizing our hunting rights along the foothills in the way they had been understood by the people at Treaty Seven.

But, as we have seen, the seeds of discontent and injustice had been sown at the making of Treaty Seven and during the original survey. These were not only the misunderstanding as to what "not interfering with our traditional way of life" would mean, but also the confusion over the location of our reserve land, how many reserves there would be, and who would choose the location. When, as described in Chapter Five, the whiteman began to take over our vast traditional hunting grounds, when much of the game was driven away, when the government began to enforce policies that held us to the reserve and restricted our hunting rights, when it was discovered that the Morley Reserve was both poorly suited to agriculture and offered little game, when the government cut back on the rations it had promised us in time of need, then the seeds of inequity flowered and the problem of land became very serious indeed. It was not only a question of principle; it was a question of whether we had the wherewithal to survive.

As early as 1889—five years before Peter Wesley led his band to the Kootenay Plains—the Tribal Council at Morleyville petitioned the Indian Affairs Branch to enlarge the reserve. A committee comprised of the three Stoney Chiefs, Reverend John McDougall, and E. J. Bangs (acting agent, 1897–1900) was formed to press for an extension to the existing reserve on the north side of the Bow River.[1] In support of its claim the committee explained that: (a) the residents on the north side of the Bow River had a smaller area of land in proportion to those living on the south side; (b) the reserve was not heavily timbered; (c) additional pasturage was required if the band was to establish a viable ranching industry; (d) the tract requested was small and of such poor quality it would not likely be developed by anyone else; and (e) the enlarged reserve would be clearly defined by natural boundaries (i.e., the mountains, the Ghost River, Stoney Creek, and the Kananaskis River).[2]

The immediate reaction from the Indian Affairs Branch was to turn down the request. The Commission pointed out that the bands had received their full land entitlement as outlined in the treaty, and besides, the land applied for was of no better quality than their present reserve. As an alternative, however, Commissioner A. E. Forget was willing to extend the western boundary of the reserve to the base of the mountains and south to the Kananaskis River.[3]

After sending his reply, the Commissioner was visited by John McDougall, as chairman of the committee. The missionary explained that the only realistic means of self-support on the reserve was ranching and not agriculture. More land was required if the bands' herds were to be enlarged. The per capita area of land fixed by treaty, he said, was ample for farming, but it was not sufficient for ranching, particularly because the reserve contained little of the hay and grasslands needed to sustain a large number of horses or cattle.

Thereupon Commissioner Forget approved the original proposal

Typical dress of Stoney women at the turn of the nineteenth century.

as he was now convinced that the Stoney claim was "reasonable and well grounded."[4] The proposed new area was estimated to be fifty-five square miles.

But the Indian Affairs Branch could not grant or even lease land to a band on its own recognizance. If it decided that a request for an addition to a reserve was reasonable, the Superintendent General of Indian Affairs had to submit a memorandum to the government, through the Department of the Interior, which made the final decision.

In this case, upon receiving the Indian Commissioner's application, the Department of the Interior conducted a title search of the tract requested and discovered that it was included in a timber berth and in a grazing lease. The lessee was in arrears for rent and if he did not pay, the lease could be cancelled, but until such time however, the land was not available to the Indian Affairs Branch.[5]

We waited.

The question of granting additional land to us was again raised in 1901. By now the Indian Commissioner was David Laird, the man who had represented the Dominion Government and Her Majesty, the Queen of England in concluding Treaty Seven. He recommended that the fifty-five-square-mile tract be reserved for the tribe if the timber berth and grazing lease were not still in force. His argument was the same one McDougall had used two years before: the present reserve land was admittedly of little use for agriculture, but before any cattle industry could achieve a firm basis, more hay lands were necessary to augment the existing fields.[6] The tract requested also contained prime timber, which could be sold to augment stock raising.

The request was referred to the Chief Surveyor of Indian Reserves, A. W. Ponton, who pointed out that on the basis of the 1900 census count, the Stoney Tribe at Morley was entitled to an additional sixteen square miles of land, but no more if the quantity allowed by treaty was not to be exceeded. (The increase in population was attributed to families from other bands migrating to Morley because of its proximity to the hunting grounds in the mountains.) The Chief Surveyor also suggested that if the tract applied for was not covered by timber and grazing leases, a five-year lease on it might be issued to the Stoneys. This short-term measure, he said, would give the Indian Affairs Branch sufficient time to decide whether to apply for a permanent addition to the reserve.[7] (The use of title searches and short-term land leases were standard delaying tactics in dealing with Indian land claims at the time. The bureaucrats in the Department of the Interior found them a useful way of denying requests without actually saying "no.")

But Commissioner Laird's representation to the Department of the Interior had been very strong. So Chief Surveyor Ponton submitted another report arguing that the Stoneys did not require additional land. He based his opinion on conversations held with the Stoney farm instructor, H. E. Sibbald, who had formerly been a stock foreman for G. K. Leeson, a prominent and wealthy Calgary businessman. There is every indication that Sibbald's observations were clouded by personal sympathies because an enlargement of the reserve would have precluded use of the grazing meadows for neighbouring ranchers. (In later years, a cattlemen's association did complain that the Indians were tying up valuable grazing lands.)

Surveyor Ponton opposed any extension of land until the needs of the bands were outlined in more detail. He added that if they were granted, "any lands reserved should be for the benefit of the Department, for as long as required, and in which the Indians would have no title, as it is possible and, I think, even probably, *that valuable coal seams and other minerals* [sic] *veins will be found inside the proposed extension* [italics added]."[8]

A United States president once described an Indian reservation as a land set aside for Indian people, surrounded by land thieves. To many of my people this description comes close to the truth. In view of this statement, it is significant that Surveyor Ponton was instructed to determine "the extent and value of the grazing lands and timber" both on the reserve and in the proposed extension.[9] The insistence in his own statement that the Department should retain title and mineral rights to the land, even if the Stoneys were given the use of it, is equally interesting. It is typical of the attitude that the Indians, who once owned all these lands, including their minerals and natural resources, were now intruders asking for someone else's land and someone else's coal.

The 1901 request for an addition to the Morley Reserve was stalemated when the Department of the Interior conducted another title search and replied that the land was still reserved.[10] But the battle for more land continued, led partly by Indian Commissioner Laird, who lauded any proposal which would create an incentive for my people rather than "pamper" us by maintaining ration houses. Although a large number of residents from Morleyville continued to migrate to the traditional camp grounds along the banks of the Red Deer and North Saskatchewan Rivers each summer and fall to hunt, this, he supposed, was a passing way of life. Ranching and lumbering were the only alternatives he saw.

Despite the successful return of Peter Wesley and his band to a free, hunting life, Commissioner Laird was not alone in his estimate that the days of our traditional life were over. For example, in 1901, Chief Surveyor S. Bray, in a memorandum to the Indian Affairs Branch, noted:

> The Stoney Indians have in the past chiefly supported themselves by hunting; but now that the B.C. Legislature has forbidden them to hunt across the Rocky Mountains, and Banff National Park has been extended, and strict game laws have been passed in the Territories, the Indians are naturally anxious about the future.[11]

Most Indian Affairs officials at the time seem to have made the same assumptions and concluded that we needed to be helped to a new means of livelihood. The differences seem to have been mainly whether they saw the problem as one of justice or one of charity (or departmental self-interest). Some department officials, such as Commissioner Laird, believed that we were entitled to additional land to fulfill the intent, if not the precise terms, of the treaty. Others, such as Surveyor Ponton, disagreed with this interpretation, but they did concede that something must be done for my people to enable them to become "self-supporting" through ranching and manufacturing timber products (but not by farming *or* hunting).

Whatever the various officials' motives, contemporary Indian Affairs files contain voluminous correspondence which reflects their attempts to find suitable areas, free from settlers, for the Stoney reserves. Innumerable land title searches were conducted to discover what areas might be made available to the tribe. In the majority of cases, the surrounding territory was already under grazing leases, reserved as a timber berth, owned by the Hudson's Bay Company, or set aside as a school section. Each alternative area suggested by the Indian Affairs Branch was turned down by the Department of the Interior. A substantial area was lost when Rocky Mountain Park (Banff) was enlarged in 1902.

Indian Affairs' efforts finally seemed to bear fruit in 1904, when application was made to transfer several sections northeast of the reserve (Twp. 26, Range 7, West of the 5th Med.) to the Stoney Tribe. Upon closer inspection, the soil was discovered to be of poor quality while the adjoining grazing areas were already under lease. Nevertheless, a ten-and-one-half-square-mile section was reserved in 1905 under a five-year lease to provide timber for the band. (The lease was renewed every five years until 1920, when the Regional Inspector reported that the area was not being used by the Indians and that it included grazing land which might be opened to returned soldiers.[12] Stoney Agent E. H. Yeomans confirmed that the tract was no longer needed by the band.[13] I have often wondered

A group of Stoneys at Banff in 1908. Left to right, James Swampy, Hector Crawler, Jonas Twoyoungmen, John Bearspaw, Peter Wesley, Amos Bigstoney, John Mark (or John Ear). *(Glenbow Archives NA-1263-13)*

how someone who was supposed to be helping us and assisting in acquiring more land could have held such a view. Nevertheless, the result was that the land set aside in 1905 under temporary leases reverted back to the Crown on March 31, 1922.)

Apparently after 1905 no further action was taken to extend the reserve at Morley until 1914.

The history of the Kootenay Plains area was a very different story.[14] The negotiations discussed above had not involved those of my people living there. They had left Morley in 1894 because the quality of life on the reserve was so poor and, furthermore, because they believed the Commissioner had promised that band land on the Kootenay Plains during the Treaty Seven gathering. It is unlikely that Peter Wesley's group would have returned to the Morley Reserve even if the Indian Affairs Branch had made substantial improvements there because their first love was the great outdoors and the pursuit of the Stoney traditional way of life.

For some time they lived happily, sustaining themselves on these traditional hunting grounds, where the game was plentiful, where the grassy slopes were open in winter, and where there were only itinerant white people.

But they knew they were able to live there only because of the tacit consent of the government, which took no steps to force them back to the Morley Reserve, and they never forgot that the tribe had been promised land in the area at Treaty Seven. In the spring of 1909 Moses House, on behalf of ninety-nine Wesley Band members and supported by Reverend John McDougall, petitioned the Indian Affairs Branch for a reserve in the Kootenay Plains, near the North Saskatchewan River.

Moses had heard of the Promised Land, and the man who had promised land at Kootenay Plains was the Indian Commissioner David Laird, who had signed Treaty Seven over thirty years before. But Ottawa's response was negative. It replied that since the tribe had already received the land due to them under the treaty, if a reserve were to be set aside on the North Saskatchewan, an equivalent area would have to be surrendered from the Morley Reserve. "The Department is adverse to making these continuous changes. However, I presume, if the change is very much desired, it can be carried out on the above lines."[15]

The current Stoney agent, T. J. Fleetham, was asked to enquire if all the families residing in the section that would have to be surrendered would give their consent to the proposed exchange.[16] My people never liked the word "surrender." Some say it means giving away your land; others say it's giving up your land and your rights and your game and all that you have. Simply, it means giving up everything forever. This was not what any of us wanted to do. On the contrary, we were trying to get additional land, not to give it away.

In response to being asked to suggest the surrender of land for an exchange, Agent Fleetham replied that "there would be great difficulties in making any arrangements with the Indians of the Bearspaw and Chiniquay Bands to give up their lands for such a purpose." The land north of the Bow River was rocky but contained good timber while the area south of the Bow River held excellent hay land. At this time, the agent explained, Moses House and the other members of the Wesley Band were in the north hunting, so he proposed that he discuss the situation with them when they returned to Morley.[17] Nothing more seems to have been heard about a land exchange.

A few weeks after the correspondence with Agent Fleetham, letters were sent to Ottawa supporting a reserve in the Kootenay Plains by two tribe leaders: John Abraham, a leading Councillor, and Chief Jonas Bigstoney, former head of what was now the Wesley Band, whose father had signed Treaty Seven. In his letter, dated May 31, 1909, John Abraham described the inadequacy of the Morley Reserve—the scarcity of firewood, the poor road conditions, the hay lands insufficient for cattle, the short growing season, and the restrictions barring the people from the best hunting grounds. He then went on to describe his personal attachment to the Kootenay Plains and his desire to live in the land of his ancestors. His father, he explained, had lived on the Kootenay Plains before the signing of the treaty because it was the best location for growing vegetables and hunting game. John Abraham continued:

> He went up in the mountains to what is now known by the name of Kootenay Plains on the Saskatchewan River and there settled, growing vegetables with success. This land is inside of one range of mountains—outside of the extended National Park Line—*and over the summit* [underlined by a departmental official]. Therefore the climate is such that will produce vegetables and roots . . . *Later on my father told the commissioner and Rev. John McDougall that he was taking treaty for that land at the head of the Saskatchewan in the Mountains* [italics mine]. This was before the surveying and granting of

what is now known as Morley Stoney Reserve. The year after Treaty No. 7 was made [,] my father died and his last living request was that I settle down on the land he had taken in the Mountains. I have gone there and stayed periodically, but owing to some of my children being in the Morley School [I] could not stay altogether; but now as the above school is disbanded, I ask you in all fairness to allow me to carry out the wish of my dead parent.[18]

John Abraham's clear statement was that his father had claimed the Kootenay Plains at Treaty Seven negotiations. Chief Jonas Bigstoney, in his letter of the same date as Abraham's, further elaborated our people's understanding of the treaty:

It was not on account of this land [at Morley] that they took treaty in 77 at Blackfoot Crossing but for the lands which our fathers held upon the North Branch of the Saskatchewan in the Mountains. One of our Chiefs only [,] John Chiniquay [,] took treaty for this land, as Revd. McDougall knows and this man is now dead.[19]

But my people's explanation of their understanding of the land promised by the treaty went for nothing. The Indian Affairs Branch

John Abraham in 1904 *(Glenbow Archives NA-1263-6)*

rejected the request on the grounds the treaty had been concluded more than thirty years before and it clearly stated that the Stoney reserve "shall be in the vicinity of Morleyville." The officials argued that neither of the treaty commissioners, David Laird nor Colonel Macleod, had mentioned a Stoney claim to land in the north. Moreover, the area now requested "is within the bounds of Treaty Six" and by signing Treaty Seven the three Stoney Chiefs had relinquished all "rights, titles, and privileges to all other lands in the North West Territories." Therefore, the Secretary of the Department concluded that there was "no just ground of complaint against the treaty commissioners or the Indian Department."[20]

The problems described in Chapters Three and Four about the signing of the treaty and surveying of the reserves—the error in having the Stoneys sign Treaty Seven, which the Order-in-Council had specified was for the tribes living south of the Red Deer River; the oversight in omitting the Kootenay Plains area from any treaty territory until 1899 and Treaty Eight (which my people were not asked to sign); the misunderstanding as to the verbal promises of the commissioners concerning the location of each band's land; the actions of John McDougall, who was apparently working to serve his mission at Morleyville while he served as translator and adviser during the negotiations and survey—all were now climaxing in the denial of any right to our traditional land. Because of the government's misunderstanding of my people, to this day the Bighorn–Kootenay Plains band owns no legal reserve land in the Kootenay Plains area.

Indian Affairs had even more arguments against the establishment of a reserve on the Kootenay Plains than the exact wording of the treaty. Following a second letter from John Abraham, a reply was sent:

> This Department is apparently unable to take any action to secure for you the land you desire as you say it is situated on the other side of the summit of the [Rocky] Mountains; it would therefore probably be under the jurisdiction of the Province of British Columbia.[21]

(In actual fact, the "summit" of the mountains mentioned in Abraham's letters referred to the Bighorn Range, in Alberta, which partly encircles the Kootenay Plains.) John Abraham was informed, however, that the government was attempting to obtain additional land for the Stoneys near the Morley Reserve even though tribal land claims elsewhere could not be accepted.

The two letters from Morley, along with the Department's reply, were forwarded to Indian Commissioner David Laird for his comments. Laird replied that "the Commissioners at Treaty Seven had not heard of any request for land at the headwaters of the North Saskatchewan River."[22] (Given Laird's other, more sympathetic reactions during his career, I wonder what would have happened if he had been able to speak to the Stoneys in their own language. I am sure that he would have had a better understanding that some of my people at the treaty came from the Bighorn-Kootenay Plains, and that they had requested land in their traditional hunting grounds to be set aside as a reserve. But Laird did not speak Stoney and my people did not speak English. An interpreter had to be used, and our chief interpreter had been John McDougall. With his interest in settling us on land in the Morleyville area, I wonder if he ever interpreted my people's request for land in the Bighorn-Kootenay Plains.)

In his comment on the letters from John Abraham and Chief Jonas Bigstoney, Laird further stated that he had noted, in reading a report of Surveyor John C. Nelson, dated December 28, 1882, "apparently some Stoneys were not satisfied with the Morley Reserve when it was surveyed in 1879." Some tribal spokesmen had asked Nelson to survey a reserve for them on the Red Deer River but no mention was made of the North Saskatchewan district.[23]

Furthermore, Commissioner Laird pointed out, if the requested area was "over the summit," as described in John Abraham's letter, and over one hundred miles from the Indian Agency at Morley, it would be impossible to administer the new reserve effectively.[24] (In fact my people on the Kootenay Plains were making a good living without government rations—about all the government was providing at that time. Surely it would not have made any difference if they were a hundred miles away from the agent and the ration house. It was only another excuse.)

But although Commissioner Laird rejected the Stoneys' claim to the Kootenay Plains area, he did agree that the complaints of our forefathers were justified: "I am decidedly of [the] opinion that they have a strong claim to more and better land than they now hold."[25]

Commissioner Laird supported his opinion on the basis that (1) the Stoney population had increased markedly since the treaty and based on the 1908 census, was eligible to receive another 12,160 acres (nineteen square miles); (2) the quality of land at Morley was "so very inferior for agriculture and grazing purposes, that it is impossible for these Indians to support themselves unless they are allowed a much larger acreage than the treaty provided for." The band should be given good grazing land in order that they "may have a fair opportunity of becoming self-supporting." If no land was available near Morley, he suggested that perhaps "unoccupied lands on the upper waters of the Red Deer or Clearwater Rivers" might be considered.[26]

In light of Commissioner Laird's strong endorsement, the Indian Affairs Branch asked the Department of the Interior to grant us "an additional area of not less than 19 square miles of agricultural land, or at least good grazing land, or an entire township."[27]

The Department of the Interior replied that the lands adjacent to the Red Deer and Clearwater Rivers were not available because they were within the limits of the Rocky Mountain Park; instead, a small tract south of Morley might be considered.[28] This proposed area plus the sections set aside under lease in 1905 were to constitute part of our permanent land allotment and a formal application for us made to the Department of the Interior.[29]

It is interesting to note that the government continued to insist on looking for agricultural or grazing land for my people, although we were requesting lands in our traditional hunting area. There were good hunting areas available along the foothills but the government refused to consider these alternatives, although the treaty had never stated that we would all have to become agriculturists or ranchers.

Ironically, it was the government itself that next suggested that the new lands to be granted my people might be in the Kootenay Plains. This came about because the Indian Affairs Branch, in its efforts to locate a sufficiently large tract for us, kept running into the problem that so much of the land was already under lease or reserved by other departments. After the discovery that the lands adjacent to the Red Deer and Clearwater Rivers were not available, the Chief Surveyor in Ottawa suggested that the Kootenay Plains should be considered as a possible alternative site.[30]

Stoney Indian Agent Fleetham replied to this suggestion that the Indian people had indeed told him that grain crops and vegetables could be grown there, but he believed that the Stoneys wanted it "merely for hunting purposes." In addition, he contended that it would be difficult to distribute rations there, although the residents claimed that they could live without government assistance.

Reluctantly, however, he did conclude that "with the land on Kootenay Plains, and the land south of the reserve the *conditions of the treaty* could be fulfilled [italics added]."[31]

It is interesting to note that missionary John McDougall not only supported the request for the Kootenay Plains land but at this time did so on the basis that it was due us in the spirit of the treaty. On March 31, 1910, he wrote that the Kootenay Plains were "the original home country of these people and they have always clung to it . . . [I]*t was by force of circumstances over which these men had not control that They were given [a] Reserve near Morley* [italics added]."[32]

Why this change of attitude on McDougall's part? It is impossible to say. Perhaps he had grown wiser after many years of attempting to establish an agricultural base in the unsuitable land at Morley. Or perhaps he had come to realize that the Bighorn residents had not been fully represented at the treaty making and during the first survey and that he had not interpreted their wishes clearly.

Whatever his reasons, they are not very important, for the government was not really listening to him anymore. At first the Europeans had relied upon him for information when it came to decision making about the location of the reserve and other policy matters related to the Stoney Tribe. But after Treaty Seven was concluded and the survey made, John McDougall was not as influential with the government or the Indian Affairs Branch as he had been with the treaty commissioners.

But although John McDougall no longer had much influence on the government, others did, and the Indian Affairs Branch was apparently really eager to settle the problem of the Bighorn Stoneys. As a result, in April 1910, Ottawa directed the local Indian agent "to ascertain as accurately as possible the locality and extent of land which it is desired should be obtained for the Wesley Band on the Kootenay Plains at the headwaters of the Saskatchewan."[33] The Indian Affairs Branch was prepared to make the necessary application to the Department of the Interior once the land's precise location was known and a legal description was shown on a map.

Agent Fleetham was unable to describe the area except in general terms because he had never visited the area. But he suggested that D. B. Dowling and other members of the Geological Survey Branch might provide the information required since they had been in the area on several occasions.[34] Dowling thereupon provided a detailed "plan showing Kootenay Plains" which noted all cabins in the valley built by white travellers and by the Stoneys on the Kootenay Plains. A few Stoney families apparently had "small gardens though these do not amount to much" and they were raising several head of cattle. The only other improvements were a horse ranch managed by Tom Wilson, a white trader from Banff, and a house belonging to another white rancher (unnamed) below the mouth of the Siffleur River.[35]

Now that Indian Affairs knew where the proposed reserve was located, it renewed its efforts to obtain the land for the Bighorn Stoneys.[36]

In response to the Indian Affairs Branch's request to set aside a reserve in the Kootenay Plains, the Department of the Interior enquired whether the tribe had not received its reserve as described in the treaty.[37] But Indian Affairs reiterated its position that we were entitled to a larger reserve, particularly agricultural land, as recommended in David Laird's comprehensive letter of the previous year, and suggested that the Kootenay Plains might be made a permanent addition to our reserve in lieu of the area set aside under lease in 1905.[38] A map enclosed by J. D. McLean, Secretary of the Indian Affairs Branch, recommended that the 23,680 acres in the Kootenay Plains be applied for in lieu of the 6,702 acres leased on the northeast corner of the Morley Reserve. In order to arrive at a speedy decision, he urged the Superintendent General of Indian Affairs to meet personally with the Minister of the Interior.[39]

At such a meeting, in Winnipeg, the Minister of the Interior "signified his willingness to consent to the setting apart of such additional lands as may properly be reserved for these Indians."[40]

The Wesley Band appeared to have won its claim at last.

If we had indeed won, if the decision to make a permanent reserve at the Kootenay Plains had been carried out at that time, I would not be writing this book in this manner. The treaty promises regarding reserve land would have been fulfilled and there would be no need for me to try to point out in critical terms the way my people have been treated.

But before the final terms for setting up the reserve were drawn, before the area was surveyed, the political climate changed in Ottawa, leading to the reversal of the Minister's decision. It was like a photo finish in a race. It seemed that our horse finished first, but the proving photo showed that the government beat us to the line. Therefore, we lost the race: once again, we lost the land to the Ottawa bureaucrats and politicians.

This is how the race was lost.

Instructions were given to the Land Patents Branch to start a title search on the three tracts applied for by the Indian Affairs Branch once again. In March 1911, the Lands Branch replied, recommending that several of the sections near Morley be protected by annexing them to the Rocky Mountain Forest Reserve. Another tract was already reserved for reservoir purposes by the Irrigation Branch. As for the Kootenay Plains, it was within the Rocky Mountain Forest Reserve and remained "unsurveyed and undisposed of, excepting the land is Timber Berth 1219 . . . [and lands] under lease for coal mining purposes."[41]

After examining the reports of its field staff, the Department of the Interior concluded that none of the land applied for was fit for agricultural development.[42] It therefore enquired whether the Indian Affairs Branch was indirectly asking it to imply (as my people interpret now):"We have no land available for the Stoney Indians. Do you still want to press their application?"

The Indian Affairs Branch replied that the area south of the reserve and the Kootenay Plains were required for grazing land and it asked that "immediate attention" be given to its proposal.[43] Meanwhile, the Wesley Band had again petitioned the government for a reserve in the Kootenay Plains.[44]

In June 1911, J. K. McLean, District Land Surveyor, was ordered by the Indian Affairs Branch to proceed to the Kootenay Plains. But when the Indian Affairs Branch requested a blueprint of the survey to Timber Berth 1219 from the Department of the Interior, the latter replied that it must be notified before any further steps were taken.[45] And a telegram was sent to Surveyor McLean to postpone plans to survey the Kootenay Plains.

During the summer of 1911, the Department of the Interior was reorganized. New administrative branches were created, and others were elevated in status. During the course of establishing new policy guidelines, doubts were raised by some of the new governmental bodies as to the advisability of granting a reserve in the Kootenay Plains. Again my people were left landless in our ancestral homeland.

Truly the trek was a long, rocky trail. Many a moccasin wore out. But my people put on new moccasins and continued the trek to rediscover and retain the life we had once known and loved. Everything we had owned was gone, and our lingering hope in the midst of government red tape, conflicting and contradicting government Indian policy, and false accusations from the newspapers was

Samson Beaver and Lily Beaver in 1909 at the Kootenay Plains.

that the Indian braves' spirit within us was still alive—that spirit which had once known freedom like the winds on this beautiful land.

The Immigrant Society Closes In, 1910–1945

Those members of the Wesley Band living on the Kootenay Plains were disappointed by the sudden failure to obtain land there, especially after we had been so close to winning it in 1910-11. But we did not give up: in the whiteman's eyes we were squatters, but in our own way of thinking we were on our own land, living there under the rights guaranteed us by Treaty Seven in 1877. So, often in the face of threatened eviction, we continued our battle to get the government to honour its promises for the next several decades.

Before we can examine the story of these decades, it is necessary to backtrack a bit to examine my people's relations with one of the government agencies that had been instrumental in defeating their request in 1911 and was to become an even stronger opposing force in the next few years.

The identity of this agency was particularly ironic; it was the Forestry Branch of the federal Department of the Interior—a body charged with protecting the natural environment.

The creation of this branch and of protected areas such as the national parks was the outgrowth of the conservation movement which swept Canada and the United States in the first decade of the twentieth century, winning many influential converts.

This movement should have been a great help and joy to my people. We have always been conservationists regarding the earth, wildlife, and plant life. Ever since the arrival of the Europeans in the New World, my people had been trying to express conservation ideals to that society. Our ideals were—and still are—retaining and preserving wildlife and natural beauty and protecting the natural environment, instead of polluting and destroying our Mother Earth. (It was only after the coming of the whiteman that some of the Great Island's original inhabitants, some animals, birds, and fish, were placed in danger of being eliminated from the face of the earth forever. Animals such as the seal, polar bear, the arctic fox, the eagle, and the whooping crane are now near extinction. Even our fellow tribesmen, the Beothuk tribe of Newfoundland, have been slaughtered and become extinct because of the greed and self-interest of the whiteman.)

The philosophy of the Stoney Tribe is to live in harmony with nature and in accordance with the Great Spirit, respecting all things He has created. If you destroy nature or the environment, you are ultimately destroying yourself. If you protect and preserve nature and the environment, you are protecting yourself.

Therefore, with the growth of the conservation movement, my people might have felt that at last we were getting our message across. Surely this movement would help preserve what little we had left that was natural and beautiful. Perhaps it was not too late!

But the conservationist movement and the hopes of its non-Indian supporters were very different from what my people had envisioned. Although legislation was passed to preserve certain areas for conservationist purposes, other government departments continued their mass destruction of the beautiful forests, the open prairies, and the mountainous areas of this continent. And the movement itself was to prevent us from going to our ceremonial and sacred places, which all ended up in a park or another restricted area. It was later to spoil the sacred mountains by creating attractions for the collection of tourist dollars.

The problem was that the conservationist movement emerged from a money-oriented society which never learned our ways, our values, our traditions. The sacred waters, the hot springs that we used for healing and cleansing, were to become tourist resorts; our sacred mountains were to become ski areas and parks where we no longer have the right to pursue our religious practice. The pipestones that we got from the mountains and the natural earth paints that we used in our religious ceremonies and for other special occasions were bulldozed over and concrete now covers them.

On June 8, 1911, the Dominion Forest Reserves and Parks Acts was passed, setting aside forest reserves and national parks for the protection of timber stands, the conservation of minerals, and the safeguarding of water resources. A few months before, the bureaucratic machinery to administer these goals had been set up. In 1910, the Rocky Mountain Forest Reserve, encompassing the entire eastern slope of Alberta, was established to centralize the federal government's water, timber, mineral, and wildlife management programs.

After its reorganization in 1911, the Department of the Interior was comprised of many branches (such as Indian Affairs, Forestry, Irrigation, and Dominion Lands Branches), which occasionally resulted in a great deal of interdepartmental feuding. The Forestry Branch, which had the responsibility of managing the Rocky Mountain Forest Reserve, was looking for good hay or grazing lands where it could position its rangers to conduct patrols and forest management. One area it decided it wanted was the Kootenay Plains, because of its central location within the Forest Reserve. As a result, the Ministry of the Interior now had two branches—Indian Affairs and Forestry—vying for the Kootenay Plains.

In a lengthy report to his director in July 1911, Chief Forest Ranger Albert Helmer strongly urged that the grazing lands at Kootenay Plains be reserved for the Forestry Branch. The boundaries of Banff National Park had recently been reduced and he feared that game previously protected by park authorities might be "destroyed" by the Stoneys. He recommended that a closed season be declared on all big game in the Forest Reserve and that these "animals should not be allowed to be destroyed even by the Indians." [1]

As a result, the Department of the Interior notified Indian Affairs Branch that:

> as it might make the enforcement of the Game Laws very difficult, it is not considered advisable to permit the Indians to locate so far within the boundaries of the Rocky Mountain Forest Reserve, in which the [Kootenay Plains] lands are included. [2]

The many years of effort to have the Kootenay Plains reserved for my people were simply swept aside without any investigation into the damaging accusations laid against us. Furthermore, the Forestry Branch started exerting every effort to remove my people from the Plains, where the Indian Affairs Branch had more or less ignored them for more than fifteen years after their return to the land of their fathers.

In such efforts at removal, the Forestry Branch was supported by the conservation group who protested against my people being permitted to roam the mountains. Their cries of outrage were supported by the influential Banff newspaper, *The Crag and Canyon*, which remarked:

> The Indians are now clamoring for more money and other privileges, among the latter was a lease of . . . the [Kootenay Plains] Prairies on the North fork of the Saskatchewan River, a little over 165 miles northwest of the [Stoney] Indian Reservation, and trailing through the eastern and northwestern boundaries of the Park, a paradise for large and small game . . . it is only a blind to allow them free passage to and fro, with all the attributing country, between the Reserve and these supposed grazing grounds. Good-by [sic] to the game. In two years there would not be a hoof left . . . at one stroke of the pen, a very large portion of this protected area is going to be thrown open to a race of people, who do not consider the tomorrow. Hundreds of square miles of the finest breeding ground of *wild game would be desolated with the slaughter of the Indian*, and all the game guardians in Alberta could not prevent it, if the Indians are allowed free access to the trails of the eastern and northern boundaries, inside and out of the Rocky Mountain Park [italics added].[3]

The fact that the above extract was in the Indian Affairs' files and brought to the attention of the Deputy Minister of the Interior is indicative of the government's sensitivity to public criticism of the Indian Affairs Branch's scheme to grant the Stoney Indians a reserve in the Kootenay Plains.

Of course we were not given an opportunity to defend ourselves against such charges and accusations. We could have done so easily, not only by speaking to our own traditional values of living in accord with nature, but in terms even the whiteman could understand easily. For example, we could have reminded the

At the Calgary Stampede, in the 1920s.
To the whiteman, there was no such thing as Indian culture, and our traditions were of value only for shows and entertainments.
(Glenbow Archives NA-667-195)

critics that there were simply not that many families on the Kootenay Plains, maybe ninety-nine people including men, women, and children. They would not have had a drastic effect on the game population. Nor did these people even stay on the Kootenay Plains all year round; they hunted west, north, east, and south along the vast foothills area. They only wintered on the Plains, where there was less snow and where game from other areas came to feed at that time. Nevertheless, the extremist attitudes, combined with the government's general endorsement of conservationist principles, served to override our claim to the Kootenay Plains.

The warning to Chief Ranger Helmer that the Indians would "destroy" the game animals supposed to be protected by the national parks came from one of the false white friends my people had the misfortune to encounter every so often. He was T. E. (Tom) Wilson, a white squatter in the area, known to and apparently friendly with many of the Stoneys, especially those living on the Kootenay Plains.

Tom Wilson was one of the first settlers to live at the present site of Banff, Alberta. He improved a homestead near Morley from 1886 to 1893. When it was surveyed, however, it was found to be a school section, and he was refused title.[4] Consequently, in 1902, Wilson established a ranch and trading post on the Kootenay Plains. Several cabins and a horse corral had been built there already by Silas Abraham, a Stoney Indian. These were located at the confluence of White Rabbit Creek and the North Saskatchewan River. Since the cabins and corrals were already established, Wilson asked to borrow them from my people. These were lent to him by us on the understanding that the buildings would be returned to us when he left the Plains. He agreed and also promised my people that he would bring food and tobacco into the Plains to trade for furs. We agreed to this since the trader was going to leave the Plains after a few years and even put up another building for him.

As it turned out, when Wilson left,

Silas Abraham in 1912. He built some of the first log cabins at Abraham Lake, west of the Bighorn Reserve.

the local authorities refused to acknowledge the Stoneys' claim to the buildings, and the forest rangers exerted every effort to remove the Indian "squatters." John Abraham, today over eighty years old, is one of the Stoney elders on the Bighorn Reserve who has personal knowledge of the events. He recently described them in an interview:

In my time I saw my old people when they were alive and how they were used to this land . . . The people went to Banff for the Annual Indian Days. They came across a certain white man [Tom Wilson], who said that he was willing to put up a Trading Post at Kootenay Plains, if the Indians would sell him all the fur they trap, including the Big Horn sheep's head. This man presented his proposal in a meeting and they discussed the matter until everyone agreed on the trading post. When he got here they built him a cabin just east of here. After that the old people started dealing with him. They purchased groceries and paid with horses. The old Indian people made this white man a rich man in no time . . . When he left the area, we started using the land again. He also said I could use the cabins that he left behind, but the forest ranger would not allow me to use it . . . At that time he [Tom Wilson] stamped my name on the cabins but the ranger tore it out and threw it away.[5]

If Wilson had not won the friendship and trust of the people living on the Kootenay Plains, it would not have been possible for him to have enjoyed such success. With their help he built his ranch. The Stoneys built other cabins nearby and planted vegetable gardens. At first Wilson clearly did have the close cooperation of the people, perhaps mainly because he was their main supplier of food and ammunition in return for the furs and hides they brought in. Our tribal records include old letters from Paul Beaver to Tom Wilson asking for supplies, and another, dated 1902, in which Morley Beaver sadly informed his friend about the death of their mutual friend "Johnnie."[6]

Moses House also wrote to Wilson on three occasions, reminding him to bring food, "a number of 44 caridge [cartridge] and tocca [tobacco]" up to the Kootenay Plains trading house,[7] and Peter Wesley asked Wilson to take some cattle up to the Plains.[8] All these letters were written to Wilson between 1902 and 1905 when he was just starting to build up his ranch. Once the ranch was firmly established, he apparently sought to remove the very families who had helped him and who had come to trust him through their trading activities.

In another interview, John Abraham has explained why Wilson tried to coerce our forefathers into leaving the Plains area:

> This is all the plowed patches and fields I can remember in this area at Kootenay Plains where we had lived at that time. Then the white man [Wilson] said he had to graze his horses at this place until he sells them all and asked us to move to another place and we moved away leaving the house which was built for a store and other small storage cabins. All of these buildings were built by our old people whom I mentioned. In fact, in these days our people went hunting to other places and brought back whatever was to be sold. They were making a good living but the horses were getting to be too many.[9]

Another tribal member from the Bighorn Reserve, Nat House, was more to the point:

> During the original time when our forefathers came to Rabbit River, if Wilson did [sic] not force us to leave the Rabbit River area, we would still have it as our own land.[10]

By 1909 Wilson reportedly had 150 horses feeding on the Kootenay Plains.[11] He applied to the Dominion Lands Branch to secure an exclusive grazing lease to the grasslands; he objected to my people keeping their horses on the grass ranges, and he wanted permission to erect a fence to keep them out.[12]

The Department of the Interior refused to register his homestead claim, but Wilson was assured by officials that "your interest would not be materially affected whether you were protected by a leasehold or not."[13] In 1920 Tom Wilson relinquished all claims and rights to the land and the buildings he had occupied on the Plains. In compensation he received a section of land in the Peace River area.[14]

The Department of the Interior recognized Tom Wilson's right as a squatter, but the rights of his Indian neighbours, who had preceded him to the Plains, who had built his home, and whose descendants still live there, were ignored. The only reason given for this discriminatory policy was the unproven accusation that the Stoneys would kill all the game in the Forest Reserve.

The Indian Affairs Branch did keep trying to find land for the

Wesley Band. Owing to the Forestry Branch's objections to having an Indian reserve established at Kootenay Plains, Surveyor J. K. McLean was instructed to ask us to select another tract:

> especially where there is fair agricultural land . . . If you can induce the Indians to make a selection you should proceed to survey it and notify the local Land agent in order that squatters may be warned not to enter on the land.[15]

But after discussing the matter with us, Surveyor McLean reported:

> They will await a decision regarding the lands at Kootenay Plains and are very anxious to have an area set aside there as soon as convenient, to be surveyed when possible.[16]

The surveyor believed that we wanted the Plains "for the sake of the hunting" and explained that the Plains residents contended

> that the treaty did not take away their hunting rights and that they did not recognize the local government or its rights to make regulations affecting them in any way, that their dealings were entirely with the Dominion Government.[17]

In other words, my people questioned whether a government department or the province had the power to override a treaty made with the federal government.

But Ottawa retorted that if the Indians wanted the land solely for hunting, then a reserve could not be secured for them. The Indian Affairs Branch told the surveyor to tell them that they would have to choose another site because

> the preservation of the game is to be made a principle [sic] feature of the Forest Reserve in which the Kootenay Plains are situated and that the hunting operations of the Indians are decided objectionable.[18]

My people refused to consider any alternative area and maintained that our freedom to hunt in the surrendered area was guaranteed by treaty. In a letter to the Indian Affairs Branch, Surveyor McLean observed:

A number of them have made their home there for a considerable time and according to their own statement have about
100 head of cattle and a greater number of horses. One Indian
has 11 head, and the moving of these people will be a hardship, others of course want these lands for the purpose of
hunting only. There is a great dissatisfaction regarding any cur-
tailing of their hunting privileges. They contend that the
understanding when the treaty was made was that they were
to have these privileges with reasonable regulations, and they
were not to be entirely taken from them as now appears to be
the case by the Forestry regulations. They also state that the
smooth land fit for settlement is all taken; that they always
observed the treaty and never interfered with the settlement,
but now the rough land unfit for settlers is to be taken also and
they are deprived of all hunting grounds and that this is contrary to the treaty and their understanding of it.[19]

The Indian Affairs Branch was impressed with our argument and
again petitioned the Department of the Interior:

> to consent to the laying out an Indian Reserve at Kootenay
> Plains . . . and that the Stoney Indians may be allowed to carry
> on their hunting operations under such special regulations as
> may be considered to be just and within the proper under-
> standing of the Treaty made with them.[20]

The Department of the Interior remained unpersuaded and
refused to reverse its decision because it would necessitate an Act of
Parliament to withdraw the land from the Forest Reserve. The
Indians would derive no revenue from timber since the valley
"would only be suitable for grazing purposes," which in the department's judgement was not an adequate reason to grant the
request.[21]

The situation remained at a stalemate. Each time the question was
raised—by petitions signed by my tribal members, by letters from
John McDougall, by the Inspector of Indian Agencies, J. A. Markle, or
by the Indian Affairs Branch itself—the Department of the Interior
adamantly refused to grant us land in the Forest Reserve. Our people pointed out that we had already built houses and planted gardens; we had numerous horses and cattle there. Our fathers and children were buried there. This was our homeland. We were not asking

the government to give us somebody else's land; this was land promised to us at the time of treaty and later by the Indian Affairs Branch. We were only asking the government to recognize our right to this land and to register title or patent to it.

The same points were raised time after time but to no avail. The Indian Affairs Branch conceded that the Wesley Band was entitled to more land but it had to choose it in an area not already leased, sold, or reserved for some other purpose, and preferably of good agricultural potential.

The Chief Inspector of Indian Agencies, Glen Campbell, personally visited Chief Peter Wesley to reach a final solution. He showed the people a map outlining alternative locations that they might choose, but the band remained firm in its opinion of land in the traditional area. The Inspector interviewed R. H. Campbell, the Chief of Forestry, who finally admitted that Indians might be an asset to his department in the Forest Reserve since they were very careful in preventing forest fires.[22]

Nevertheless, the Minister of the Interior refused to present legislation withdrawing the area from the Forest Reserve for the Stoneys.[23] No reason was given for the decision and it was thought that we would merely select another area. Other sections were considered, but it was discovered that there were no suitable lands near Morley which were not already occupied or leased by ranchers. There was no system of redress by which the Indian Affairs Branch could reverse a decision made by the Minister of the Interior.

Several families from the Wesley Band continued to live on the Plains, and the area was frequently visited by the two-thirds or three-quarters of the Wesley Band members who continued to live at Morley. Over one hundred head of cattle were moved to the area because of the depleted grazing land at Morley. But as far as Ottawa was concerned we had no legal claim to the territory.

The government did not treat the problem as a legal question since it assumed that all members of the Wesley Band had been represented at Treaty Seven and had received treaty entitlement at Morley. Rather, it saw it as a question of providing us additional land in order that we might have the same opportunity as other tribes to raise cattle and grow crops so that we might eventually become "self-sustaining." But we, of course, viewed it as a problem of getting the government to keep a promise made by the Queen's representatives at the treaty negotiations. It was our land, and we refused to consider an alternative area.

The question lay in abeyance for about a year. The Indian agent continued to make application for new grazing lands near the reserve. A number of Stoney people continued to live on the Plains heedless of the agent's work at Morley.

Then, in the fall of 1913, the forest ranger in charge of the Clearwater Division of the Rocky Mountain Forest Reserve protested against my people's fencing in a pasture for their horses. The fencing blocked the main trails (originally blazed by my people) along the Saskatchewan River which were used by the rangers, hunters, and other visitors. The Indian Affairs Branch was instructed by the Department of the Interior "to take the necessary steps" to avoid further friction and to end the Stoneys' "unauthorized occupation," which interfered with the administration of the Forest Reserve.[24] In turn, the Indian Affairs Branch instructed the Stoney agent to have the fence removed and to notify the tribe not to interfere with the administration of the Forest Reserve.[25]

The agent did not want to have a confrontation with the Wesley Band, because the members living on the Plains were independent of the ration house. If they were brought to Morley, it would increase expenses since many of the band would be destitute. He estimated that two hundred people were living on the Plains with approximately forty homes. It would likely be necessary to call in the North West Mounted Police to force them out. Rather than precipitate trouble, the agent decided not to disturb the families.[26] Apparently, no one forced him to change his decision at that time.

During 1913 and 1914, the Indian Affairs Branch made several successive attempts to obtain more land near the Morley Reserve for the tribe. In the spring of 1914, Deputy Superintendent General Scott visited the reserve at Morley and was deeply moved by my tribe's desperate need for better land:

> It seems to me that there is no Indian Band in the west whose situation is more precarious in a sense than the Indians of the Stoney Reserve. They depend largely on the wood industry which cannot last forever, and to what are they to turn their attention for a permanent source of livelihood?[27]

Scott's worry about finding an industry for my people is interesting because it is so typical of Indian Affairs thinking. "Christianize, civilize, and control" were the constant goals of even those individuals who obviously meant well. To this end all Indian children were supposed to be educated in federally supported schools run by the Churches. (In actual fact attendance was low and irregular.) Most such schools were residential schools, kept in session for most of the year; the idea was to keep growing minds under European control as much as possible so as to develop habits of "industry" and "perseverance" (according to the whiteman's definition of the words).

At Morley, John McDougall had built the first such residential school in the 1880s. The second residential school, which I attended in my youth, was built in 1925.

Meanwhile, after Scott's inspection of the Morley Reserve in 1914, the Department of the Interior agreed to set aside 12,742.6 acres located a few miles north of the Morley Reserve by Salter Lake (Twp 27, Range 6, west of the 5th Med.). The Order-in-Council (P.C. 947) was passed April 7, 1914 establishing Stoney Indian Reserve 142B.

The land was certainly needed by the Morley Reserve, but it did nothing to help members of the Wesley Band on the Kootenay Plains. There, during the summer of 1914, the relationship between my people and the Forestry Branch deteriorated to its lowest level. Forestry officials had permitted us to use Forestry ranches, upon payment of the usual fee, and the provincial Department of Agriculture had

The new residential school in Morley, which opened in 1925. Students had to have their hair cut when they enrolled.
(Glenbow Archives NA-1448-46)

Chief David Bearspaw

issued us licenses to hunt in the regular open season. Now, following a meeting between the new Supervisor of Forest Reserves, E. H. Findlayson, and the Wesley Band, the agent informed Ottawa that "It is now impossible to issue permits to the Stonies in the Forest Reserve as when he [Findlayson] visited them lately they were very cheeky, and informed him that they had the land before he did, and they would not take any notice of him or his regulations."[28]

Then Findlayson approached Ottawa to remove us from the Forest Reserve because we were "destroying" the game. The Deputy Superintendent of Indian Affairs was willing to make the attempt, but did point out to J. W. Waddy, agent at the Morley Reserve, that there would be many problems in doing so. Not the least was that before the land could be effectively brought under the provisions of the provincial game laws, it would be necessary to provide on the reserve "such occupation as will enable them to maintain themselves."[29]

Agent Waddy had informed my people repeatedly that we had no right to the Kootenay Plains. Waddy now believed that the best recourse was to evict us forcibly and compensate those who had their homes there. In a communication to D. C. Scott of Indian Affairs, he stated:

I think it advisable to send in a few of the R.N.W.M.P. under some old Sergeant, who will not take any insolence from the Indians, and make them all return to their Reserve. The Stonies will make trouble if the Forrestry [sic] men try to do the work; as they have worked with most of the rangers and do not look on them as officers of the law. After they return it will of course be up to the Forrestry [sic] Dept. to see they do not return, [and] they can easily do this.[30]

The agent was instructed to evaluate the buildings and improvements at Kootenay Plains and to suggest what arrangements might be made for the families to be returned to Morley. However, the agent was to proceed "with discretion, as any arbitrary proceedings would undoubtedly antagonize the Indians."[31]

Agent Waddy could not suggest any profitable means of livelihood for the returned families but stated "they are the most self-reliant of the band and I do not think we will have much trouble from lack of work, as they are in the habit of getting out and helping themselves."[32]

(During the nineteenth century whitemen often viewed this independence and self-reliancy of the Wesley people with consternation. We were called the least "progressive" members of the tribe because we wouldn't settle on the reserve but now, twenty years later, our independent qualities had not only proved themselves necessary for our survival in the wilderness area, but were seen as positive values by the agent envisioning us on the impoverished Morley Reserve. Sometimes I think the government spent years trying to destroy in us the very same qualities that it was attempting to instill in most other Indians.)

When Supervisor Findlayson's threats and the plans to remove the families living on the Kootenay Plains were made known there, a contemporary letter from a member of the band reveals that there was a split among my people as to how to respond. Jonas Benjamin wrote, "Some members led by Chief Peter Wesley would not accept anything . . . less than the large tract they had always requested. Others were willing to accept small, individual lots if the government would lease the lots to them."[33]

But the division was not serious or permanent. The government has used the divide and conquer approach very effectively, but it did not work at that time with my people.

As Benjamin continued, they remained united on the main point: "In either case, no one wanted to move to Morley because it would be hard for them to make a living there."[34]

Superintendent Duncan Scott's reply to Benjamin may easily have encouraged the unity of opposition: "I am sorry you are having this trouble, but I think it is the fault of those Indians who went to Kootenay Plains and would not listen to advice."[35]

The government was moving softly but with great determination. For example, the province had several charges for violations of the game laws pending against Chief Peter Wesley, but he was not prosecuted for fear that it might jeopardize the Indian Affairs Branch's efforts to remove the Stoneys from the Forest Reserve.[36]

During the summer of 1915, District Forestry Inspector E. H. Findlayson and Indian Agent Jack Waddy proceeded to compile a comprehensive list of which families were entitled to compensation. The list of improvements and their location was completed by the government in February, 1916. Joshua Wildman, on behalf of the band, submitted his own evaluation. That summer, Agent Waddy resigned his post and the new officer, E. H. Yeomans, was instructed to arrive at a compromise between the two estimates.

Acting Agent Yeomans believed that if Chief Peter Wesley could be convinced to remain at Morley, the rest of the band would follow his example.[37] The agent discussed the situation with the people on several occasions, and arrangements were completed with the province f or compensating them and for removing their belongings to Morley.

In the spring of 1918, a memorandum was presented to the Minister of the Interior and the Superintendent General of Indian Affairs, Arthur Meighen, outlining the plan drafted by the Forestry and Indian Affairs Branches to remove my people from the Kootenay Plains. It requested that $1,800 be provided for transportation of household effects, machinery, horses, and cattle from Kootenay Plains via rail from Nordegg to Morley, and that another $7,000 be requisitioned to compensate the people for the value of the improvements. The two departments requested this latter, special provision "with the object of preventing the destruction of the game and especially in view of the attitude of the provincial authorities, [and] it would be good public policy to provide for the removal of the Indians immediately." The Indians would leave "peaceably," provided they were allowed the above benefits.[38]

The Minister approved the scheme, but directed that the entire expense be borne by the Indian Affairs Branch rather than that it be shared with the Forestry Branch. Deputy Superintendent Duncan Scott included the supplementary amount of $10,000 in his budget estimate for that current year to cover the cost of removal. After four years of interdepartmental discussion, a final solution was accepted by all branches which the government believed would meet the approval of my people.

Chief Peter Wesley was notified that the government officials would meet his people to make final arrangements for their removal from the Plains.[39] A cheque for $2,000 was forwarded to J. A. Markle, Inspector of Indian Agencies, to meet the immediate costs of removal. He was authorized to accompany Agent Yeomans and Forester

Findlayson. To meet the rest of the expenses, a cheque for the final amount would be forwarded once the settlement was known.[40]

This arrangement was proceeding smoothly when, unexpectedly, Indian Commissioner W. M. Graham telegraphed Indian Affairs Deputy Superintendent Scott that "It would be a great mistake to bring Stoney Indians down to Morley at present time [.] Understand they have two hundred head cattle . . . only limited quantity hay on Morley Reserve [.] would ask that arrangements be made deferring action till spring."[41] Ottawa agreed to the postponement and Agent Yeomans was ordered to remain at Morley.

My people have said many times that the "Great Spirit has created us for a purpose, and placed us here on this good land." It seems that His unseen hand intervened here, postponing our removal.

Forestry Inspector E. H. Findlayson, of course, protested the decision and pointed out that the Wesley Band members on the Kootenay Plains would tie up valuable range which could be leased to ranchers for their stock. He maintained that there was sufficient range at Morley to meet our needs and that the Plains should be opened to others to relieve the feed shortage.[42] A bitter argument resulted between Indian Commissioner Graham, who preferred that we not be removed until the spring of 1919, and Supervisor Findlayson, who wanted to see us removed in order that district ranchers and farmers might lease the grazing lands. Both sides presented their case to the Minister of the Interior who sided with Commissioner Graham in delaying removal until spring. The $2,000 requisitioned to meet the costs was subsequently returned to Ottawa.[43]

Although Graham had only requested that the removal wait until spring 1919, the question of removal does not seem to have been raised again until 1920. Again the instigator was the Forestry Branch, plus B. Lawton, Chief Game Warden for Alberta. The Indian Affairs Branch completely reversed its previous stance and declined to take any action on the matter since the department had made no appropriation to cover the expenses of removing us.[44] This decision appears to have been the final word and there was no further discussion of the issue until the late 1920s.

The question of Indians squatting in the Rocky Mountain Park was reopened in 1928 when the Supervisor of the Clearwater Forest Reserve notified Ottawa that two groups from the Chippewa Tribe had visited the reserve in search of camping ground. The Royal Canadian Mounted Police had warned the visitors that they were trespassing and the Native groups left.[45]

With trapping, hunting, and seasonal work in the coal mines, the mountains could more easily provide us a living than the land around Morley.

During the following year, when the boundaries of Banff National Park were extended to the Cline River, the National Parks Branch became concerned over our presence in the Saskatchewan River Valley. The Park wardens were unable to explain the new circumstances to the Native residents living inside the park and it was left to the Indian Affairs Branch to handle the situation.[46]

About the same time, the Inspector of Indian Agencies, M. Christianson, was asked to report on the presence of Stoney families camping in the Rocky Mountain National Park area. The inspector reiterated our basic argument: we could make a living more easily in that area than on our tribe's reserve at Morley because of the plentiful game and the seasonal work that was available in the coal mines. He also refuted the argument of the park officials that the families were wantonly destroying wildlife in the area:

> In looking over the files here, which have copies of letters on them from officials of the Department of the Interior, I find that *no charge is made against the Indians* to the effect that they are giving any trouble whatever, *it is simply a matter of the Parks Branch* wanting to get rid of them [italics added].[47]

Inspector Christianson also stated that he believed that "if the Stoney Indians are to be moved back to their reserve at Morley it will have to be done by force and the argument they put forward is that they have lived there more or less all their lives." If, however, the small band was left unmolested, he expected that the younger generation would move back to Morley as the older people died, thereby avoiding force.[48]

This report was forwarded to Ottawa with the desultory comment by Indian Commissioner W. M. Graham, "If they are moved back to Morley by force it will mean a large expenditure of money and then many of them will drift back to their present location."[49] The general feeling was that we might as well be left alone with no commitments being entered into by the federal government.

There are only a few spotty documents which record the events for the period from 1920 to 1945.

In 1934 members of the Wesley Band again petitioned the Indian Affairs Branch to establish an Indian reserve on Kootenay Plains.[50] The agent at Morley endorsed the request because "they make a better living than the Indians here as they are nearer to the source of fur and game animals."[51] Ottawa replied that the Band had received its land entitlement according to the terms of treaty, but that the Band Council could pass a resolution asking the Indian Affairs Branch to purchase a tract in the area from the Band's capital funds. Indian Affairs would then approach the province, which now owned the land in accordance with the 1930 Alberta Natural Resources Act, to obtain its agreement to selling the territory. However, the letter added, obtaining such agreement was unlikely as the land was located in the Clearwater Forest Reserve.[52]

In other words, the transfer of Crown land to the province had let Ottawa off the hook. The federal government no longer had to give a direct answer. Now the province could be blamed for not giving up land to my people. Apparently no further action on this request was taken either by the Band Council or the Indian Affairs Branch. There were very few band funds at that time.

The question was again revived in 1938 when the Wesley Band hired R. Mulcaster, K. C., a lawyer practising in Prince Albert, Saskatchewan, to press our land claim in the Kootenay Plains. At this time my people were concerned about the new Lake Louise-Jasper Highway and a road from Nordegg joining it; it would cut through our hunting territory[53] and interfere with our land claim. This time the Morley agent advised the Indian Affairs Branch against buying the land because this would be repeating a mistake that was made when the reserve was established at Morley, i.e. acquiring land for hunting, then finding the land useless when the hunting was finished . . . I informed them that I would recommend that some arrangements be made whereby they would have exclusive hunting rights over an area there in the Kootenay Plains locality.[54]

The agent also urged the Department to approach the province to grant a ten-year lease to the headwaters of the Saskatchewan River for the exclusive use of the band.

As far as departmental officials were concerned, the situation was at an impasse: the province wanted my people removed; the Indians Affairs Branch wanted to avoid confrontation but had no intention of obtaining land for us; and my people refused to consider living outside our traditional homeland. The status quo was succinctly and frankly summarized by Mr. Christianson:

This is a question which has come up repeatedly during the last twenty-five years . . . These Indians [on the Kootenay Plains] are law abiding and give no trouble whatever. They are visited by the Agent from Morley once or twice a year, and they visit Morley annually. Whenever a new Forest Ranger takes charge in that part of the country, he immediately starts to take steps to get the Indians out of that territory. A few letters are exchanged and that ends the matter for the time being . . .

I personally know that there would be absolutely no chance of getting a Reserve set aside for these Indians by the Provincial Government, although very anxious to get them out of that district. The Indians refuse to move, and I would advise that the matter be left in abeyance as long as possible. The moment we start asking for a reserve for them, we will be starting something which we will never be able to finish. I have told the Provincial Government repeatedly that we could not move the Indians out of the district, as they have lived there so long.[55]

Throughout these decades, the actions and attitudes of the Indian Affairs Branch left much to be desired. It had been set up to be our trustee, to look after our affairs, and to protect our rights. Instead, it swayed with every wind of pressure from the non-Indian society—the conservationist movement, the new government forestry regulations, the newspapers—all of which interfered with our hunting, our fishing, our religion, and our traditional way of life. Again, we were left as strangers in our homeland.

The feeling of my people was perhaps best expressed by an old woman, Mrs. Jake Rabbit, now over eighty years old, who was born on the Kootenay Plains. Throughout her entire life she has witnessed the fight to establish our land claims there and the government's whittling away of treaty rights. Recently some young Stoneys were gathering information by tape recording interviews conducted in the Stoney language.

Mrs. Rabbit was visited in her home, and a young man tried to explain that the interview would be taped and translated into the English language, then presented to the federal government for fulfillment of treaty land claims.

The old Stoney woman replied in a flat voice: "Are you going to take my voice, and give it to the government? No, the government has taken my land, and everything that I have, and now it wants my voice. That is the only thing that I have left and now the government wants my speech. I say no! I will die keeping my voice. The government is going too far! I don't think the government will ever be satisfied."

A Place to Spread Our Blankets, 1945–1948

B etween 1945 and 1948 the Indian Affairs Branch finally did take action to provide the Stoney Tribe with more land: an addition to the impoverished Morley Reserve; a reserve for a group of Bearspaw Band members who had been "squatting" south of Morley for many years; and land rights for the Wesley Band members living on the Kootenay Plains. The major problems with these actions were that the first was very costly for the tribe, the second gave us only a small piece of land, and the third did not give us the reserve land we needed or believed we were entitled to.

In 1945, Indian Affairs, following a lengthy report by D. J. Allan, Superintendent of Reserves and Trusts, on the desperate land situation at Morley Reserve, decided to purchase more land for the Stoneys near that reserve.[1] (In the preceding decades some additions had been made to Morley as the population increased—some Crown lands were transferred in 1914[2] and land from the Ethol M. Potts estate was purchased with tribal funds in 1929. But this was not nearly enough for the needs of what was now a population estimated at 1,200 to 1,500.)

So that the tribe could pay for the new land, the government agreed to loan it a sum of $500,000 for an indefinite period at three percent interest per annum ($15,000 per year without any repayment on the principal). This interest would be collected from the fees paid to the tribe by Calgary Power Limited, who were renting the three dams on the Morley Reserve: Kananaskis Dam, Horseshoe Dam, and the Ghost Dam. This money was almost the only income to our band funds and we were to use a substantial proportion of it to pay the government every year for this land.

The scheme was presented to a meeting of the three bands' members on March 16, 1946. The government representatives explained to those present that because the annual interest payment would be deducted from the revenue obtained from Calgary Power, the loan would not "cost" the tribe anything. (This explanation was neither clear nor accurate; it is costing us a lot of money to repay that loan. Since 1946, we have been paying an annual sum of $15,000, and it is now 1976. We have paid $450,000 to date on the interest alone and the loan of $500,000 is still there. If we were to pay off this loan this year, it would have cost us $950,000. We would be paying the government almost twice as much as the original loan. Some people think that the government helps us purchase land at little cost but it certainly will cost us a lot by the time we are through paying our loan.) Nevertheless, after the government's explanation, a majority of the tribal members at the meeting authorized the government to purchase both the Ralph C. Coppock "Merino" Ranch near Cochrane and the Arthur Crawford Ranch adjoining the Morley Reserve.[3] (This brought the total size of the Morley reserve to 143.3 square miles, approximately what it is today.)

At about the same time, the government finally provided land for a special group of my tribe—members of the Bearspaw Band who had moved away from the Morley Reserve more than twenty-five years before. The return of Peter Wesley (*Ta-otha*) with his band of followers to the Kootenay Plains in 1894 had been the first split from the reserve at Morley. To escape the ravages of the influenza epidemic in 1918, a group of Bearspaw Band members had also left Morley to establish more permanent camps on their traditional hunting areas to the south, along the Highwood and Pekisko Rivers. Like the Wesley Band members on the Kootenay Plains, this group had requested that the government establish a reserve for the Bearspaw Band, as had been promised at the time of the signing of the treaty. The government had not been responsive to the requests of my people at that time.

For the next twenty-five years, this group had lived in encampments in this area and gained a livelihood from seasonal work on the nearby ranches, supplemented by hunting in the surrounding area and the mountains.

After World War II, the pressure for a reserve was renewed so that houses could be built for the families. In 1946 a developed ranch on the Highwood River was purchased for this purpose and converted

Our children were reared to respect the values and traditions of our people.
(Glenbow Archives NA-714-141)

to special reserve status for my people. The 5,000 acres of this reserve was too small to offer much hope for economic development, but its natural beauty and the fact that it was the first real home for this group of my people support the name of this Stoney reserve—Eden Valley.

The Stoney families still "squatting" on the Kootenay Plains were not helped by the additions to Morley or the new Eden Valley Reserve. However, at the 1946 meeting when the Morley additions were authorized, there were Kootenay Plains representatives present and their situation discussed. They were told that Indian Affairs was continuing its talks with the province aimed at getting title for land in their area. For the moment, however, there was little likelihood that the province would sanction the establishment of a permanent Indian settlement in the Clearwater Forest Reserve. Therefore, we were free to continue living in the Forest Reserve and to trap furs on our lines registered with the province.[4] There was no pressure from the Indian Affairs representatives to get the people of the Kootenay Plains (or Nordegg, as it was now often called) to move back to the reserve. Indeed, it was made clear that even with the new land at Morley, our removal would only serve to add further pressure to the already inadequate living conditions on the reserve.[5]

Apparently Ottawa had gained a little wisdom over the years. The government realized that my people at Bighorn–Kootenay Plains would not leave the traditional homeland where they had been born and where their fathers and relatives were buried. Now that additional land had been obtained for the people at Morley, the Department turned its attention to the Wesley Band members at Nordegg (Kootenay Plains).

On January 4, 1947, John Laurie, Secretary of the Indian Association of Alberta (IAA) and long-time friend of the Stoneys, submitted a report recommending a separate reserve alongside the Nordegg River for the people residing in that district. He stressed the urgent need to guard our land claims because (1) the route of the David Thompson Highway had now been surveyed and the area near the confluence of the Bighorn and North Saskatchewan Rivers was a prime location desired by private developers for an auto camp; (2) my people would need many years to adopt a livelihood other than trapping, guiding, and hunting; (3) the recent land extension to the Morley Reserve was inadequate and the Bighorn residents had not received any portion of any benefits from the government loan.[6]

The Inspector of Indian Agencies for Alberta forwarded Laurie's report to Ottawa with the recommendation that, unless other lands were known to be available and to be more suitable for the Bighorn Stoneys, the Government of Alberta, through one of its ministers, should be approached to make negotiations. The provincial Department of Mines and Resources might get sufficient land to make a small reserve, or at least withhold a suitable area until negotiations could be made on behalf of my people.

This suggestion to open discussions with the province was endorsed by R. A. Hoey, Director of the Indian Affairs Branch. It was the first positive response by a high-ranking government official since the Minister of the Interior's approval of the Stoney land claim on the Kootenay Plains in 1911.

Ottawa had no knowledge of the geography or of the topographical features of the area, so the Indian Affairs Regional Inspector was instructed to approach the authorities in the Provincial Land Branch to ascertain what area could be made available to us. The field staff was to assess what acreage would meet the needs of the Kootenay Plains people in order that the appropriate funds could be included in the yearly estimate. Director Hoey wrote: "We quite appreciate that they require land at or near their present settlement and are prepared to acquire them on their behalf if suitable lands can be obtained at a reasonable price."[7]

A meeting was held January 24, 1947, with N. E. Tanner, provincial Minister of Lands and Mines, and C. W. Jackson, Chief Executive Officer of the Department of Mines and Resources, Ottawa. At this meeting, John Laurie suggested that approximately 5,000 acres, suitable for "small farms, small ranches and for community grazing," were required by the Stoneys of the Kootenay Plains.[8] And that suggestion was a serious mistake with far-reaching consequences.

The error was surely made in good faith, for John Laurie was a true friend of my people. He used to stay on the Stoney Reserve at Morley. I remember when he used to live with Chief Enos Hunter, Chief of the Wesley Band, during the 1940s and 1950s. He used to eat bannock, lard, and dried meat, and drink tea with us in our humble cabins. That was the best we could offer him at the time. There was no indoor plumbing or central heating in our homes, but he was always welcome and happy to come. There was no doubt that he experienced the warmth of friendship in our log houses. In the winter months when we took our team of horses and sleigh into the forest for firewood for our shacks and cabins, he used to help us load the wood into the sleigh. At that time he was trying to learn the Stoney language. (Although he never did master our language, he learned enough to follow our conversations.)

John Laurie really tried to help us in our fights against great odds for education, land claims, and our treaty rights. He lived among us. He was adopted into the home of Chief Enos Hunter. He knew our hardships and joined us in our pow-wows and joyous occasions. He also lived with various other tribes in Alberta. He attended many IAA meetings and worked hard as an officer of that organization. He knew the problems we were experiencing in trying to find our place in the Canadian society.

Because John Laurie was our friend and knew us so well, it is difficult to understand why he suggested a reserve of 5,000 acres. He knew that such a small area—less than eight square miles—was totally insufficient for our needs. He also knew that my people at Bighorn-Kootenay Plains were requesting the 23,680 acres agreed upon in 1909. Perhaps he thought that if he requested more than 5,000 acres, he might scare off the provincial government and we would end up with nothing again. He may also have envisioned the reserve as a small central area, where a field staff could provide medical, educational, and welfare services and from which my people could fan out to continue their lives of hunting in the larger Forest Reserve. After all, although the province objected to our presence in the reserve now, it did issue us registered traplines. Perhaps with my people under close supervision on a small reserve, rather than "footloose and nomadic," the province would be more amenable to other accommodation.

Whatever John Laurie's reasons for suggesting such a small area and whatever hardships have come to us because of it, we remain grateful for having had such a white friend who helped us in so many other ways.

In accord with Laurie's recommendation, the Indian Affairs Branch decided in January 1947 that the province should be approached about selling a block of 5,000 acres for the use of the Stoneys.[9]

As it happened, Alberta Minister of Lands and Mines N. E. Tanner was in the capital at this time; he advised Director Hoey that his Forestry officers would undoubtedly object to an Indian community deep in the Forest Reserve. The area suggested by John Laurie, he said, was not for sale. However, he continued, his office was willing to reach some accommodation with Ottawa over our claim.

Director Hoey replied that the Indian Affairs Branch was prepared to purchase "out of public funds" enough land to meet the needs of the Stoney people on the Kootenay Plains and that further talks would be necessary. He thereupon directed his Regional Inspector, G. H. Gooderham, to open negotiations with Edmonton to determine "how much land they would be willing to sell us and at what price ... Anything you can do to further this matter with the Province and to break down their resistance to selling us the land we require to meet our obligations to the Indians and to enable them to establish permanent residence in the district of their choice will be appreciated."[10]

The federal government now fully acknowledged its responsibility to us. The only major hurdle that remained was the province's reluctance to have an Indian reserve in the Saskatchewan River valley.

The Alberta government counted that no individual or company representing any group would be granted land in the Clearwater Forest Reserve. The province was just formulating a policy governing the reforestation and preservation of the eastern mountain slopes, and the Department of Lands and Mines was reluctant to relinquish any land in the forest reserves, particularly to a permanent Indian community which would cut timber and raise cattle and horses. Furthermore, Imperial Oil Limited had just established an oil well not too far away at Leduc, and there was a flurry of activity in search of additional sites. After hearing these arguments, Inspector Gooderham wrote his superior on February 14, 1947, that the Indian Affairs Branch would be unable to reach any immediate agreement with the province but that the talks were to continue later at a more propitious time.[11]

No records of the proceedings between February and September 1947 were made available to our researchers.[12]

But sometime during that interval, apparently the province consented to allocate, without cost, a 5,000-acre reserve for our use in the vicinity of Nordegg east of the Kootenay Plains. Before approving the grant, the province imposed several conditions (some of which were later employed by Ottawa to turn down requests that the Bighorn Reserve be enlarged). Additionally during that summer, arrangements were concluded with the Surveyor General's Department to obtain a legal description of the proposed reserve.[13]

The area selected was to include within its boundaries as many existing Indian homes as possible. Adequate meadows for hay and pasturage were to be provided, including two areas on either side of the North Saskatchewan River that had previously been described by John Laurie. The Indian Affairs Branch would fence the area to keep horses out of the Forest Reserve since wild horses might be shot by forest rangers.[14] Land suitable for cultivation, for growing of winter feed, and for gardening was to be chosen. The site was to be convenient to the highway leading to Nordegg, in consideration of the school, nursing station, warehouse, and staff residence. Finally, my people were to assist in the selection of the land to reduce any dissatisfaction.[15]

The stipulations were agreed to by the Indian Affairs Branch and by the Alberta Cabinet. The only requirement before an Order-In-Council could be passed was to retain a qualified surveyor to outline the reserve boundaries.[16] (It was later discovered that the Bighorn area had already been surveyed in 1910 in connection with some coal mine leases.)

On October 16 and 17, 1947, a reconnaisance of the proposed reserve area was made by J. E. Pugh (Superintendent of the Stoney Sarcee Agency), P. B. Baptie (Land Surveyor for Calgary), Mr. Suter (Indian Affairs representative at Nordegg), a Royal Canadian Mounted Police constable, and P. Campbell, the local provincial forest ranger. "*All agreed that a block confined to 5,000 acres was totally inadequate,* because there was less than 1,200 acres of land fit to live upon, crop and graze [italics added]."[17]

The party therefore reconnoitered an area exceeding 12,000 acres which straddled both the North Saskatchewan River and the proposed David Thompson Highway. Superintendent Pugh advised the regional office that "he would not recommend an area as small as 5,000 acres because it would mean the starving out of these people in a very limited time." Pugh concluded that when John Laurie had made the original suggestion of 5,000 acres, "he must have erred in suggesting such a small area, and that his letter had been misleading."[18]

The impression the reconnaisance party left with the Bighorn people was that they would receive a sizable grant of land. "He [a representative from Indian Affairs] told us that his job was to work on the issue of setting up the reserve but he informed us that he would stop them because he thought the land was too small and that the Bighorn people needed a larger area of land."[19]

The Wesley Band assumed such informal comments by Superintendent Pugh and other government officers describing the inadequacy of 5,000 acres were a promise to obtain more land for us. We were, of course, mistaken.

This is not to say, however, that at least some employees of Indian Affairs did not attempt to obtain a more reasonable amount of land for us. In such an attempt to obtain a more reasonable land allotment, Superintendent Pugh, Regional Supervisor of Indian Agencies G. H. Gooderham, and John Laurie met with Alberta's Minister Tanner. Tanner stated that he had always believed the acreage requested by Ottawa to be insufficient unless it were of exceptionally high quality. But 5,000 acres was all that had been requested by the federal authorities and he had not questioned it. He agreed that a more amenable arrangement must be made and that he would discuss the question with the officers in his department. This discussion was reported to Director Hoey in Ottawa by Supervisor Gooderham.[20] Following this meeting in Edmonton, Superintendent Pugh submitted to his superior, Supervisor Gooderham, a report on it and the reconnaisance that had preceded it.[21]

In this report, dated November 6, 1947, Pugh described the topography of the area in question as a very rugged hill country covered with brush and trees with only a few hundred acres suitable for grazing or for raising crops. He also pointed out that there were a large number of Indian cabins situated outside the proposed 5,000-acre reserve.

In accordance with the instructions from the Director, he said, the Stoneys were consulted in selecting the land. My people first pointed out that 5,000 acres would not take care of our needs, and then that we were thinking of the 23,680 acres originally agreed to by the Department of Indian Affairs in 1909.

As to location, Pugh reported that some of my people had at first requested land on the Kootenay Plains proper, but were told that it would be very difficult to have that land set aside as an Indian Reserve. In addition, the Kootenay Plains area was not considered suitable by the non-Indian advisers because grasshoppers and several dry seasons had completely denuded the grasslands.

In light of what was happening, my people had then suggested three alternative areas: (1) a reserve along both sides of the North Saskatchewan River, from New Haven Creek to Whirlpool Point Rapids; (2) an area stretching along the riverbanks from White Goat (Cline) River (instead of New Haven Creek) to Whirlpool Point Rapids; or (3) an area stretching from the grasslands across the Saskatchewan River at the proposed Bighorn River site to a flat clearing, north of the David Thompson Highway.

In the first two instances, Superintendent Pugh reported that he had explained to my people that the province would not abide such large requests. Also, he had told us that our selection must be confined to the area adjacent to the proposed settlement. (In other words, although my people had been requested to suggest locations for the reserve, Indian Affairs insisted that it be adjacent to Bighorn Creek and the North Saskatchewan River, where some of us were already living.)

To Superintendent Pugh the most reasonable solution seemed to be the third proposal, with the settlement area extended to include most of the existing homes; this would incorporate about 15,000 acres.

Superintendent Pugh concluded his report, which he understood to be a "preliminary survey" to determine the suitability of the proposed site, with the warning:

> *the writer would feel unjustified in stating that the proposed area of 5,000 acres would be a solution to the problem of locating this band of Indians,* [italics added] taking into consideration a long term view of occupation, carrying the horses and cattle in such a confined area consistent with the type of terrain and land, with its heavy timber and lack of suitable vegetation and the location of the homes of the Indians concerned, and if requested for a recommendation in the matter the writer feels that he could not conscientiously recommend that these Indians be confined to the above area, under the conditions that are set forth for consideration in making this preliminary survey.[22]

Supervisor Gooderham forwarded this report to Indian Affairs Director R. A. Hoey in Ottawa. Although it had no effect on Hoey's decisions about the new Stoney reserve, Ottawa was "more than a little disturbed" by the events the report detailed and the recommendation it included.

The reasons that Director Hoey was so "disturbed" seem to have been at least threefold:

1) He had already made up his mind as to the location of the new reserve and had written instructions based on this decision to Supervisor Gooderham on November 3. (Superintendent Pugh's report, it will be remembered, was dated November 6; apparently the two letters crossed in the mail). This directive stated that a firm decision had been reached between Edmonton and Ottawa. The field officers were to inform my people of the decision and to survey the boundaries in a specific area: the confluence of the Bighorn and North Saskatchewan Rivers.[23]

2) Director Hoey was very worried about disturbing federal-provincial relations. For example, during the negotiations, Alberta Minister Tanner had stated that he could not approve the establishment of a regular reserve for ranching and farming purposes for fear that more Indians and their livestock would move into the district, a move that would be unfair to white settlers who had been already forcibly removed from the Forestry Reserve. In his directive to Gooderham, Director Hoey said the Indian Affairs Branch had assured the provincial government that the Bighorn residents would not be the nucleus of more Indian families moving into the provincial Forest Reserve. Bearing this in mind, Director Hoey said, the advantages of establishing a permanent reserve were twofold:

> a) to concentrate the Indians presently in the Forest Reserve where they were squatting on Crown Lands on a modest block of land which they could call their own and where they would have undisputed ownership and control of their homesites;
>
> b) to gather them together in one community where we would have control of the land on which we could establish a community centre consisting of a school and teacherage, a nursing station and ration house, all of which were necessary if we were to furnish the group with education, medical and welfare services . . . These purposes could have been accomplished on a quarter section [160 acres or about one-quarter square mile]. It was, however, recognized that the group required grazing and winter feed for a definitely limited number of horses used in connection with their hunting and trapping activities and this was the sole reason for enlarging the area 5,000 acres . . .[24]

These advantages placated the province since the reserve they presupposed would not permit the development of a large ranching or farming community within the Forest Reserve.

3) As is suggested in the above quotation, the Director had accepted, sight unseen, the estimate of 5,000 acres as being quite sufficient. Any objections, however valid, were now too late as far as Ottawa was concerned. My people did not have a choice of where to live and how to plan for the future; we were to be confined to a small piece of land on which to subsist.

Whether my interpretation of Director Hoey's motives is correct or complete, one thing is absolutely clear: he considered that a final plan had been made and he was in no mood to brook counter-suggestions, even from his own employees. Gooderham and Pugh were severely chastised for the report of November 6. Supervisor Gooderham was reprimanded for not proceeding with the original instructions to survey the 5,000 acres. The department "did not either ask for or expect recommendations from the field staff, much less independent negotiations with the province . . .you and your field staff . . . have risked the whole settlement and the immediate completion of the whole survey in the hope, however well-founded, that you could win better terms."[25]

Gooderham, however, maintained that he had not exceeded his instructions which, in his view, had authorized him to conclude the necessary final arrangement for surveying the land. He was merely reiterating Superintendent Pugh's statement that a parcel of 5,000 acres could not conceivably contain all of those items mentioned in the letter from the Director, dated September 16, 1947 (i.e., hay pasturage, land for gardening and cultivation, a school, warehouse, staff residence and homes). These facts were simply relayed to the provincial authorities in order that the survey work might commence before the winter set in.[26]

Superintendent Pugh's defense of his report and its recommendation was somewhat more spirited, showing an understanding of the reality of the physical situation and a concern for my people. "Recommendation of the proposed (5,000) acreage would be unfair to the Branch, to the Indians and to those who would administer this territory." It was not expected that my people would engage in ranching or farming, but the acreage promised was not even sufficient for accommodating the present number of horses and cattle. Some feed must be grown for the winter months and to support natural growth of the herds. We would continue to earn our livelihood from the sale of furs, but Pugh added prophetically, "This proved satisfactory with game plentiful and fur prices good, but should prices become depressed and game supplies wane, their livelihood would be almost gone."[27] (Today, the clearing of the river valley for the Bighorn Dam has indeed wiped out several registered traplines and driven the game away.)

Others also tried to get Ottawa to reconsider. Gooderham wrote Director Hoey that the land surveyor, P. B. Baptie, was still available; he also passed on a report from John Laurie that the Stoney families he had talked to were in favour of the 15,000 acres suggested by Superintendent Pugh.[28] Even the provincial Deputy Minister of Lands and Mines, John Harvie, wrote that the province "was still of open mind and prepared to consider favourably any reasonable suggestion that you [Director Hoey] might be prepared to make on behalf of these Indians."

But the Indian Affairs Branch had made up its mind. Instead of investigating the objections raised by its field officers and others on the scene, it apologized to the province for any embarrassment its regional representatives might have caused by requesting more land for the Stoneys.[29] Then it went ahead with its plan to obtain the use of only 5,000 acres at the confluence of the Bighorn and North Saskatchewan Rivers.

Indeed, in at least one respect, the plan was cut back. Director Hoey had stated in his letter of November 3 to Supervisor Gooderham that the province had agreed to include the Indian dwellings situated on the south side of the North Saskatchewan River.[30] But the Indian Affairs Branch in Ottawa decided this was inconsistent with the government's objective of gathering the various families into one compact area where the Branch "could undertake to keep them under control and regulate their activities."[31] So this area across the river was deleted from the final terms of transfer on the grounds of difficulties in transporting children across the river to school. (It is not mentioned in the correspondence whether my people received additional land north of the river in compensation, but it is evident that, for the sake of expediency, we lost one of the two major hay pastures described in John Laurie's field report.)

The final terms of transfer were explained to the band. Many members who heard this explanation are still alive today, and their comments suggest both their view of the government's motives and their understanding of what they were being promised. Nat House, who was raised at Bighorn, explains:

We usually lived with him [his grandfather, One Side Moccasin] on the south side of the Saskatchewan River, until the school was built on the north side of the Saskatchewan River. Then we moved to the north side of the river, closer to where the school is now located. We lived here since the school was brought here.[32]

Several residents living south of the river were also required to settle in the new area.

According to Killian Wildman, another Stoney born and raised on the Kootenay Plains, a school and a band hall were promised to the people when the final terms of the agreement were explained. He regards the government's promise of a reserve as a ploy to get those families living on the Kootenay Plains to move down to the Bighorn area.[33]

A participant in the meeting held at Bighorn was John Abraham, who is acknowledged by my people as the most authoritative "old-timer" on the early history of our tribe. John Abraham recalls that the Kootenay Plains was one of "three written papers" discussed with government representatives:

At that time they [government representatives] brought in three written papers and set it on the table. We were going to discuss the proposed reserve and they asked us which one of these areas we wanted. One was Kootenay Plains. The people made their intentions known about the Kootenay Plains at the meeting. Indications was that they agreed to settle at Bighorn for the time being on account of wanting a school. Their thoughts were that the Bighorn reserve is just a "waiting place." That was the reason why they have settled at Bighorn River because they thought that negotiation was still going on for the Kootenay Plains. At that time they informed us that the rangers also supported this statement. This is all I know about Bighorn reserve and I don't care to discuss it![34]

In short, my people, the Wesley Band, approved the proposal for the small Bighorn reserve with the understanding that they would receive additional lands in the near future, and that in the meantime they could continue making their livelihood from the Plains region. The local officials they spoke with had, of course, no authority to make an official pronouncement, but my people cannot be faulted for believing the field officers' reassurances that the reserve would be enlarged.

Ottawa now considered that it had a final settlement and it requested the province to take official action. This was done on December 16, 1947, when an Order-In-Council set aside the stipulated 5,000 acres "for the use of the Dominion of Canada so long as the same shall be required in the interests of the Stoney Indians and their descendants, reserving thereout and there from all Mines and Minerals . . ."[35]

In the summer of 1948, the Government of Canada passed an Order-In-Council establishing the special Bighorn Reserve 144A. One of the conditions officially set out was "That the Stoney Band of Indians has no claim to the land in question, having received grants of land consistent with the terms of its treaty (number seven)."[36]

There are several interesting points to be noticed in these negotiations and their conclusion—points that speak to the differing viewpoints and interests of the various parties involved. These are not matters of mere intellectual curiosity but vital differences that have continued to cause problems and hardships for my people to this very day.

The first such point is that treaty Indians in general, and the Stoneys in particular, have become a political football to be tossed between the federal and provincial governments. I shall deal with this problem generally later. Here it is sufficient to point out that part of this problem should not exist at all since under the terms of the 1930 Natural Resources Act (which transferred most Crown land to the provinces) the Province of Alberta is obligated to provide land to fulfill outstanding treaty obligations whenever it is requested to do so by the Indian Affairs Branch.

Nevertheless, Indian Affairs Director Hoey entered into discussions about the Bighorn Reserve with the provincial authorities on the premise that he must accept whatever the province conceded. In a letter to the Regional Supervisor of Indian Agencies, he stated very clearly:

It must be borne in mind, that we have no legal claim on Alberta to furnish any land whatever to this group and we are, therefore, in no position to bargain for better terms than those freely offered to us.[37]

And it was later viewed by Indian Affairs that it was only owing to provincial Minister N. E. Tanner's "commendable generosity and understanding" that the federal government was able to get the 5,000 acres.[38]

The federal-provincial football game also shows up in the connected point about hunting rights. Indian Affairs Director Hoey agreed to negotiate a reserve for my people at Bighorn in order that they could maintain their horses for "their hunting and trapping activities."[39] This was an implicit acknowledgement of my peoples' right to trap and hunt in the Kootenay Plains. And, according to the treaties with the Dominion Government, we do have the right to hunt, to fish, and to continue our traditional way of life on unoccupied Crown land. But when these lands were transferred to the province, the federal government gave up any effective enforcement of these rights. For the most part the Government of Alberta has stuck to the agreement that my people could hunt in the Rocky Mountain Forest Reserve, but it has hedged that agreement with many restrictions and taken other actions that have reduced our ability to support ourselves by the hunt. For example, one of the conditions the province imposed on the transfer agreement in 1947 was that the number of horses to which Indian ownership could be claimed should be reduced to a minimum so that the nuisance of wild or semiwild horses then roaming over provincial lands might ultimately be abated.[40]

Later, the Forest Rangers took on the objective of killing off the wild horses in the Forest Reserves because they were eating up valuable hay. Simultaneously, they decided on another objective of killing off the packs of wolves and coyotes roaming in the forest reserves. The rangers tried to do the trick by killing two birds with one stone, thereby saving time and money. They shot the wild horses and put poison on them to kill the wolves and coyotes.

This killed more than two birds with one stone! What had probably been planned as a conservation measure killed many eagles and other animals, instead of getting rid of the coyotes and wolves. The eagles and other animals ate the poisoned horse meat and died. When there were fewer eagles reported, we Indians were blamed for killing the eagles for feathers. We did preserve many of the feathers from the poisoned birds, but we had not killed them.

In addition to killing many animals, this "conservation measure" meant that forest fires began to spark and flare because there was so much grass in the forest; in the past the wild horses had eaten the grass, keeping it down and preventing fires. (Long ago when there were many deer, elk, and other smaller grass-eating animals, they kept the grass down in the forest. But since the coming of trophy hunters and sportsmen during open season for non-Indians, there are fewer of these animals and fires are easily kindled. The wild horses had been helping us keep the forest fires down.)

More recently, a substantial area of the natural habitat has been destroyed as a result of the Bighorn Dam built on the Kootenay Plains by the province and Calgary Power. Much of our traditional hunting grounds lies under a twenty-seven-mile man-made lake. Our livelihood from guiding hunters and trapping wildlife has been wiped out by the hydro-electric development, with no consideration for our hunting rights or for compensation or retraining for employment in the new environment. About 95 percent of my people on the Bighorn Reserve have been on welfare since the completion of the dam.

Over the past seven years, as Chief of the Wesley Band, I have tried every peaceful avenue possible to try to bring this matter to the attention of the Government of Alberta and the Indian Affairs Department, so that my people in the Bighorn area might be retrained for this new environment and be able to take advantage of the new opportunities brought about by the construction of the Bighorn Dam.

But to no avail. No one from the provincial government really wants to discuss with us any future plans for my people at Bighorn–Kootenay Plains. And the federal government sees it as a provincial problem. For example, in 1976, the tribe wanted to build a gasoline service station and convenience store on the Bighorn Reserve. But the federal government told us that the province would not permit it because there was another service station just outside the reserve.

Another point that must be made about the Bighorn Reserve is that the tribe does not hold title to it nor do we hold the mineral rights. (Indeed these were specifically exempted by the province's Order-in-Council which reserved the land for us through the federal government in 1947.) This is not true of the other lands the tribe received in fulfillment of treaty obligations nor of those we purchased.

It is not clear from the documents made available to us why the Kootenay Plains residents were given a leased reserve with the province retaining all mineral rights, rather than a regular reserve. But it is possible to guess why. When the land negotiations were conducted, the provincial government was aware of the rich potential of the mineral resources in the North Saskatchewan Valley. If the Bighorn Reserve had been established as a regular reserve and if gas and oil had been found there, at that time we would have received about 14 percent of the income. (The other 86 percent would have gone to the oil company and the provincial and federal governments.) So from the viewpoint of the province it is understandable why the authorities insisted that we be given only a leased reserve with all mineral rights reserved.

But in 1947 we understood that the Bighorn Reserve was to be a regular reserve as promised by the treaty commissioners. Instead, we were told that the "Bighorn will be leased to you only four feet from the surface according to the written statement of this regulation, for some time only . . . They also told us that all of this area, the coal company had bought it."[41] (The question of whether my people at Bighorn should be given full title to the land as originally promised is all the more pressing today because there is renewed interest in the coal reserves in the North Saskatchewan Valley at Nordegg.[42])

Behind all these points is the most basic one of all: What are the Stoneys of the Kootenay Plains due, under the promises of Treaty Seven? Or, to put it another way: was the Bighorn Reserve the beginning of the fulfillment of a promise or was it an added gift from a benevolent government to a band of Indians who needed (and still need) help?

As we saw in Chapter Six, during the negotiations of 1910 to 1911, Indian Commission David Laird clearly treated the provision of additional land in the Kootenay Plains area as an obligation of the government to fulfill its treaty promises. This was the attitude of a man who had represented the Queen and the Dominion Government at Treaty Seven and he came very close to getting the Department of the Interior to act on his view.

But Laird seems to have been the last high government official to be convinced that our requests for land were a petition for justice, not charity or appeasement. Clearly the two governments involved in 1947-48—the Government of the Province of Alberta and the Dominion Government as represented by the Indian Affairs Branch, the trustees of the Indian people—approached our land claim as a "problem." They did not view it as their obligation to fulfill a just cause and a treaty right. Their agreement was based on the premise that the Stoneys had received their land entitlement as set down in Treaty Seven; there was no consideration of the former promise for

additional land, nor that there might be a legitimate grievance arising out of some misunderstanding in the past. The federal government—and perhaps the provincial one as well—was concerned
with coming to some expedient solution that would quell embarrassing protests.[43] Although it was interested in alleviating the worst
conditions on the Stoney Reserve, the government did not wish to
set a dangerous precedent that might lead to claims by other groups.

The Indian Affairs position was that the province had made a generous offer which should be gratefully accepted by my people and
perhaps later added to, without risking the loss of the 5,000 acres.
The Deputy Minister stated:

> It is felt that, considering all the angles of the question, a rea-
> sonably satisfactory settlement has been achieved and that
> with careful planning a permanent solution to the problem
> which this isolated group has presented to the Department for
> many years can be built even on this imperfect foundation.[44]

There never has been, of course, subsequent "careful planning
. . . on this imperfect foundation," and whatever shaky basis there
was for the agreement in 1948 has since been undermined by the
building of the Bighorn Dam.

On the other hand, my people—the Stoney Tribe, and the Wesley
Band in particular—see the gaining of land in our traditional territory of the Kootenay Plains as something to which Treaty Seven enti-
tles us. We never regarded the settlement reached in 1948 between
Alberta and Ottawa, as final. The minutes of the Indian Association
of Alberta (IAA) for the years 1948 to 1957 amply document that my
people at Bighorn were unhappy with the agreement from the
beginning. In 1948, the year the reserve was established, the IAA
passed a resolution: "Resolved that all lawful means be employed to
enlarge the new Bighorn Reserve to 14,000 acres."[45] The band asked
that the reserve be extended east to Haven Creek, west to the
Kootenay Plains and south to the Saskatchewan River as originally
promised.[46] Essentially the same resolution has been passed year
after year, although sometimes additional points have been raised,
such as asking the province to confirm the band's traplines and to
stop the wild horse roundup in the Kootenay Plains.[47] The government's response to these resolutions is unknown.

Another impasse of misunderstanding had been reached in
1947–48. My people at Bighorn believed that the agreement was a

start, however faulty, for negotiations to fulfill the treaty promises, whereas the Indian Affairs Branch thought that it had found a "final solution" to a long-simmering dispute.

It had been seventy years since the signing of Treaty Seven, but the communications gap between my people and the government was wider than ever. Neither did the whiteman's government show any greater spirit of co-operation or respect for us than it had in 1877. During the treaty negotiations an interpreter was used to convince us that it was in our interest to sign a document ceding the greater part of the land to the government. During the setting aside of the Special Bighorn Reserve in 1947–48, the Indian Affairs Branch interpreted what was going on to us and assumed what was in our best interest in making the arrangements. None of my people actually took part in the negotiations. Technically, we were consulted, but no one with authority paid any attention to our requests or understood that we were asking for justice.

The original Morleyville settlement in 1885. This settlement was started in 1875 by the McDougall family. This picture show David McDougall's ranch and trading post (in the foreground), and across Jacob's Creek (in the background) is the Methodist Mission site. (*Glenbow Archives*)

Part IV
Rediscovering the Path

Self-Government Comes to the Stoney Reserve, 1930–1969

The seventy or eighty years following the signing of the treaties were years of near cultural genocide for the Indians of the Canadian West. Our forefathers had signed these agreements in good faith, in the expectation that the newly dominant society would honour its promises, protect our way of life, treat us in the same spirit of brotherhood with which we had welcomed them into our land. Instead, as we have seen from the detailed history of the Stoney experience, the newcomers relentlessly hemmed us in, interpreted the treaties according to the narrowest letter of the written word when they were not abrogated entirely, and never examined, much less attempted to protect, our traditional culture.

Much of the preceding history of the Stoneys has dealt with our attempts to prevent abrogation of our land claims and hunting rights because these are basic to our continued existence as a people—as such rights are basic to all the treaty Indians. But, as has been suggested from time to time in these chapters, our problems were not only a question of having to fight, usually unsuccessfully, for these rights. There were countless other problems that resulted from the newly dominant society's attitude toward my people, an attitude that resulted in an "Indian policy" that nearly destroyed our livelihood, our culture, our self-respect, and our ability to determine our own fate.

Until very recently, it can honestly be said, Canadian Indian policy consisted primarily of an attempt to see that we did not bother anybody, that we did not interfere with the physical and social development of the immigrants to our land. (Since we were mostly confined to reserves, dependent for our very livelihood on government handouts—whether they were called "ration houses" or "welfare benefits"—and became unused to making our own decisions, it was not too difficult for the government to achieve this control.)

Beyond providing us with a subsistence diet, the government's Indian Affairs Branch provided the people for whom it was supposed to be acting as trustee with two, and *only* two programs: agriculture and education. But the agricultural program took no notice of differing soil and climate conditions on different reserves or of preferences among different tribes for ways of life other than farming. Considering that the government gave the Churches an exclusive monopoly over Indian education and considering the curriculum provided, it is reasonable to ask whether the intent was ever as much to provide education as to enforce conversion to Christianity. Certainly Christianization (which was equated with assimilation to Western civilization) was a major part of the education program, and the Canadian government heartily endorsed the Churches' methods. For example, Lieutenant-Governor Morris wrote in 1880:

> Let us have Christianity and Civilization to leaven the mass of heathenism among the Indian tribes . . .[1]

This policy of assimilation was obviously the case when an Indian agent stated in his 1991 departmental report:

> I think that when we succeed in getting the Stonies really convinced that the road towards Christianity and advanced civilization is the right path for them they will become the best Indians in the west.[2]

As Mr. Justice Berger recently said:

> When the first Europeans came to North America they brought with them a set of attitudes and values that were quite different from those of the original peoples of the continent. At the heart of the difference was land. To white Europeans, the land was a resource waiting to be settled and cultivated. They believed that it was a form of private property, and that private property was linked to political responsibility. This

political theory about land was coupled with religious and economic assumptions. Europeans believed that the conditions for civilized existence could be satisfied only through the practice of the Christian religion and cultivation of the land. As an early missionary phrased it, "Those who come to Christ turn to agriculture."[3]

This is not to say that there were not individual white men and women who, at least according to their own rights, did not devote a good deal of time and effort to helping the Indian people. A few, such as John Laurie, even made genuine efforts to understand our real needs. But as for government policy, during the seven or eight decades after Treaties One to Seven were signed, nothing positive was done to benefit Canada's native Indians. No attempt was made to coordinate government programs with the realities of Indian life or to fit the traditional patterns of Indian society. Nothing was done to assure that native Indians had similar rights to those freely extended to newly arrived immigrants—for example, freedom of religion, assured most others, was denied to aboriginal Canadians. And almost nothing was done to honour the many treaty promises and verbal agreements made between Her Majesty's representatives and our forefathers.

Then, following the Second World War, a new social conscience seemed to emerge among the general public. Around 1950 it forced Ottawa to revise the obviously inadequate Indian Act and to reform a thoroughly discredited Indian policy.[4] Unfortunately, the nature of politics being what it is, all too often these revisions were made with a view to the desires of the politicians and non-Indian public rather than for the needs of the native people.

Another twenty years were to pass before Canadian Indian policy looked to the Indian people themselves to provide some of the answers and solutions to their problems.

To explain to the reader the changes that have occurred in Indian affairs during the past quarter-century, the easiest way is to offer the story of my own life. It was my generation that was born and raised when the old policies of Christianize, civilize, and ignore were still very much in force, when my people had no choice but to eke out an existence while the Indian Affairs Branch exercised dictatorial control over our lives. It is also the generation that has come to its time of assuming leadership at the very moment when we have an opportunity to grasp a chance at self-determination, to pull ourselves out of the morass of subsistence living and paralysing dependency into which we have been forced, to rescue our culture and regain our traditional pride as children of the Great Spirit.

I was born on the Stoney Indian Reserve at Morley during the Depression years—the hungry 1930s. For Canada at large it was an economic depression. For the Indian people, the Depression was economic, cultural, social, and religious, and it lasted many years both before and after the 1930s.

My parents have told me that I was born on a very cold night in January 1933. My first bed was a traditional Indian moss bag of buckskin and beads (a "cradle" into which a baby is laced; the moss serves as a disposable diaper). All our family were reared in moss bags. I received my Indian name, *Intabeja Mani*, meaning Walking Seal, from one of my great-grandfathers, Jonas Goodstoney, one of the old hereditary Chiefs of our tribe and the son of Chief Jacob Goodstoney, who had signed Treaty Seven for the Wesley Band. This name was given to me just a few days after I was born and before I received my English name, a common practice among our people in those days.

One of my great-grandmothers, Mary Goodstoney, who lived to an old age on the reserve, told and retold me many legends and tales of the Stoney people. These included stories of the signing of Treaty Seven and of how I received my name, Walking Seal, in a ceremony held by my band.

Stanley Rollinmud in a traditional moss bag, or cradleboard.

She would begin the latter story by saying: "During a pow-wow held by the tribe, the old Chief said, 'Walking Seal has come.' Some of the tribal members began to ask, 'Who is this Walking Seal?' They thought a visitor from another tribe had come." Then she would go on to tell me that, after the people became curious, "Old Chief Jonas Goodstoney announced at the pow-wow, 'A son is born to Tom Snow and his wife, and his name is Walking Seal.'" This was how I received my name from the old Chief. It was the name everyone called me by in my childhood days.

I was the fifth of eleven children—seven girls and four boys. My mother's name was Cora. She never attended a whiteman's school, but she was well-versed in Indian legends, in tanning hides, in drying meat, and in caring for her family. My father, the late Chief Tom Snow, had very little formal schooling—a half-year in an Indian day school at Morley—but he was well educated in Indian traditions, religion, and ways of life.

My mother and father were good parents. They taught us about the Great Spirit. They told us to respect the elders. They told us that when an elder speaks you must be silent and listen. "Don't argue and don't say things as though you know more than the elders," they would tell us.

Times were hard in those days, although a man could still keep food on the family table by hunting hard enough. There were hardly any employment opportunities available on the reserve except carpentry, logging, ranching, and odd jobs. Like most band members, my family earned some income through hunting and trapping and some by cutting timber for rails, posts, and firewood. My father's trapline was along the foothills just north of the Morley Reserve, and he would catch lynx, silver fox, red and cross fox, coyotes, marten, mink, and squirrels.

Our family's worldly goods were about average for the reserve. Most of it was the vehicles and animals we needed for our livelihood. We had two wagons, a buggy, a big wagon for hauling logs, and a sleigh. We had three teams of horses, about fifteen saddle and pack horses, and about a dozen head of cattle.

There was no such thing as a modern house on the reserve. (The only modern buildings in Morleyville were the United Church and manse, built in 1921, and the residential school, built in 1925.) No home had electricity, central heating, running water, or indoor plumbing. Quite typically our entire family lived in a one-room cabin, with a wood-burning stove for heating and cooking. Sometimes in the winter the pail of water in our cabin froze during the night and had to be heated before we could drink.

But we were accustomed to such living conditions and thankful for our poor cabin and our way of life. At mealtimes we all gathered around the table and prayed and ate together. We thanked the Great Spirit for what he had provided. When we shot game, we thanked the Creator and, even though there was little money, we had dried meat, pemmican, wild meat, rabbits, grouse, and bannock to eat. Somehow, we always managed to get by.

It was a demanding life, but one that kept our family close together and aware of our cultural roots. However, when I was eight years old I was suddenly uprooted from the security of home life to join the fifty to eighty pupils in the residential school at the Morley townsite.

In theory, all reserve children were supposed to attend this school from about the ages of eight to sixteen. In practice, most, although not all the children of my generation did enter the primary grades but few stayed for long and there was little official objection if a student left. My family, however, had a tradition of respect for education; although neither of my parents had received much, other family members had had more, and we children were encouraged to get as much as we could stand.

It was very difficult. The residential school was funded by the federal government but operated by the United Church of Canada for the purpose of "Christianizing the heathen" and "civilizing the savage." We were totally removed from our family and culture for ten months of the year. School started in September and we remained in residence until the end of June, with only two days' holiday at Christmas and another two at New Year's during which we could visit our parents. Non-Indians took care of us and supervised our chores, which were extensive, especially as we grew older. The few pupils who stayed as long as age fourteen were expected to put in a half-day's work to maintain ourselves in addition to a half-day's studying. Boys plowed the school's land, cared for it and the gardens, milked cows, tended cows, pigs, chickens, and mink. Girls did the housekeeping and looked after the younger children.

From the beginning the language used at school had to be English. Of course, the language spoken at my home and in general use throughout the reserve was the traditional Stoney dialect of the Sioux language. Consequently, when I entered school, I, like most Stoney children, knew hardly a word of English. Yet that was the language in which I was to receive my education from the very start.

That education consisted of nothing that had any relationship to our homes and culture. Indeed, Stoney culture was condemned explicitly and implicitly. Our classes consisted of teachings in Protestant religion and ethics, the three Rs, and European and Church history.

From listening to these teachings it seemed to me that the only good people on earth were non-Indians and specifically white Christians. We were taught that the work and knowledge of our med-

This truck, pictured here with students in 1950, was used by the Morley Residential School to transport students, school supplies, and feed for livestock.

icine men and women were of the Devil. We were taught that when people died they went to Heaven and walked streets paved with gold or to Hell and forever roasted in a lake of fire. We were taught that only by believing in a righteous man named Jesus, who lived two thousand years ago, could we be saved from that fire. (No one at the mission seemed to have thought of the intelligent approach of saying: the Great Spirit, the Creator whom you worship, has revealed himself in the person of Jesus Christ.) We were taught that Christianity was the only true religion and that all others—including the faith of our fathers—were false and of the Devil.

This was real indoctrination and some of the students dreaded going to church, but they were given no choice. These were confusing times for all of us when we were taught at home to respect the beliefs of our elders and at school to have disrespect for their values.

In later years when I was doing research work, I looked over the files of the teachers at the Morley Residential School. I found that the two teachers who taught when I attended were both non-certified. One had a high school education and the other had not even completed high school. In those wartime years, perhaps that was all the United Church could find to teach us, but it seems more likely that these two teachers were hired after consideration of their Christian calling to work among Indians, rather than for their academic qualifications. This would fall in with the point I have made elsewhere: the government and the Church considered their mission to be Christianizing the savage, rather than providing a good education to meet realistic, practical needs for the future.

Because of the inferior quality of the education, the poor qualifications of many of the teachers, and the strangeness of the curriculum, it is little wonder that the dropout rate was (and remains) astronomically high—almost 100 percent by Grade Eight. In fact, the school really only went through Grade Six, with a very few pupils staying the extra two years. In theory, secondary education was available in regular schools in nearby towns. In practice, our poor preparation, the difficulties of transportation, and, above all, the lack of encouragement from non-Indian officialdom made continuing education all but impossible. Yet if we had had qualified teachers and a say in the curriculum of our schools in the past, I am sure that by now many Stoney students would have acquired a good standard of education and even college or university degrees.[5]

In July and August we Stoney schoolchildren had our summer holidays; we returned to our homes and some measure of Indian traditional culture and values. One of the important events of the summer was the religious observances in the Sacred Lodge—the Sun Dance as it is called by English-speaking people. This observance has been misunderstood, misinterpreted, and grossly distorted by whitemen. I have even heard commentators at the Calgary Stampede describe the Indians who practise it as "sun worshippers." Nothing could be further from the truth. The Stoney phrase which describes this religious observance is almost impossible to translate into English. This phrase is "*ti-jarabi-chûbi*"; it literally translates as "making a lodge dwelling for a religious ceremony." The words "sun" and "dance" are not even used in the description of this sacred ceremony conducted by our religious elders.

We do not worship the sun. The dance is an expression of the joy and ecstasy of a religious life, of being thankful for life, the beautiful creation, the rain, the sun, and the changing seasons. The medicine men or women performing the ritual express their gratitude to the Great Spirit for all these things and pray for a good future, health, strength, and prosperity for the tribe.

During August, my parents usually took us on fishing and hunting trips to the North Ghost River near the Rockies. We younger children travelled by wagon while my older brother, sisters, and cousins rode on horseback.

Much of what I learned of our Stoney values came from my grandfather, William Snow, who was a medicine man. He is shown here as he looked when I was a child in the 1930s. *(Glenbow Archives NA-7-54)*

Father hunted big game and Mother prepared dried meat and pemmican for the winter months. We picked wild berries and dried them, fished, and hunted grouse and small game—and, as children, thoroughly enjoyed the wilderness. Then, just before school was scheduled to reopen, we would return to Morley.

Like all students, I left the residential school at the age of sixteen and returned to my parents and our one-room home. I helped supplement the family income by doing various jobs, and my father taught me much about big-game hunting and trapping, wildlife, the forests, and the rugged mountain country. He taught me the traditional custom of sharing the hunter's kill: which parts of the animal were the hunter's and which other parts of the animal were to belong to the other tribal members. For example, if a hunter killed a moose, the hide, head, and a certain part in the back of the animal would belong to him, while all the other meat would belong to the tribe. The Stoneys were a sharing community. Therefore, even a hunter's kill was subject to the custom of sharing the meat with other families of the tribe. Also, we had a tradition of leaving some small parts of the animal for the birds, our feathered brothers.

One year I worked with a group of Stoneys who were rounding up wild horses along the eastern slopes of the Rockies. In order to survive in the wilderness, I had to learn the traditional customs of living in the wilds. I learned to identify the various edible plants and herbs, to read the weather, and to identify direction and landmarks so as to find my way home, even at night.

During this period of my life, I visited many homes on the reserve and learned the traditional legends and their meanings, the philosophies and religious thoughts, and the history of my people. But I also attended church services quite regularly and helped the current missionary, Reverend Edwin Kempling, on the Morley Reserve. We had Bible studies and cottage prayer meetings in various homes, and sometimes I would translate the messages into the Stoney tongue for him.

During this period, too, I tried desperately to further my education, even to the point of attempting a Grade Nine provincial correspondence course. I attempted to enroll in a technical school in Calgary but the red tape—which almost seemed to be designed to back up the lack of encouragement I received from the local non-Indian counsellors—prevented me. So I decided that I had to make my way by helping myself. In this I was much influenced by my father, who had always taught me self-respect and determination. Often he would say, "If someone else does something that seems good to you, do not think that you cannot do it also."

In the spring of 1957, I was converted to the Christian faith; I took a stand and accepted the Lord Jesus Christ as my personal saviour. By this time I had an idea of the true mission of the Church and was hopeful that I could help my people in a real way through it.

Some of the Christian people in the reserve community did indeed

My father, Chief Tom Snow.

help me in searching for a place where I might continue my education and prepare myself for the future. But it was difficult to find a school that would meet my needs and the goals I had in mind. Upon the recommendation of friends and advisers, I applied to the Cook Christian Training School in Phoenix, Arizona. Cook specializes in Indian education and has a curriculum designed to train Indians for leadership with a view to having its graduates return to the Indian community. At the time it was the only school of its kind in

North America; there are still none in Canada.

I was very anxious to attend this specialized school but had to save money to pay for my education. To do this I worked for a year as a boys' supervisor at the Morley Residential School. Then, in 1958, I was accepted by Cook for the fall semester. The instructors were very understanding and were aware of Indian culture and Indian religious thought.

I spent four years in Arizona studying at Cook and at Phoenix College. While I was there I met a fellow student, Alva Townsend, whom I married in 1960. I received my diploma in the spring of 1962, the first member of the Stoney Tribe to have done so, then enrolled at St. Stephens Theological College in Edmonton in the fall of that year to complete my training in preparation for the Christian ministry.

While attending Cook School, I did work as a part-time janitor to pay for my first three years of education there. I am very grateful to the United Church of Canada for paying for my last year of training at Cook and my year's theological education at St. Stephen's, as well as giving me other financial assistance.

After a year's study at St. Stephen's, I was recommended by the United Church of Canada's Alberta Conference for ordination to the Christian ministry. In the spring of 1963, I was ordained along with five non-Indian classmates in a ceremony at the Northern Alberta Jubilee Auditorium in Edmonton.

I then spent the next five years working among native people as well as with white congregations.

Shortly after ordination, I was stationed at Wolseley, Saskatchewan, where I worked as assistant to an experienced and understanding minister, Reverend Harvey Clarke, who served a rural white congregation as well as the Assiniboine Indians at Sintaluta. After serving at Wolseley for two years, I returned to Phoenix for an additional year of studies at Arizona State University. While studying there, I also served as a minister in the U.S. Presbyterian Church, working with Apache and Pima Indian congregations at Fort McDowell and Lehi. I enjoyed my work there and received considerable inspiration from their accomplished pianists and excellent choirs. In the summer of 1966, I returned to Alberta and was stationed at Ashmont, where I served the Cree Indian Churches of Goodfish and Saddle Lake, as well as the local white congregation.

Then, in 1968, I returned to my home on the Morley Reserve.

Returning home after a long absence and many new experiences is always strange. It is difficult to sort out what has really changed and what one is seeing with new eyes.

There had been a few physical changes since my boyhood. A new, modern elementary school had been built in 1954, replacing the first day school, which was started in 1945. A community hall had been put up in 1958, just before I left the reserve. Now there were five modern houses under construction at Morley—the first homes on the reserve to have central heating, running water, and indoor plumbing. The rest of the houses were the small cabins I remembered, but most had had electricity installed in 1967. (The telephone line was not to reach the reserve until 1971, about the same time that indoor plumbing became more common. To this day, there is no garbage collection, and many homes still depend on wood-burning stoves for both heat and cooking.)

Economically the situation had worsened because, in contrast to my father's time, it had become almost impossible to feed a family by hunting. The reserve population had increased to nearly 2,000 with a very large proportion of children; the herds of game were mostly within the confines of parks and "protected" wilderness areas; the ever more oppressive hunting regulations restricted a man's opportunities to put food on his table by his own efforts. In consequence, families lived primarily on the welfare cheques that the majority of the adults received, the Family Allowances that had been recently introduced by the federal government, and the five-dollar-per-year treaty payment each tribal member continued to receive. Only a very little could be garnered from traplines, fishing, and the occasional hunting of big game.

Jobs were few and hard to come by—mostly casual labour in ranching or lumbering. The skilled jobs available went to whitemen. This was perhaps no longer so much because of direct prejudice as because the day school, although no longer run by the Church and somewhat improved from the residential indoctrination centre of my day, did not train for employment. (White officials blamed the failure of the school on the high dropout rate, but who can expect students to stay when the curriculum is irrelevant and jobs so few. The same non-Indian officials gave—as they still do today—scant encouragement to any good student who was interested in furthering his or her education to the secondary level or beyond.) Even on the reserve itself, all the full-time jobs were filled by non-Indians. In 1968 the only Stoneys employed there were a part-time janitor to clean out the Indian agent's office and the nursing station, and two office workers—Ray Baptiste, who was the welfare administrator, and Claris Kootenay, who was the Band Council secretary.

Psychologically, the time of my return to Morley Reserve was the worst of times for my people. Canada had celebrated its centennial by granting the Indian people full citizen status and with it the right to cast a ballot in elections, to consume alcohol in bars, and to stand in line for welfare cheques. The Stoney world had been turned around and, at the same time, had become smaller. Thirty years before, every Stoney man could provide most of his family's food from the forests, the plains, the hills, and the rivers; on top of that he would be able to make a little spending money from trapping or helping out a neighbouring rancher. Such cash income was rarely required for absolute necessities but could be used to make a bleak life more bearable; if a little of it went to buy a bottle of cheap whisky, purchased illegally, how much harm could it do? But by 1968, most of our food had to come from the stores. The game herds were so depleted and driven back that a man could only hunt a deer or moose for a treat, for those special times when his womenfolk told him they were hungry for wild meat. Only then did he have reason to go out into the wilderness doing the things that a man should do.

Several very important changes in our cultural patterns began to be apparent. Some families bought deep freezers. When the man returned with game he no longer shared it willingly, as was the traditional way; he butchered the carcass for freezing.

Despite the decline of the hunt, money income, which had always been used for the little luxuries of life—candy for the kids, the extra groceries for all, pretty thread and cloth for the woman, and a bottle (legal or not) for the man—was still used in the same way. The welfare and Family Allowance cheques were often spent entirely on these luxuries while the nutrition of many families suffered. For the first time we saw, with horror, evidence of neglected children and the first signs of a loss of moral responsibility among our people.

It was apparent that external bodies—the governments, the government departments, the Church—could not do a great deal to improve our critical situation, even if they were willing to try. It was doubtful whether they could even see the problems they were causing by the solutions they offered. Clearly, it was time that the Stoney people took over the helm to steer their own ship through the troubled waters.

Two new circumstances at this time made it possible for us to begin to rediscover the path on which we can find our way back to being a people with self-respect, a people who determine our own destiny, a people who have amalgamated ourselves into the larger society without losing our traditional culture and values.

These two new factors were the Department of Indian Affairs' new policy of promoting integrated education for Indian children and the anticipated introduction of self-government to the reserve in 1969, about five months after my return to Morley.[6]

When I returned to Morley in July 1968, the federal school integration policy was in full swing. The Department's theory behind this policy was that the sooner you got the Indian off the reserve and into Canadian society-at-large, the better it would be for the Indian. Education was to be one of the major means of achieving this integration.

As usual, the Indian Affairs officials had never discussed their new education policy with us nor asked us about our future wants. The curriculum was never questioned. No consideration was given as to whether or not it was suited to the real needs and desires of the people, or relevant to Stoney society, Stoney values, and Stoney religious philosophy.

In order to induce the Stoneys to have their children educated off the reserve, the federal government resorted to some very enticing pressure tactics. For example, it introduced a clothing allowance for students registering in off-reserve, integrated schools. Each student going to an off-reserve school received fifty dollars from the general welfare funds allocated to the entire band; students remaining in the reserve school received no such allowance.

This enticement of children to leave the reserve caused great concern among the tribe. Not only were my people worried that the whiteman's curriculum plus physical absence from Stoney society would eradicate our children's traditional values, we were also under no illusions about how our children would fare in these schools and what would happen to them when they reached school-leaving age. As bad as services and conditions might often be on our reserve, it offers more than the urban slums.

Another basic objection to this policy was that it was a one-way street. There was no consideration given to integrating off-reserve, non-Indian students into the reserve schools. Furthermore, on looking into the government's educational plans for our children, I discovered that Indian Affairs had made arrangements with nearby towns for the education of our children without consulting the Tribal

Council. Municipal schools were being given capital expenditure money that had been allocated to the *reserve* school, and this money was being used to expand their facilities or to build additional classrooms, theoretically to accommodate increased numbers of Stoney students.

Some of the non-Indian communities took advantage of the offer. Probably the worst example of departmental stupidity and lack of control can be illustrated by the case of the non-Indian community near the reserve that accepted money for additional construction on the understanding that Stoney children would be admitted. Then, on completion of the work, the school announced that it did not want to have the Stoney children attend.

The sad irony of the new policy was that money was being expended on it just when many Stoneys were requesting much-needed capital improvements to the educational facilities on the reserve. In addition, as we thought through the implications of integrated education and rejected it, some of us began to see the need for and to request a general upgrading of the reserve school's educational materials and the immediate removal of biased social studies books that condemned Indians and Indian ways and values. In the meantime, some of the students who had received clothing allowances and enrolled in off-reserve schools began returning and re-registering at the Morley Indian School. These manoeuvres took place in September 1968, but it was to be another year before we were able to make the Indian Affairs Department hear our verdict on integrated education.

While the Department of Indian Affairs was attempting to go its own dictatorial way on education policy, it also introduced its most positive program ever—local reserve self-government. The Stoney tribe was one of the first Alberta Indian communities to assume self-government. It was to prove a real challenge for the Stoney people and the beginning of a new era.

When the program was first announced, it was not well received by all members of the tribe. In fact, when I returned to Morley—after the program had been announced but before it had been implemented—I found that self-government for the bands was the subject of many discussions. The Indian Affairs Department was applying various pressures for the Stoney Tribe to assume self-government very rapidly. Many individual Stoneys felt that if self-government was refused the government might withdraw various services; the tribe, which was financially poor at the time, could not afford this. Others feared that, as a result of accepting self-government, we might lose our treaty and aboriginal rights. Others held the view that it was time we took on the responsibilities and met the demands of our times, became independent, made our own decisions, and planned for the future of our own children.

It was clear to everyone that self-government would be a tremendous challenge. For generations we had been brainwashed into believing that Indians were not capable of handling their own affairs—a view that justified perpetuating the Indian Affairs bureaucracy. Almost overnight we were being told to handle our own affairs ourselves.

We knew that we lacked the training or preparation for the job. We knew that those who spoke against the scheme might be right in suspecting that the government will someday try to use self-government to abridge our rights. Yet the majority felt that we had to accept this challenge or be accused of being afraid to accept the responsibility and control we had been demanding for years. There was a foreboding silence from the Department of Indian Affairs. Although it had introduced the program, it was apparent it had done so with reluctance. It made no attempt to prepare or train the Councils for their new roles. (A few years later it did distribute a pamphlet, "Local Government on Indian Reserves," which informed Chiefs and Councillors about their respective roles and responsibilities.) We sensed that the Department was waiting for us to make mistakes and fail, so it could criticize us. There was an expectation that we would not make it. It seemed to be trying to create a situation that would assure failure and a justification for reestablishing departmental control.

Self-government might easily have ended up as another of Indian Affairs' "successful failures," except that we knew we could not afford to fail once again. One protective force that helped us through the difficult years of adjustment and learning was the strength and wisdom of our elders. We were aware that the Great Spirit created us for a purpose and placed us on this Great Island. Our elders reminded us to have faith in the Creator, and that everything would fall into place as though it were planned.

Another protection was that from the time we accepted the idea of self-government we began to plan that the Chiefs and Tribal Council that would be elected would combine the best of the available talent and experience. The challenge of the modern age would be met under leadership that included both the traditional wisdom and experience of some of our elders and the administrative and "outside-world" experience of some of the tribe's younger, educated members.

As one of the latter—and perhaps because I was the son of a former Chief—some of the Wesley Band elders approached me not long after my return to Morley and asked if I would consider seeking the band Chieftainship in the upcoming elections of December 1968. At first, after discussing the matter with my family, I decided to remain with Church work where, I thought, I might best help my people. I had been appointed minister of the McDougall Indian Mission Church at Morley. While serving as clergyman, I intended to help my people, not only in spiritual matters, but in social and economic ways as well. The need for improved medical services, education, economic development, housing, and job opportunities presented a challenge I found impossible to ignore. At the time I was quite confident that the Christian Church would be involved in helping correct these many social ills.

Unfortunately, I came to discover the Church neither was fully aware, nor sufficiently understood the importance of modern Indian issues and problems. Furthermore, it didn't seem that the Church really wanted to become involved. Its main social concern seemed limited to the issuing of used clothing to my people.

I think that the turning point for me came late one Wednesday afternoon when, during one of my pastoral visits, I stopped in at the Morley nursing station. Some Stoney people were waiting there for the doctor to come after he had seen patients at Cochrane, some twenty miles to the east. While I was talking to the people, the telephone rang; after a brief conversation, the nurse in charge politely and apologetically informed those waiting that the doctor was not coming that day, but would be there one week later.

Many of these people had no cars—one was a woman who had walked in with her sick baby on her back and was obviously worried. Clearly, the medical services were grossly inadequate, if not discriminatory.

As a clergyman serving my people on the reserve, I had already approached Indian Affairs officials to point out my concern regarding the integrated education policy. Now I offered suggestions as to how medical services could be improved. Each time, however, I was simply told, "Keep to your preaching; we listen only to the elected representatives on the reserve."

After repeated but useless attempts to talk with Indian Affairs personnel, I became convinced that unless I held elected office, I would never be heard and my concern for my people could only be a fruitless effort.

Consequently, when several elders asked me to reconsider and run for the Chieftainship in our first elections under self-government, I accepted their advice and consented.

I was elected and took office as Chief of the Wesley Band in January 1969. Tom Twoyoungmen was chosen as Chief of the Bearspaw Band and Frank Powderface as Chief of the Chiniquay Band. With twelve Councillors, representing the three bands and three reserves of the Stoneys, we formed the first Tribal Council under reserve self-government.

There was no shortage of challenges.

The overall goal of the new Tribal Council had to be a better quality of life for our people to meet the demands and stresses of the modern society. Our first priorities were to provide full-time jobs for tribal members, to offer ways of upgrading skills, to improve education, to raise the general standard of living and social services, and to increase our revenue to enable us to invest in economic development projects. Groundwork had to be laid in all major areas of community growth—jobs and training, education, recreation, health, preventative social services, and housing. The federal government's programs in all these areas had been inadequate (or nonexistent) for much too long.

To help us determine our own priorities, we commissioned a Calgary consulting firm (Underwood, McLelland and Associates Ltd.) to prepare a land use study (and later a recreation resource study). These studies highlighted the recreational and tourist possibilities of the Morley area and the employment opportunities that would develop if we could establish viable production enterprises.

While this was an important advance, in that for the first time we were discussing our real problems and setting our own goals and priorities, it became apparent that our own people lacked the necessary trade skills and management and professional training to accomplish what we wanted to do. We came to realize that we needed training programs for our people, but also sympathetic outside help until we had sufficient personnel of our own.

But before this planning was anywhere near complete, before the Tribal Council was really comfortable in its new role, and long before the people had become used to the challenges and disciplines self-government demands, a crisis arose that could have destroyed us. Because my people met the challenge, because the tribe acted in a unified and determined manner in the face of an action by the Indian Affairs Department—those bureaucrats who had ordered our lives for so long—that crisis turned out to be one of the best things that ever happened to us. But nobody knew that while it was going on.

The crisis arose over one of the problems that had long plagued us: education. Even before the institution of self-government, many of my people had come to realize how harmful an education totally oriented to the dominant white society was to our children. This was why we so disliked the integrated off-reserve school program.

When the Tribal Council first took office and began to work out priorities and goals, we agreed that the school system had to be reworked.

In June 1969 the Morley Education Committee met with district Indian Affairs officials and informed them of our education plans and aspirations. We announced our intention of rebuilding our inadequate educational facilities, and we made it very clear that we opposed the integration policy in its present form. (Our early opposition to the government's *enforced* integration policy—especially in education—is now generally in tune with the views of most social planners and social activists. Such wasn't originally the case, and pressure from white experts and their supporters to a great degree forced the government's hand. Time has done much to vindicate Stoney judgement.)

At this meeting we also requested what seem in retrospect two very small steps toward greater orientation of the school to Stoney needs: (1) that the Education Committee be involved in the selection of the next school principal (due to be chosen for the upcoming fall session); and (2) that a community-minded principal be chosen—specifically one who would live on the reserve and be part of the reserve community. (In the past, Morley School principals had lived off the reserve, in Calgary or elsewhere, and they had rushed with the children for the door at three-thirty, leaving the community entirely until the beginning of the next school day.)

The district education officials agreed to these requests and left the meeting. We were quite happy that our concerns had been favourably received and our initial requests approved.

Then came August of 1969.

The Morley school was scheduled to reopen during the first week of September. Less than a month before that date, we suddenly discovered that the Indian Affairs District Officer had hired a principal, Stewart Robertson, without consulting the Tribal Council or the Education Committee. Furthermore, Mr. Robertson was to live off the reserve. This was in direct opposition to what had been agreed by the district Indian Affairs officials and the Stoney Tribal Council in June.

We were willing to overlook the fact that the Education Committee had not been consulted in selecting Mr. Robertson, but the Tribal Council reiterated our request that the principal of the Morley School live on the reserve. Mr. Robertson refused to do this. Unfortunately, E. R. Daniels, the Department official then responsible for Indian education in Alberta, chose to side with him rather than with the elected representatives of the Stoney Tribe. It was apparent that, regardless of the wishes of the people, Indian Affairs was determined to bulldoze its way through as it had so often in the past.

But this time, the Stoney Tribal Council was prepared to test the strength of self-government; we were determined that we were not going to be pushed around. The Stoney people were in unanimous agreement with Council's attitude.

The Council talked about various ways of dealing with the school crisis, and one suggestion appeared acceptable to all: a school boycott. It was unanimously agreed that our children would not attend school until our simple request was met. (With the type of education our children were receiving, we thought that missing a week or two would not be much of a loss anyway.)

On the first day of school, the newly appointed principal arrived, but only about thirty of the three hundred children enrolled attended. The majority of those who showed up came from families who were unaware of the boycott. The next day only a handful returned.

Despite this firm community stand, initial negotiations produced no satisfactory results. The *Calgary Herald* reported on September 4:

> Talks to end a boycott by 300 Indian school children at Morley broke up today with no prospect of settlement.
> . . . "They're not listening to us," Chief John Snow complained of the federal officials. "Nothing happened in the talks. Nothing," he reported.
> The 14 members of the Stoney band council unanimously supported a request that the newly-appointed school principal

be required to live on the reserve. This is the third day of the boycott of classes and Stoney leaders say children will stay away from school "until this is settled, and by that we mean until we receive assurance the principal will reside on the reserve."

Stewart Robertson, the newly-appointed principal, repeated today he intends to live on his ranch near Calgary.

Frank Powderface, another Stoney chief, asked for the resignation of Mr. Robertson, who left the meeting before its conclusion.

. . . "We've made a simple and reasonable request—that the principal live here with us. We want someone who is interested in our community, not someone who rushes off every day at three-thirty," Chief Snow said.

"We're fed up with the whole school system here . . ."

During the boycott, I telephoned Ottawa and spoke with top education officials in Indian Affairs; I discovered they were under the impression that the new school principal was to live on the reserve. Somewhere along the way, bureaucratic wires had obviously become crossed. Furthermore, Indian Affairs officials showed little willingness to alter entrenched indifference to Indian aspirations. On September 5, an editorial in the *Calgary Albertan* took the Department to task on this matter:

> The children on the Morley Indian Reserve between Calgary and Banff are not furthering their education at the moment. The officials of the Indian Affairs Department are, or should be, because from what has been said on both sides, it seems pretty clear that if the departmental officials had exercised intelligence and understanding in good time, the current boycott of the reserve school would not have occurred. Indeed Chief John Snow is quoted as having told one departmental official:"It is because you cannot even reason with us, we have to force you to talk to us by boycotting the school."

The boycott lasted eight days. By that time it was evident that hard feelings had increased to the point where any reasonable possibility of a satisfactory relationship between Mr. Robertson and the Stoneys at any time in the future had disappeared. The Indian Affairs Department gave in and allowed us to appoint a principal who was prepared to live on the reserve. The first school boycott on an Indian reserve in Alberta was ended, and the Stoney students returned to classes at the Morley School.

Appointing our own principal—and one who was prepared to live on the reserve—marked the beginning of our involvement in the education of our own children and at least the start of the development of a school that would adequately meet requirements of the Stoney students. It marked the beginning of a realistic belief that we, as Indian people, could have a say in how our schools should be run, and who our teachers should be, and what kind of curriculum would be used in our education programs.

But our victory went much further than the field of education. We began to get a feeling of what self-government was all about. For the past one hundred years we had been unable to break through the bureaucratic red tape that enslaved us.

For many generations we had had decisions made for us—supposedly for our own good—and many changes had been arbitrarily imposed upon my people. Most decisions affecting us were decided in Ottawa or in local Indian Affairs offices, and the Indian agent simply announced the new directive or policy. If an official agreement was involved, he presented the document to the Tribal or Band Council for a rubber-stamp signature. Now, even though we realized our status under self-government was only semi-autonomous and subject to the final control of the Indian Affairs Department, we knew we had the right to control many of our own affairs, to publicly protest those policies we question, to present our own alternatives—and to win. As the late Ron Campbell, principal of the Morley School in the 1950s, commented, the school boycott was "the first battle the Indians won since Custer and Little Bighorn." In that knowledge we could see a glimmer of hope and possibly the dawn of a new day.

Under Self-Government: Indian Culture Begins Again, 1969–1977

The history of the development of this land and its natural resources would have been written differently if our forefathers had refused to sign the treaty one hundred years ago. They signed, but they did not sign to get rich. Nor did they invite the whiteman to share the country just to exploit it and make himself a profit. They signed the treaty in a spirit of peace, cooperation, and trust, expecting that the written and spoken promises of the Commissioners would be fulfilled.

These promises included the right to land and its resources (including the resources to be gained from hunting and fishing, which our forefathers knew the value of, and those from underground mineral wealth, which my people learned about later). The promises also included the right to continue our traditional life, with its culture and values that differ so sharply from those of the immigrants.

But our forefathers, despite their lack of experience with the whiteman and some very poor "advice" from those they trusted, were not naïve about what this right to our tradition meant. When the treaties were signed, they knew full well that contact with the whiteman—with his artifacts, with his new technology, with his different economy—had already made some difference in our lives. They also realized that the buffalo were beginning to disappear. They could foresee that the future would necessitate a new way of life and, to the best of their ability, they attempted to provide for this in the treaty, too. They could not have forecast the shape life would take in the twentieth century (no more than the Commissioners could have), but they clearly knew that before long their people would have to make a living from the land at least partly from agriculture and the new concept of industry. For that reason they saw to it that the treaty also included promises that the government would supply us with equipment and with teachers and schoolhouses so that we could learn the new technology we would need to make the necessary adaptation.

Whether or not these promises were immediately fulfilled in the letter and the spirit of our forefathers expected is beside the point in some contexts today. What is really important for both Indian and non-Indian to understand is that the treaty, signed in perpetuity ("for as long as the sun shines, rivers flow, and grass grows") guaranteed both that we would be free within our own tradition and that we would have the means of reaching accommodation with the other society.

This has not yet happened, but with goodwill, hard work, and careful planning on the part of both Indians and government, there is no reason why the promise of the treaties cannot be met—even if it has suffered a hundred years' delay.

When the Stoney Tribe first accepted self-government and selected our first Tribal Council, few were completely aware of the challenges and responsibilities to come, but nearly all sensed that change—for better or for worse—was in the air.

The reader may imagine the mixed feelings of the members of the three Stoney bands as they gathered at the polling places on our three reserves at Morley, Bighorn, and Eden Valley. We were to elect a fifteen-member Council: one Chief and three Councillors to represent each of the three bands at Morley; two Councillors to represent tribal members at Eden Valley; and one Councillor to represent members at Bighorn. Most of the Chiniquay Band members lived at Morley. The Bearspaw Band members were split, with some being at Morley and some at Eden Valley. Most of the Wesley Band members lived at Morley, but almost a hundred of them had chosen to live at Bighorn on the Kootenay Plains.

That polling day in December 1968, the members of the three bands were to select the group which would steer our people into reserve self-government. It was, at the same time, a challenge and a threat. Democracy through the ballot box was still a new idea, and many votes were cast with respect for the old hereditary chieftainship system. Many others saw a need to put into positions of responsibility men who had a broad experience in the other society. And many believed in following the customary pattern of placing a family representative on the Council. It would be fair to say that when the ballots were counted, the newly elected Council was fairly representative of all these different opinions.

As soon as we took office, the Tribal Council began to discuss many good ideas and plans for the future of our people on the reserve. But as we pondered them, we began to realize more and more how deep rooted our problems were and how deep rooted the solutions had to be.

The basic problem, we realized, was to rebuild the shattered Stoney tribal society. It was a must to rebuild our once proud society if we were to be successful in the new venture.

Part of the solution to this was that the harsh realities of the twentieth century had to be faced squarely by our people. We could no longer hide behind the none-too-benevolent dictatorship of the Indian Affairs Department and accept our miserable lot while bemoaning the loss of our traditional nomadic life. Alternatives to the traditional economy had to be found and programs planned and instituted that would provide a good future for our children.

But, although we had to accept the dominant economy, technology, and legal system surrounding us, we did not have to accept all its cultural assumptions. The Stoney Indians', culture, language, and religion have been threatened ever since the whiteman arrived on this Great Island. With his excessive dependence on technology, restrictive legislation, greedy individualism, and smug certainty that he knows all the answers—even in religion—he has been a real and constant threat to our cooperative communal outlook, our respect for nature, and our value system. With the coming of self-government and a measure of self-determination, we did not have to accept this.

In other words, we came to understand that it was not an either/or choice: acculturation to the dominant society or clinging to our old ways in a world where they could no longer offer us and our children a good life. We came to understand that there was a third way—the way of *biculturalism*. We came to understand that we could still follow Stoney tribal custom but, at the same time, adjust to a technological age on our own terms. Our hope was (and still is) to retain the best in the Stoney culture and to take the best in the dominant culture.

We had no illusions that this would be an easy task, or a short one. We would have to take an embittered, despondent, confused people and point them toward rediscovering, recapturing, and revitalizing our cultural philosophies and values, while adapting this traditional culture to modern times. And to give our people the hope to do this, we would have to discover or invent employment programs and opportunities whereby they could put bread on their tables without degradation.

Parallel to this effort would be the task of reminding government and Church of their treaty promises and obligations. It would not be easy to communicate our ideas to the larger, alien society or to convince it of the worth of our programs, but it was essential that the challenge be met if we were to venture into the future with success.

As the Tribal Council started to grapple with the challenges of responsible government—which we had decided meant instituting programs leading to this new biculturalism while carefully insisting on our treaty rights—we came to realize that one of the difficulties which has long faced Indian people has been our ignorance of Canada's constitutional framework and the workings of the parliamentary system of government.

Originally our people believed that the Great Queen Mother was the real political authority. Everything was done in her name, and, in those days, the attachment of all whitemen to the Crown was apparent. Government compartmentalization, bureaucracy, interdepartmental feuding, even the distinctions between levels of government were foreign and unclear to us. Therefore, it was difficult for our people to understand many events and changes that occurred over the past hundred years.

For a long long time we could not understand why the Queen would allow the Canadian Parliament to break the promises made by her official representatives. Only after many years of protesting about the injustices inherent in the outlawing of religious ceremonies (such as our Sun Dance), the constant introduction and change of game regulations, and the transfer of the control of Crown forestry lands from federal to provincial jurisdiction in 1930, did we finally come to realize that our lives were really being controlled by politicians in Ottawa. And still more gradually did we realize that the politicians were largely influenced by public opinion, and that government-set policy is usually administered by bureaucrats, with the top level often unaware of "routine" decisions that affect hundreds of lives.

Another fact of Canadian government which we found difficult to understand and which has caused us many problems was the intervention of the provincial level. While we were still very much under the impression that we were under the direct protection of the Crown, the authority of the Province of Alberta was imposed on us without consultation or much consideration of the effect it would have on Canada's treaty obligations.

From the signing of the treaties until 1905, the North West Territories were under the direct jurisdiction of the federal government. When Alberta and Saskatchewan achieved provincial autonomy, the treaty Indians living within the borders of the new provinces were without the franchise. Consequently, politicians saw no necessity to consult us about the new division of Crown authority. As we have seen in previous chapters, whenever there have been problems concerning treaty Indians, the province has found it convenient to deny direct responsibility and has referred the matter to the federal government. Too often the federal government has attempted to toss all or part of the responsibility back on the province.

The worst problems with the province have occurred since 1930, when the Imperial Parliament in Britain gave effect to Canada's Natural Resources Transfer Agreement. Even after the prairie provinces had been created in 1905, the federal government had retained ownership of the Crown lands and natural resources. In 1930, however, control was transferred to the provinces of Alberta, Saskatchewan, and Manitoba. In theory this should have made no difference whatsoever to our treaty rights and land claims. Section 10 of the Natural Resources Act states clearly:

All lands included in the Indian reserves within the Province, including those selected and surveyed but not yet confirmed, as well as those confirmed, shall continue to be vested in the Crown and administered by the Government of Canada, and the Province will from time to time, upon the request of the Superintendent General of Indian Affairs, set aside, out of the unoccupied Crown lands hereby transferred to its administration, such further areas as the said Superintendent General may, in agreement with the Minister of Mines and Natural Resources of the Province, select as necessary to enable Canada to fulfill its obligations under the treaties with the Indians of the Province, and such areas shall thereafter be administered by Canada in the same way in all respects as if they had never passed to the Province under the provisions thereof.

The Act was also supposed to guarantee the treaty Indians of Alberta their treaty hunting rights, according to the terms set out in Section 12:

> In order to secure to the Indians of the Province the continuance of the supply of game and fish for their support and subsistence, Canada agrees that the laws respecting game in force in the Province from time to time shall apply to the Indians within the boundaries thereof, provided, however, that the said Indians shall have the right, which the Province hereby assures them, of hunting, trapping, and fishing game and fish for food at all seasons of the year on all unoccupied Crown lands and on any other lands to which the said Indians may have the right to access.

Alberta's track record in honouring these two provisions has been, to say the least, inconsistent. Numerous provincial acts and statutes which infringe on our treaty rights have been passed without regard to Crown promises. When any such breach of trust is questioned, the action is always justified by the same argument— that it has been done for the benefit of the larger society.

Even when the federal government has wanted to meet a land claim, Indian Affairs has felt it necessary to walk very softly, negotiating with the province for transfer of any Crown land.

The Alberta Forestry Service personnel and Fish and Wildlife officers have harassed and pressured Stoneys and other Indians hunting on Crown lands. Treaty Indians have been repeatedly charged with hunting out of season or trapping in closed areas, but the courts have invariably dismissed the charges whenever the accused are defended. (Unfortunately, there have been, and still are, many instances when our people were too afraid to criticize or oppose the government's authority and simply pleaded guilty to the charges, unaware that they were entitled to legal aid, and that the charges against them were also charges against our treaty rights.) With this sort of confusion, it becomes clearer why it took many generations before the Indian people finally became aware of how the Canadian system of government works. But today many educated Indians are beginning to understand the mechanisms of the bureaucracy and the legislative system. We have not totally mastered them—it seems that maybe we never will—but in many ways we are learning to cut the bureaucratic red tape of the Indian Affairs Department and to let our voice be heard at the appropriate level and department of government—and sometimes, also, by the public at large.

If nothing else, the coming of self-government has forced us to learn this. Unlike other groups in Canadian society, we have only semi-autonomous status under the final control of the Indian Affairs Department. And since we are still under federal jurisdiction, we continue to be hampered by bureaucratic interference and confined within the limitations permitted by federal Indian policies. Self-government, however, allows us to protest these policies with some effectiveness and present our own alternatives.

It is this method of protesting poor policies and infringement of treaty rights while working out new programs to help our people that the Stoney Tribal Council has followed for the past eight years.

Not surprisingly, many of our protests have been directed against the Province of Alberta.

Despite the many complaints we have about the federal Indian Affairs Department, it has become the position of Alberta's Treaty Indians to reject any transfer of any service programs from the federal to the provincial government, even in areas which are normally under provincial direction—areas such as education, medical services, hunting rights, social programs, and services commonly available to local municipalities. The British North America Act clearly states that Indian people will remain under the jurisdiction of the federal government. It is that body with which we signed the treaties and which has the responsibility of honouring our treaty rights.

The manoeuvring around these areas of jurisdiction is constant since the legislature and bureaucracy of the province have historically displayed a disregard for our interests and rights. Take, for example, the matter of taxes. Treaty Indians are exempt from paying income tax as long as they live on a reserve. We firmly believe that this is just since we prepaid for government services when our forefathers signed Treaty Seven. But there are a series of hidden provincial taxes (such as sales taxes) which we are forced to pay. The Indian Association of Alberta (IAA) has protested this but achieved nothing as yet.

On another provincial-federal question, protest proved more successful.

In 1971 the federal government brought in its universal Medicare program. We were concerned as to how this would be integrated under the treaty promise to provide a "medicine chest," especially since the provinces were to administer the program. The government of Alberta, through its enabling legislation, was making it clear that it had no intention of making any distinction between treaty Indians and the others Medicare would cover. Since more and more Alberta Indians were becoming employed during these years, we foresaw a problem with paycheque deductions.

At the time I was Director of Research for the IAA's newly established Treaty and Aboriginal Rights Program (which I shall describe later in more detail). With my staff I prepared a position paper on the Medicare problem to present to the All Chiefs Conference of 1971. It outlined the fears of the native people when it said:

> We are here because many of our Indian people have been informed by letter that they must not expect the Department of National Health and Welfare to pay Medicare premiums for Treaty Indians who are employed full time.
>
> We are here because the Government of the Province of Alberta has passed legislation requiring all employers of five or more people to make payroll deductions for Medicare premiums on behalf of all their employees. This legislation does not exclude Treaty Indians . . .

It stated positively that:

> Health services for our people are not a form of welfare. Health services for our people are a right, pre-paid at the signing of the treaties.
> . . . Medical services were promised to our people by the Queen's representatives not only for today but for tomorrow and for as long as the sun shines, rivers flow and grass grows. In other words, this Treaty agreement was to last forever. This is a Treaty right that we have our medical services paid for, paid with our land.

The paper accused both the provincial and federal governments of breaking the treaties. We got the results we wished: having medical services assured and deductions stopped.

About the same time, the same organization prepared a position paper against several new pieces of provincial legislation regarding land use, in which there appeared no recognition of special rights traditionally enjoyed by the Indian people. The bills restricted or prohibited hunting on Crown lands. I presented this protest to the Alberta Legislature on behalf of the Alberta Chiefs. It stated that:

> The treaty Indians of Alberta are opposed to Bill 66, "An Act to Amend the Public Lands Act," and Bill 67, "The Wilderness Areas Act," as we feel that they are an infringement and a restriction upon both our constitutional and our treaty rights. We believe that these bills, as they are presently written, will suppress our traditional way of life and adversely affect the social patterns of Alberta's Native people.

The protest brought to the legislators' attention the assurances given by Crown representatives, when the treaties were signed, that our traditional culture and social patterns would not be greatly affected, that we were promised complete and free access to all unoccupied Crown lands; it pointed out that these guarantees were reaffirmed by the Alberta Natural Resource Act of 1930:

> . . . the government of Alberta is proposing new legislation which will curtail these rights. This legislation is a good example of the manner in which new laws change old laws in such ways that they benefit the dominant society with drastic consequences to the Native people in this province.

It catalogued modern complaints about governmental disregard of the treaty rights, cultural values, and social patterns of Alberta's treaty Indians. And it further stated:

> The government is well aware of the fact that the Indians consider certain areas of Crown land to have religious significance. These areas are holy grounds where we Indians can go to communicate with the Great Spirit. We hold special pow-wows, dances, and most of all, Sun Dance ceremonies in these areas. The government knows about these facts . . .

The paper objected to a number of specific sections of the Acts and recommended that:

. . . the aforementioned legislation be revoked because of its curtailment of our freedom and right to utilize the existing unoccupied Crown lands. The government of Alberta must honour and safeguard our treaty rights. However, we realize that it will take time to repeal this legislation. The treaty Indians of Alberta therefore ask the province that they be exempt from the provisions of this piece of legislation until such time as the bill may be rescinded by the government.

Unfortunately, we were not successful with these requests.

For the Stoney Tribe in particular, the greatest battle for land rights in recent years was also with the Province of Alberta. It was also unsuccessful, climaxing in one of the blackest days of our history and the virtual destruction of any possibility of a decent livelihood for those of my people living on the Special Bighorn Reserve on Kootenay Plains.

When I assumed the Chieftainship in January 1969, I was only too well aware of the Bighorn-Kootenay Plains land claim. I had also heard of provincial government plans to build a dam somewhere on the North Saskatchewan River, but I thought it was another long-range scheme for the future development of provincial water resources and electric power. Being a rookie politician, I was not aware that plans for the construction of the dam were already well underway. Before I discovered how far this had gone, work crews had moved in with heavy equipment and begun massive destruction of the beautiful North Saskatchewan valley, near the Bighorn Reserve. Wesley Band members from the reserve came to Morley and told me of bulldozers knocking over Indian log cabins, destroying Indian graves, and ruining traplines as well as traditional hunting areas.

I went to the Bighorn-Kootenay Plains area to look over the situation for myself. What I saw was unbelievable. Land that had belonged to the Stoneys—land that the Stoney Indians still claimed—was being bulldozed without consideration for, or consultation with, my people. As a consequence of what I saw, I held a meeting with Wesley Band members living in the area. As a result of this meeting, the Tribal Council took a position of unanimous opposition of the construction of the Bighorn Dam unless and until the Stoneys' land claims in the area were settled.

To bring this opposition to the government's attention, I addressed the following letter to Premier Strom:

Dear Premier Strom:

On behalf of the Stoney Indian Council at Morley I am writing to you concerning the Bighorn Dam project. It has been thought up, planned, and is now actually being built without at any time consulting the Indian people on the Bighorn Indian Reserve. It appears that the Government has once again ignored the Indian people on this very important matter that directly affects their way of life.

The people of the Bighorn Reserve are part of the Wesley Band of Stoney Indians at Morley. The Stoney Band Council at Morley is very concerned about what is happening and we are requesting that you and the Cabinet Ministers concerned with the project meet with our band representatives to discuss the various problems that have arisen and will continue to rise. Indian graves have already been destroyed by bulldozers clearing the land. All clearing must be stopped immediately so that these graves can be relocated, before the markings are destroyed and the locations lost forever. Many of these graves cannot be located with the snow covering the markers. There is an urgency due to the problems that are being even now created.

Therefore, we request a meeting before the end of March 1969. We do not want to talk to representatives who do not have authority to make decisions.

We have talked with one of your representatives in our council meeting on March 11th and all he could tell us was that he had no authority and would have to talk to other people about this.

We want to talk to our elected legislators who are responsible for making policy. We prefer if you could come to Morley to discuss these problems but we recognize that you are very busy and we would be willing to send a delegation to meet with you in your office.

We are opposed to the construction of the Dam because of the problems it will create. Some of the problems are as follows:

1. Indian Graves.
2. Indian homes to be flooded.
3. Indian land to be flooded.
4. Hunting area.
5. Grazing land for horses.
6. Traplines.

7. Sun Dance and Recreation Area.

8. Historical and Cultural significance to the Indian people of the flooded area.

9. Disruption of Indian way of life through development of area.

10. Fear of living below the dam.

Please arrange this meeting at once and let us know when you will meet with us. Your help and co-operation in this important matter will be greatly appreciated. Thank you kindly.

Sincerely yours,

Chief John Snow
Chief of the Wesley Band

Copies of this letter were sent to key people in the provincial and federal governments, Calgary Power, and the IAA. Pressure was also brought to bear on the Social Credit Association of Alberta (the party then in power) and the Conservative Opposition.

As a result of this protest, I was given the opportunity to address the Alberta Legislature during the spring session of 1969. In speaking to the assembled members, I bluntly asked this question:

> Why did the Provincial Government not inform the Indian people about the plans for this construction of the dam at Bighorn? Was this ignorance on the part of the Government? Was it disrespect on the part of the Government to the native people who have lived in the Bighorn area for centuries?

I outlined the damage that was being done, then continued:

> Mr. Fred Colborne, Chairman, Human Resources Development Authority, has emphasized that we as Indians do not have legal rights to the land nor mineral rights. I believe we do have every right to the land to be flooded as well as the surrounding area ... Our forefathers lived and hunted in this area for generations, even centuries. We have Indian graves and Indian homes scattered throughout the land to be flooded ... There are traplines to be flooded. My people are not skilled in other fields of work ... The construction of the dam and the development will drive

back the wild animals. These animals—deer, moose, elk, goats, sheep—are our source of food and livelihood . . .

There are also many Indian homes scattered throughout this land to be flooded. I want the government to keep off my land.

The government should consider the wealthy and the poor, the strong and the weak within their country before any decisions are made. They should respect the cultures of the various nationalities. This includes minority groups. This includes the Indian people of the Bighorn Reserve.

And I went on to ask whether or not the government was trying to drive my people out of the isolated area and into the city and a way of life for which they were totally unprepared.

Unfortunately for my people, the legislators turned a deaf ear. The dam was built and much of the Stoneys' traditional hunting grounds—land to which we believe we had a valid claim under Treaty Seven—now lies under a twenty-seven-mile-long artificial lake.

The destruction of the land was a terrible thing to watch. Haze filled the air as growing things were burned off to clear the ground. Homes were swept aside by heavy machinery, graves turned over or swallowed by the new lake. (The Tribal Council did manage to get some graves moved to a new site. Only two cabins were rescued; they were moved and reconstructed on the Bighorn Reserve.)

Even more far-reaching in its result was the almost complete disappearance of game from the area. The people living on the Kootenay Plains have always been among the most independent of the Stoneys. The legacy of Peter Wesley's long rocky trail still lives. But with hunting destroyed and little employment for unskilled labour in the area, 95 percent of the Bighorn residents live on welfare today.

The damage—physical and psychological—that the building of the Bighorn Dam caused my people can never be calculated.

But, as the whitemen say, "It is an ill wind that blows no one some good." In addition to my letter to the Premier and my speech to the Legislature, I had also written Jean Chrétien, then federal Minister of Indian Affairs and Northern Development, informing him of the province's plans for the development of the Bighorn Dam and their consequences for living in the area. After much delay, the Minister reluctantly consented to provide $30,000 to research our treaty and land claims to the Kootenay Plains.

The program for which we used this money turned up a great deal of information which someday may help my people settle their claim. In addition, we learned a lot about how to set up such a program, how to best use our resources, how to conduct interviews and do research, how to write a précis of what was discovered. But above all, a number of young Stoneys learned how to take their traditional knowledge of how to work as a group and adapt that ability to accomplishing a task with modern tools and modern goals.

This research also attracted much interest among other tribes in Alberta. In April 1971 the IAA Board established its Treaty and Aboriginal Rights Program (TARR), for which I was appointed director. With a small federal grant we hired a small staff—me, an assistant director who was in charge of the office operations, one senior researcher, and two support people who did secretarial work and accounting.[1] The first major research project we were supposed to undertake was preparation of position papers stating our treaty rights in the areas of medicine, hunting, fishing and trapping, education, economic development, and the loss of tribal lands. However, before we even began researching these issues, we found ourselves faced with the urgent problems of preparing for presentation to the provincial legislature the position papers on Medicare and Bills 66 and 67 described previously.

This work and that being done at Morley on the Stoney land claims generated a lot of interest at the 1971 IAA annual meeting, held at Hobbema, and the delegates there gave us strong support and suggested valuable directions for areas of research.

Our plans were to set up a TARR field office in each treaty area, with the main research office situated on the Morley Reserve.[2] Ideally each such office would have a research coordinator, field interviewers to collect oral information from the elders, translators to transcribe that information (since we believed it essential to conduct the interviews in the native language), and the necessary secretarial support staff. It was truly exciting to initiate such a program—one that was long overdue and one that was essential if our treaty rights, under constant erosion from government legislation, are to be properly protected.

In retrospect, I do not believe that we were over-ambitious in our goals—especially given the urgency of collecting stories from Indian elders before they passed away. But we were naïve about funding. The federal grant to the Indian Association was barely adequate to meet salaries and operations for a core staff. Virtually all our time that summer was spent in drafting prospective research proposals and budget requirements to government agencies and private foundations all over North America. After weeks of follow-up requests for information, visits with foundation officials, and personal contacts with dozens of government officers, the response proved negative in every single instance. Either our research projects were too large, too limited in scope, or did not meet someone's criteria for funding.

Meanwhile, the Indian people waited for us to begin research projects in their areas. Finally, because the field interviews for the Kootenay Plains land claim report had all been completed, under our own federal grant, the Stoneys asked TARR's assistant director to complete the archival research under salary to the Stoney Tribe, while he simultaneously administered the TARR office operations.

When this research was completed, we entered a formal claim for the land on the Kootenay Plains which we believe is rightfully ours by treaty. The matter is now before the courts, and it may be years—even decades—before it is settled.

Meanwhile, the other projects at TARR went on, although very slowly because we met so many problems in funding. Despite its frustrations the work held the promise of great excitement. But in September 1971 I had to make a choice. The IAA Board of Directors passed a resolution stating that full-time employees could not hold political office. I had to resign my Chieftainship or resign from TARR. I chose the latter because I believed that I needed a strong political base from which to operate. My experience with the Indian Affairs Department has been that they will not listen to an Indian leader unless he is a Chief, as was brusquely pointed out to me in 1968, before I left the ministry to run for political office.

While TARR continued its research under new leadership (and does so to this day), the Stoneys continued their own research program. Our work on the Kootenay Plains land claim and my brief involvement with TARR had convinced the Tribal Council of the value of such work. But it was also clear that ongoing research would have to be maintained by the reserves themselves—considering the shortage of funds available for everyone's urgent needs.

That winter, the Stoneys submitted several proposals to the new federal Local Initiative Program (LIP), and one of the successful applications was the Oral History Program. We did not realize it at the time, but this interview-type project was to be another vital learning experience for our young people. They purchased tape recorders and compiled a questionnaire on topics they wanted to know about.

During the Kootenay Plains field interviews, the approach had had to be limited strictly to collecting the history of that area and the Bighorn people. Under this expanded program, our young staff approached the elders on virtually every topic—legends, religion, medicine, history, treaties, land disputes. Over the course of nine months, we collected over 300 tapes of information. The interviews were then translated into English and filed permanently. The next step was to compile the material into booklet form for use in the school. But this had barely been started when our funding ran out. (This has been our experience over and over again. A program will receive just enough money to get underway, but the government is reluctant to commit long-term funding or funding at a sufficient level to ensure the successful implementation or often even the completion of a project.)

With this program, however, the enthusiasm of our young people had truly been fired, and the new political awareness of the Tribal Council made us determined to continue the research.

Another incentive to attempting to continue the program was that we realized we had hit on a potential source of textbook material for the reserve school. This was very important to the Councils. As its Education Committee had been analyzing our educational needs, it had become increasingly aware of the degrading effect of white textbooks—especially social science textbooks. They had come to agree fully with the statement made by the American Indian Historical Society in March 1968:

> Everyone has the right to his opinion. A person has also the right to be wrong. But a textbook has no right to be wrong, or to evade the truth, falsify history, or insult and malign a whole race of people. That is what the textbooks do.
>
> There is a difference between a book for general readership, and one accepted for classroom use. In the first case, the individual has a choice, and this choice we must protect. The student has no choice. He is compelled to study from an approved book, and in this case, we have a right to insist upon truth, accuracy, and objectivity.[3]

Yet there were no Indian-oriented books with which to replace the harmful texts. If we could develop our Oral History Program further, we would have another tool with which to help our children retain our culture by teaching them history from the Indian point of

view and passing on our traditions from the elder generations.
So we continued searching for a way to develop what looked to
be a path toward bilingual, bicultural education—a path that could
reach toward our goal and use local talent and provide local employment opportunities in its making. In 1972 a new program—planned,
implemented, and operated under the direction of the Stoney Tribal
Council—was born: the Stoney Cultural Education Program (SCEP).

Fortunately we received interim funding for this dream program
from the recently established Alberta Indian Education Centre,
under the directorship of Joe Couture. It gave us much encouragement and badly needed assistance until our future was secure. We
were tired of handouts from Indian Affairs, and the insecurity created by short-term programs like LIP. Our approaches to various
foundations and the two levels of government were turned down.
Our young people had proven their abilities and willingness to
work, our program made more sense in terms of providing real,
long-range help to our people than anything we had heard of, but
no one seemed interested. Then the Indian Education Centre heard
of a new Manpower Program called the Local Employment
Assistance Program (LEAP). Under special conditions it could provide up to $200,000 per year for up to three years. We decided to
combine our separate goals in linguistics, historical research, curriculum development, and educational opportunities and coordinate them under one program.

Following the submission of a carefully prepared presentation
outlining our three-year objectives, our request was favourably
received by the Manpower officials.

Once SCEP was underway, four basic interrelated departments
were established: Curriculum Development and Teacher Training;
Graphic Arts and Printing; Research; and Administration. We hired
three experienced resource professionals to work with and train a
Stoney staff, numbering from twenty to thirty persons. A brochure,
developed and printed by the staff, succinctly outlined our goals
and objectives:

STONEY CULTURAL EDUCATION PROGRAM
A NEW WAY
"What does it mean to be a Stoney in the 1970's?"
"Can Stoney people live in two cultures?"
"What are the best things in the Stoney and White cultures?"
"Will traditional Stoney values die out?"

Wesley Councillor and elder Jake Rabbit, schoolteacher Rod Mark, and elder Paul Wesley
facilitate a naming ceremony at the SCEP classroom.

In 1972 the Stoney Band Council created the Stoney Cultural Education Program to try to answer some of these questions.

SCEP has found that there is a lot of confusion on the Reserve about the Stoney way of life. Many people seem to be living *between* two cultures instead of *in* two cultures. They are neither completely living in the Stoney Culture nor in the White culture, and they seem to have no way of getting out of this situation.

SCEP believes that there is a way out, there is a path which will give each person the best of each culture. This path will allow each person to be happy, respect values, and survive economically.

To help reach this, SCEP believes that the wisdom of the elders must be used, that this wisdom must not be lost to the Stoneys.

AIMS AND OBJECTIVES

The main objective of SCEP is to find a way in which we the Stoneys may develop a better understanding of our history, culture, language and succeed in our personal goals as individuals.

To achieve this objective the Stoney Cultural Education Program as a community oriented project is attempting:

1. To develop a learning and training for our people in skills

and behavior in a multi-cultural setting in today's society, and which will allow us to retain our Stoney way of life.

2. To find the good in Stoney and White society in order to improve social and economic stability for families and throughout the community.

3. To improve the self image of our people by viewing our society from a fresh, new perspective—from the Indian viewpoint.

4. To return to the position of our respected elders that "a man must choose to be governed by men who are governed by God." (A saying of Walking Buffalo.)

In 1972 the Stoney Cultural Education Program took on the tremendous task of changing the learning environment of our children. The goal is to bring it into line with the community's needs and the student's language ability, while drawing from the child's rich heritage to make it work. The task is tremendous because of many different parts which must be worked on separately but within the same time frame. More than half our population of 2,000 is under the age of sixteen, so we need fifty teachers, more than half of whom should be native speakers of the child's native tongue. We need a library of more than 2,000 books in our native tongue *and* English—books which reflect our heritage and cultural values, books which recreate our own heroes. The material is available from our elders and we need a staff of interviewers, writers, editors, and production personnel to get it into written form. We need curriculum development experts to guide the work and a public relations staff to keep the parents and community informed about the goals of the program and its progress.

The challenge is enormous and will take many years to meet, but our progress to date has been very pleasing to those of us who are involved. Teacher training has begun. Curriculum materials have been developed and published. Some of our young people have learned technical skills in printing, audiovisual, and videotape technology.

A strong belief in the future of the program has grown quickly. One older member of the staff taught himself to read and write in Stoney, then spent two years in language research, collecting the words of our language. His dictionary now needs only editorial and layout work before publication. It will be the first dictionary in our language.

Hundreds of stories have been collected and preserved on tape in the Oral History Program. These are the stories of our tribal heroes, our warriors and hunters, our medicine men and wise leaders, our women and our children of the past, our heritage. The stories tell of our history, our cultural values, our ways of living within our environment, and the origins of our customs. Nearly all of these stories are suitable for publication, and they will provide the literature that will allow our children to stand tall in the realization that their heritage is worthwhile.

SCEP has begun research in other areas too. Place names and names of mountains and streams in our language have been collected and mapped. Our traditional food plants have been identified, collected, photographed, or drawn.

History, too, is being researched as the oral accounts are compared with archival research of the other society.

Training has been a vital area of SCEP activity. Printing and photography have been two areas which have required training. SCEP now has an up-to-date offset printing shop, which has provided services to our community in many different ways. Originally it was intended that its main activity would be producing curriculum materials, but job printing and the publication of a bi-weekly newsletter have also become important.

The most spectacular success in training has been with teaching staff. In 1973 the Alberta Department of Education proposed a special Language Teachers' Certificate for suitably qualified teachers of native languages. With this state certification available, SCEP enlisted the aid of the University of Calgary's Faculty of Education in providing a program through which the Stoneys themselves could produce the bilingual teachers we need so badly. This Outreach Program, which has been developed over the past four years, has broken new ground in post-secondary education for Indian students in Alberta. It is different from many university programs that seek to meet the special needs of our people in that it does not lower or change the standards on the subject matter of courses. Since the Outreach Program provides many courses on the reserve, our students can maintain contact with their families and the community on a day-to-day basis. Also important is my people's warm appreciation of an institution which met our request for help without attempting to assume control of the program.

In four short years two of our young men have achieved their goal of a Bachelor of Education degree. One of our young women will reach that same goal within a year, and with each succeeding year this tiny trickle of success will gain strength.

Since SCEP's three-year funding by LEAP was completed in 1976, new sources have been necessary. The Alberta Cultural Centre's Program of Indian Affairs will provide $50,000 in ongoing funding, and the Stoney Tribal Council's budget has allowed for $100,000. Also, several SCEP staff members have been transferred to other programs.

SCEP is by no means the only way through which the Stoney Tribe has begun to seek self-improvement and a better life for all tribal members on the reserve. Freed by self-government to search out its own road to self-respect and independence, the tribe has begun many new programs. I have dealt with SCEP at such length only because it is so illustrative of our certainty that the right road for us is one of biculturalism, of matching what we already have with the demands of today's world, of mixing the traditions of our elders with the best the new society has to offer.

Many of these new programs are attempts to better our people's very harsh lives as rapidly as possible—by making modern conveniences and services available to them and by creating employment opportunities so they need no longer suffer the degradation of living on welfare.

Some of the most promising of these programs involve developing the reserve's potential for tourism. This was the strong suggestion of the professional consultants we hired almost immediately after self-government was initiated in 1969. Although we have just begun to implement some of these ideas, the initial results are quite successful.

The Stoney Indian Park began to be promoted as a tourist attraction in 1970. Camping space is provided, as are for-rent facilities. There are riding stables, and guided trips by horseback or foot are offered into the mountains or to good fishing areas. A traditional teepee village and the archeological excavations at burnt-out Old Bow Fort also attract visitors.

Such tourist arrangements produce income and employment for my people. They also help us give the visiting whitemen a little better understanding of our traditional way of life. A more serious, intensive step in that direction was the founding of the Stoney Wilderness Centre in 1973. It is partly another phase in the provision of tourist facilities but its emphasis is on the education of white young people. Teenagers come to spend several weeks at the Centre during their summer vacation. They are taken on backpack and horseback trips where they have an opportunity to discover the glories of nature while Stoney guides teach them about our ways of finding food and surviving in the wilderness. For many it is not only their first encounter with true Indian culture but their first experience of contact with Mother Earth. Cost to these young people is kept very reasonable.

Another very new program initiated by the Tribal Council is the building of a cooperative gas station plus convenience store in the Morley townsite. To the non-Indian, such an establishment sounds very ordinary and unexciting (especially since it has yet to show a profit). But its importance to the Stoneys may be made a little clearer when it is explained that this is not only the first such retail establishment owned and operated by tribal members; it is also the first retail establishment on the reserve. Before it was built, Morley residents had to drive twenty or thirty miles to obtain gas or a loaf of bread (as they still do for most shopping and all commercial services).

A commercial project that is already in its second stage is our sawmill. For some years lumber mills from off the reserve had bought logs from tribal members. In the late 1960s a mill was established on the reserve by a white entrepreneur, employing some Stoney operators and using logs from our forests. Then a fall-off in the lumber market made it impossible for the owner to continue. In 1972, after considerable discussion, the Council established its own sawmill with old, used machinery off in the southern forest area of the reserve. This mill provided a good training ground for some of our young people. It was subject to frequent breakdowns and was never profitable, but our people learned important technical and business skills in its operation.

In 1967 we began construction of a modern mill. We hired several additional skilled white technicians, and we invited Indian Affairs forestry experts to assist us in setting up a management program for our forest reserves. The Council is very hopeful that this second stage will not only provide our people with further training, but also give us a profitable enterprise.

A few years after the purchase of the Crawford and Coppick ranches at the eastern end of the Morley Reserve and their incorporation as reserve lands, the Department of Indian Affairs had advised us to lease out the entire sixteen-square-mile area to neighbouring ranchers. For nearly twenty years, the lessees had cruelly exploited these lands by overgrazing them. In 1976 the Tribal Council decided to close all leases and redevelop the land as a large, tribe-owned ranching enterprise. Cattle purchases, fencing, corral construction, water development, housing, barn construction, and purchase of equipment were quickly attended to. Advice was sought from provincial agricultural experts and others, and a five-year plan developed by an independent consultant. Under this plan it is hoped that the project will provide food for tribal members, a model ranch for training purposes, and herd stock for interested and skilled tribal members who wish to start their own ranching enterprises.

All development projects under self-government are geared to social development in one form or other—offering job training, creating work opportunities, providing for the future, upgrading education, improving living standards. One important project in social development was the building of a modern recreation complex in 1973.

At one time there was probably no need for such a social service. For many years the Morley Reserve was basically isolated. A few people worked for neighbouring ranches or as hunting guides; families made occasional trips to town to purchase what they could not supply themselves. Our living conditions were barely adequate, but we still lived the traditional ways, and the provincial population was growing at a moderate rate. But recent years have brought many rapid changes to Morley—the right to purchase alcohol, the growing prevalence of motor vehicles, express highways through the reserve, thousands of visiting tourists to the nearby national parks, and the burgeoning growth of neighbouring towns, especially the city of Calgary, just thirty miles east. The younger population on our reserve has also burgeoned—for example, today approximately 60 percent of our total population of 2,000 Stoneys is under the age of sixteen.

Young people with nothing to do mean trouble for any society. Our boys and girls were also faced with inadequate and irrelevant education, the knowledge that the future held few chances for employment, and a poor self-image forced upon them by the dominant society.

We had been trying to combat these basic problems in the many programs instituted since we achieved self-government, but we also saw a possibility for immediate relief of some tensions by providing recreation on the reserve.

In fact, we had been requesting new recreational facilities for our young people for years. The only facilities available were an outdoor rink for skating, outdoor rodeo grounds, and a band hall, built in

1955, where dances and pow-wows could be held. The federal government refused to provide grants for capital construction, and Indian reserves were not eligible to receive the provincial grants normally available to municipalities. (Recent legislation now allows reserves to apply for such grants under certain conditions.)

Under self-government we lobbied for alternatives to combat the increasing social problems resulting from young people going into town, drinking, and breaking the law in towns. Through loans and specific limited grants, the Morley Reserve was finally able to build a modern recreation complex consisting of an enclosed ice arena and drop-in centre with an attached gymnasium and outdoor swimming pool for the school program. We now have several hockey teams, from the peewee to the senior level, that compete with the surrounding communities. Our young people are enthusiastic about all sports activities and have accumulated dozens of trophies for hockey and rodeo events.

We still face many social problems, but at least now there are proper facilities for competitive activities which do provide some outlet. When there is trouble, our band constables are able to handle the situation with an understanding of the social background. They know the individuals and can often prevent more serious situations from arising.

The Tribal Council, through its various committees, has planned,

Baseball continues to be a very popular sport among the youth in our community.

initiated, and carried through a number of other projects to construct physical facilities or renovate old ones.

Under the building program in the early 1970s the old residential school was converted into office space for the Economic Development and the SCEP Departments. Modern construction around the same time included a new, open-area primary school; a new health centre complete with nursing, ambulance, medical, and dental facilities; and a four-unit residence for the school staff.

The current emphasis in the building program is in housing. Since the inception of local self-government, successive Councils have been concerned with the poor housing in which so many Stoneys live. In 1969, when minimum Canadian living standards demanded electricity, automatic heating, and indoor plumbing, most homes on our three reserves were without them. Internal heating was achieved by radiation from the wood-fired kitchen stove, and oil lamps were usual. Water was carried from the well or the spring nearby; if these froze in winter, snow would be melted on the stove. The houses were both too few in number and too small in size—often ten or twelve people lived in eight hundred square feet. Since 1969 more than three hundred new homes have been built and more than fifty older homes remodelled with electric stoves, basements, indoor plumbing, and forced-air heating. In some of these years housing and other capital projects have been as much as half of our entire budget.

Of all the new construction carried out at Morley during the past few years, none has been more symbolically important than the administration buildings. The erection of the first was one of the earliest decisions made by the Stoney Tribal Council when self-government was initiated in 1969. Its design graphically symbolizes the road we have decided to take: it is a very modern, practical building in teepee style—a unique landmark commemorating our mingling of the best in new and old traditions. Even the ceremonies with which these new administrative offices were opened demonstrated our determination to hold on to our roots; instead of the usual ribbon-cutting, the tribe held a traditional fire-lighting. It was a great day. To many of us, having our own government offices and leaving behind forever the Indian agent's office, with all its bureaucratic, paternalistic, dictatorial, insulting, and degrading experiences of the past, marked a very important step on our journey toward regaining our traditional pride as a people.

Late in 1976, work began on our second office building, a $2.5-million construction of concrete and lumber. This new building will provide office space for the management of all projects which are developing so rapidly in our community.

We have now spent millions and millions of dollars to build for the future. Most of this development is possible because of the royalty payments from natural gas wells on our reserve lands. We have been fortunate indeed to have this revenue; it has enabled us to make capital expenditures—and often obtain matching grants for them, which are normally unobtainable by most Indian tribes.

By the time that we took over local self-government, the gas royalties had begun to flow in. Over the past eight years they have increased each year. When the Pan-Canadian Oil and Gas Company builds its new processing plant at Morley, planned for within the next two years, the flow will become even greater.

We Stoneys, and particularly those of us who are temporary stewards of our people's resources, are very aware of our great good fortune in having these wells under our reserve. It is almost as though the Great Spirit had left them there, dormant, to produce at the time of our greatest need for hope as well as money. For a hundred years we have lived at a subsistence level, taking government assistance when we wanted just our rights. Now, finally, with these wells, we can hope to build a better life for our children and our children's children.

We have thought long and hard about how to spend our newfound wealth. There have been many calls to spend it on day-to-day living expenses, so that people could go off welfare and save the government money! But too many of us have lived on welfare too long, and we know that if we spend our birthright, rather than invest it, we will be back on welfare when the gas runs out.

It is not hard for us to understand how many people would like to say, "You have all the gas money. Why not forget all those old claims, take your people off the welfare, and be glad you are prosperous now?" It is easy for us to understand, but hard to agree. We have not forgotten many of our Indian brothers of other bands who are not so fortunate as to have our luck, and who are desperate to have their claims justly met to bring them hope for the future. We have not forgotten Indian people who have spent their money as the whiteman suggested and are now again as poor as they had ever been. Our elders have advised us that, rather than make per-capita payments to tribal members, we should use our gas royalties to build a better future for generations to come.

The use of the gas reserves is a little like an experience we recently had with the buffalo. In 1969 the government gave us twenty-five head of buffalo. We fenced a large meadow for their use and budgeted to purchase hay to feed them during the winter. Some tribal members opposed our keeping them, but, as newly elected chief, I followed the advice of the elders—that we should provide a part of our land for these former monarchs of the plains.

If we look at our long history on this Great Island, we can see the very vital role that the buffalo played in supporting our way of life. In the past the buffalo had provided us with many essential things—teepee coverings, clothing, moccasins, and blanket robes from their hides; tools, knives, and spears from their bones; medicine from certain other parts. The buffalo skull was used in the religious ceremony of the Sun Dance. Indeed the buffalo had been a very important part of this Great Island and had an important role in our society. Therefore the return of the buffalo was a happy occasion. The elders performed religious ceremonies, smoked the sacred pipe, and thanked the Great Spirit that the buffalo had survived.

Since the buffalo provided us with so many essentials in our traditional life, we should not say they are expensive. The buffalo did not tell our forefathers that *they* were expensive to keep, so *we* should not say the buffalo are expensive; rather we should say they

Both the buffalo and Indigenous peoples on this continent have survived contact and colonization. We welcomed the buffalo on our reserve in the 1970s as we began to reconnect with our traditional culture and way of life. The buffalo now roam these open ranges, the shining mountains always in the background. *(Photo by Mike O'Driscoll)*

are our grandfathers. We should provide a place for them. They, too, are Natives of the Great Island.

We do not see a difference between the gas and the buffalo. It is all part of our world. As we once were helped by the buffalo and used them wisely, so we can now be helped by the gas, if we use it wisely. We believe it is best to take the goods of the earth with care, and not spend them recklessly. We are no longer alone in believing that the earth will not provide for people forever unless every resource that is used is spent with consciousness of the future.

The Indian Religious Movement

T he sun rises with a blood-red headdress of prairie clouds throwing fiery colours to the mountains. Smoke rises lazily from the teepee fires. All the living things awake around the Indian religious camp in the foothills. A lonely eagle rides the air currents, almost out of sight. Half a mile away a buffalo bull welcomes the day as he calls to his herd. A magpie announces his arrival with his chatter as he teases an old dog lying beside the teepee entrance. Below the huge teepee encampment, the rustling mountain streams can be heard. A tethered horse whinnies and stamps his hooves, and a grasshopper joins in the medley of sounds and activity of a new day.

From out of a teepee an old man stoops, carrying his pipe bag carefully. He calls out and is joined by four or five men as he walks to a small hill overlooking the camp.

On the hill, the men arrange themselves in a circle. The old man offers a prayer to the Creator, a daily thanksgiving for the glory of another summer day, as he lights the braided sweet grass and prepares the pipe.

The mountains seem closer in the morning light, enclosing the whole valley in a great cathedral which the Great Spirit built for Himself and His people. The old man's prayer speaks of the Creator's love and His protection for His red children. The pipe, now lit, is passed from hand to hand, with *reverence*, speaking of the unity and brotherhood of all in the Great Spirit's creation. In each hand the pipestem is directed to the four winds, east, south, west, and north, acknowledging the dominion of the Creator, and only the Creator, over all things. In this way man acknowledges, with humility, that he is only a part of the Creation, that he is dependent, that he, too, must submit to the natural laws of the Creator. The herbs in the pipe are consumed, the ashes are knocked out, the pipe is returned to the bag, and the men stand and return to their families in their teepees to break their fast.

Ten thousand years ago? Perhaps a century? No! This occurred last summer and the summer before and each summer for the past six years. The man and the eagle and the mountain streams are real. The setting is Morley: the home of the Indian Ecumenical Movement. Even the buffalo are real. These once proud monarchs of the plains are now restricted to a small paddock. But, like the Indian spirit, which also knew the unlimited freedom of the prairies, knew freedom like the winds, the buffalo still survive among the Stoneys, cared for through the long winters so that they might savour again the warmth of spring and the promise of summer.

The pilgrimage to the Annual Indian Ecumenical Conference, which draws more than seven thousand Indian people from all parts of North America each summer to Morley, has been hosted by the Stoney people for the past six years.

Indian people who worship in dozens of different sectarian churches every Sunday throughout the year gather together at this time to confirm that there is a Creator, and that they have followed His way for thousands of years. His protection of His Indian children has allowed their survival through who knows how many centuries. His continuing protection through the days and weeks and months to come will assure their survival into the years and centuries ahead. The annual pilgrimage to Morley, in the bosom of the sacred mountains, for a brief week of rededication recalls the mighty voice of David, the Psalmist:

> I will lift up mine eyes unto the hills, from whence cometh my help.

It is a real inspiration and challenge to live the traditional life as we view these hills and mountains, these valleys and rivers: to be close to nature and to be reminded that the Great Spirit made all these things. It is good to return to the sacred land of our forefathers.

As we look back over the past century, it has been like a long, cold winter for my people as far as our religious life is concerned here on this Great Island.

Teepees erected at Stoney Park in 1970. This area became the site of the
Indian Ecumenical Conference, hosted from 1971–1985.

The sacred fire of our religion has almost been put out by people from foreign lands who do not understand our belief in the Great Spirit, the Creator. If our sacred fire had been totally extinguished, indeed, we would have been a forgotten people who had once lived on this Great Island.

The Christian Church came to us as one of the first representatives of the whiteman's society. Its missionaries preached a gospel of peace and brotherhood which we found congenial to our native beliefs. Because they came as men of God, we believed they spoke the truth. We believed they described the role of their religion truly, and we believed they interpreted the ways of the whiteman's government truly, and we believed the advice they gave us was true and just.

Because we believed these things and then found them to be untrue, many of my people now question the Church and its mission. I still see a need for the Church in our native society, but a reformation is needed within the Church. The mission of the Church can achieve some of its original goals by studying Indian religion with an open mind, by reevaluating its position, and by starting a new kind of mission to the Indians.

Our people face tremendous pressures in adjusting to the modern society, and many of them are not able to cope with the new stresses. We see a rise in alcoholism; we experience a growing number of attempted and successful suicides among our young people; our traditional values are being undermined by the materialistic values of the wider society. The Church could help Indians develop programs to meet these serious problems, but it must first develop its own understanding of what it means to be an Indian in today's society. Historically, the missionary came to the reserves to help us adjust to a new way of life. Now, we need to modernize that noble objective, and the Church should continue to work with our religious leaders and serve our needs.

Again, there are numerous areas of practical life in which the Church could fulfill its social mission to the modern Indian. We need expertise in economic development and development in education materials. We need advice on modern technology, business, and social and cultural development programs. Certainly the Church could provide some of these things if it so wished.

But so far the established churches have shown very little interest in renewing their mission in terms of the real needs of modern life. For example, as we approach the centenary of Treaty Seven, they want to keep as far away as possible and have as little to do as possible with commemorating this historic event.

Because of this and because it is becoming more and more clear that the revival of the Indian people must come from within our own heritage, it seems to me that our religious revival must also go back to our roots.

For the last one hundred years, a few dedicated native religious leaders and medicine men and women from many reserves and communities have kept our sacred fire going. They have been in close touch with nature, the animal world, the birds of the air, and the spiritual world. They still retain the ancient truth and religion of our forefathers. We are very grateful to those who kept the religious fire burning over the long, cold century of indifference.

I was aware of this situation when I was in the Christian ministry. An Indian Ecumenical Conference had been talked about in the late 1960s by several Indian leaders. The men who organized a committee to arrange such a gathering were Dr. Bob Thomas, Wilfred Pelletier, the Reverend Ian Mackenzie, the Reverend Ernie Willie, and Ernest Tootoosis. They met in Winnipeg in 1969 and planned the first Indian Ecumenical Conference; it was held the following summer of 1970 at the Crow Agency, Montana.

There was a good representation of Native people from across the North American continent who took an active part at this historic gathering. There were Seminole Indians from the Everglades in Florida, Micmacs from the eastern coast, Dogribs from the Northwest

Territories; the tribes from the prairie provinces were also well represented. Concern was expressed about the future and the need to revive our native religion. There was also concern expressed about Indian language and culture, which are essential to our religion. At the end of the conference I extended an invitation to the religious leaders, medicine men and women, clergymen, and chiefs, to hold the next conference at the Stoney Indian Park in Morley, Alberta. The second conference was held there the next summer, in 1971, and has been held at the Stoney Reserve each summer since.

After the first conference, I returned to my home reserve with a feeling of encouragement and realization that there were many Indian leaders who were concerned with the revival of our cultural, spiritual, and religious heritage.

I was aware then that, in order to revive our religion, we would also need to retain our language and culture. Some of the delegates had told us at the conference that, in their areas in the eastern United States, they had lost their language and they had very few traditional spiritual leaders and medicine people left.

My people believe that we were created for a purpose and were placed on this beautiful land. Was it the will of the Great Spirit that we were placed on Indian reserves to isolate us so we could retain our language, to preserve our culture, and to keep the sacred fire burning? Our language, culture, and religion which are native to this Great Island have survived even in the midst of persecution, discrimination, and injustice by immigrants who do not understand our philosophy of living in harmony with nature and in accordance with the plan of the Great Spirit.

But, as some of our brothers have discovered, it is all too easy for us to lose our language, culture, and religion as we come into greater and more equal contact with the dominant society. Therefore one of my objectives as a leader of my people has been to plan programs to bring about the revival of our religion and culture. I presented a position paper on this subject to the Alberta Cultural Heritage Conference.

Today we see new hope for regaining our dignity and self-image. Events such as the Alberta Cultural Heritage Conference are giving recognition to the fact that a cultural mosaic without the colour *red* in it is no mosaic at all. But the Indian people of Alberta need much assistance from the government in bringing the colour red into its proper perspective. European cultures have had centuries to develop communication media to share their heritages. The Indian people, possessing just as rich a heritage, are just now beginning to enter the literary and audiovisual age. We need above average assistance in implementing these media (development of literacy program in the Native languages, inclusion of such programs in the education system, etc.) if we are to bring our share of cultural heritage before the total society of Alberta, and indeed of all Canada. We have much to offer, but we need help in developing the dignified, respectable means of offering it to the public at large.

Finally and most importantly, the preservation of the Indian cultures of Alberta is *a matter of life and death.* If an ethno-cultural group of European extraction fails to receive assistance and is not able to survive within our province, it is unfortunate, but not a matter of life and death. For the parent culture in Europe still continues. However, if one of the Indian cultures of Alberta fails to receive assistance needed to survive, it amounts to the death of a whole culture, for there is no other place in the world where that culture is found. We are grateful that the government policies that favoured the genocide of Indian cultures and languages are being disregarded. We are also grateful that in their place the government is implementing new policies that will lead to the enrichment of the total society of Canada through the mature recognition of the Native Indian cultures of Alberta. We ask the government of Alberta to help us now, not only to maintain our cultures as is done for those of European extraction, but even more to revitalize our cultures—those very cultures which the Governments of Alberta and of Canada once mistakenly nearly exterminated.

Of course our concern is for all the Indian people in all areas of the Great Island. We believe that the Creator made everything beautiful in his time. We believe that we must be good stewards of the Creator and not destroy nor mar His works of creation. We look upon stewardship not only in terms of money and the profit of a hundredfold, but in those of respect for the beauty of the land and of life in harmony with the succession of the seasons, so that the voices of all living things can be heard and continue to live and dwell among us. If an area is destroyed, marred, or polluted, my people say, the spirits will leave the area. If pollution continues, not only will animals, birds, and plant life disappear, but the spirits will also leave. This is one of the greatest concerns of Indian people. Many bearers of Christianity teach that only man has a soul, but we Indian people believe that forms of life other than men have souls and spirits also.

A Pima Indian student, Donna "Tina" Kisto, has expressed our views regarding nature and life:

> I am an Indian. My hair is black and my skin is brown, but I feel no inferiority before the whiteman. Brown is the color of the earth. Black is the colour of the sky before the life-giving rain falls. As the soil and rain bring forth food for life, so must I, the Lord of Nature, bring forth good into the world. All Indians are blessed at birth, with the precious heritage of independence and pride. Like a costly gem, this precious heritage must be treasured.

The Great Spirit, the Creator, in his wisdom has given to each climate its unique plant life and its unique animal life and its men and women, and He has given them a religion which is fitting to their needs. For the Hebrews who lived in the arid lands of the Middle East, with the thorny bushes and the cool, green grass near the wells and water holes for the sheep and camels, He gave a religion to suit their way of life. For the people of this Great Island, with the shining mountains, the pine-covered hills, the grassy plains, the flowing streams, and the fish-filled lakes, He made a home for the moose and the buffalo and deer and taught His red children to pray as was suited to them.

The harsh winter of our northern home is a time of trial. Some of our trees lose their leaves when the snow flies, so that only the keen observer can distinguish between the red willow and the white willow. All through the long winter, the life force of these trees retreats below the snow to await the touch of the Great Spirit in the spring. To the observer, the identities of the leafless trees are uncertain. Like these trees my people await the spring to burst again into vitality and full identity. This rebirth can only be achieved by a rededication to the religion of the Great Spirit made known to His children.

Our religion, the religion of this Great Island, is not contradictory to the teaching of the great rabbis of the Hebrews, nor is it in conflict with the great Christian teachers. Didn't Jesus say to the Pharisees:

Other sheep I have which are not of this fold; them also I must bring, and they shall hear my voice; and there shall be one fold and one shepherd [John 10:16].

Didn't He say:

In my Father's house are many mansions—I go to prepare a place for you [John 14:2].

Our religion professes faith in one Creator and acknowledges the unity and harmony of the Creation, the harmony of the whole environment—land, animals, birds, plant life, and men.

One of my grandfathers, Walking Buffalo, a Stoney philosopher who passed away some years ago, would draw examples for all men to understand the lessons of harmony from the Great Spirit's creation.

He told me one day that I must look at the beautiful forest where the trees and shrubs and tiny plants grow in a harmony of variety. He pointed out to me how some trees grow tall and straight to shelter the small trees and the misshapen ones; how the delicate flowers nestle among the grass at the foot of the trees catching the sunlight, as though the trees lean away to allow its rays to give them life. He spoke of the red trees and the white trees and the black trees, each

forming a part of a beautiful pattern in their diversity. He showed me how each stands proud and upright in its own way to honour the Maker, the Great Spirit. The diversity of plants and trees makes a beautiful forest. Why is the forest beautiful? Because it grows according to the plan of the Creator. If mankind, too, could stand humbly at the Creator's feet, mankind, too, could share in the harmony which is the Creation.

One of my grandfathers, Walking Buffalo, a Stoney philosopher who passed away in 1967.
(Glenbow Archives NB-36-1)

My people, too, must find their identity in that harmony of diversity. They, too, must once again seek their identity, humbly, in the Great Spirit's Creation. To be humble before the Creator does not mean to be trodden underfoot by others in the Creation. A man must defend himself and his companions from the perils of the wilderness.

This spring, a young Indian man from Ontario came to visit at Morley. He was here to take the vision quest in the mountains. He talked to me about his life and his understanding of the teachings from the elders he had gained while attending the Indian Ecumenical Conference. He explained that he had made preparation of fasting and praying and smoking the peace pipe before coming here. He further stated that he had been on drugs and alcohol but had given up these things since he began to study and follow the teachings of the medicine men.

He was aware now that life is a precious gift from the Creator. He had plans to search for his calling in the traditional way of going into the mountainous wilderness to be alone where perchance he would see a vision.

It was encouraging for me to have the opportunity to talk with this young man. This is one of the purposes of the Indian Ecumenical Conference—to create an awareness and challenge the young people. Many of our young people are now rediscovering our proud heritage. Some have taken up the challenge, as this young man has. They are rediscovering, as in the days of old, that in order to lead and help our people we must search the courage and wisdom of the older chiefs and medicine men.

The Stoney way of life begins with reverence for the Great Spirit and gratitude for the sacred mountains created by Him for Himself and His children. In the mountains we find many truths. As we cast our eyes toward them they seem to be different each day, and yet we know that they have always been the same, strong and unchanging.

A man must seek to emulate the mountains, strong in body and will and resolve, unchanging in his faith, yet flexible in his relations with his fellow men, compassionate with those who suffer, relentless with those who would stupidly abuse their authority, warm with his brothers and sisters.

The circle is the harmony of the Great Spirit's creation. When the grass grows lush in the summer, the deer grow fat and the hunting is good and there is the promise of easier living. When the spring rains are few, the deer are not so plentiful and man must prepare for a harder winter. These are facts and man must learn to live in this reality. The man who learns well the intricate pattern of nature will live a good life and a useful one to his people.

The way the European migrant stored food in preparation for the bad winters ahead was a thing of wonder to my people. This seemed to us an evidence of great wisdom. But when the bad winters came he did not share his storeroom; instead, he raised the price so only the rich could afford to buy the food. His poor neighbour starved. Society called him a clever businessman. My people would call him greedy. My people share in a different way. A hunter, returning with his kill, keeps the skin of the animal and distributes the best of the meat to others, keeping the poorer parts for himself. In this way he assures materials for his industrious wife and shows his generosity to others. The Holy Bible tells us to "cast our bread upon the waters." The customs of my people have told us to do the same thing for thousands of years.

The emergence of my people into close contact with the business world of the dominant society has put great pressure on our cultural values. Our traditional evaluation of a leader was made in terms of how much he gave to his people. A well-fed, well-clothed band of people mounted on good ponies was a credit to a leader. To achieve this, the leader would spend hours in prayer and meditation, for this success would, in a very large part, result from the guidance of the Creator through the leader's wisdom in placing himself in harmony with the Creation. Time to be alone in the forest or on the prairie listening to the voice of nature was most important. Sitting in Council or around the fire at night hearing his people's troubles and sharing in their joys was another part. Making decisions to shift camp when game was running out or when sickness was in the camp, to return to the winter camp, these were the duties of the leader. Today the leader's role is different. He is expected to be at a desk to direct the activities of his band, to play the politician for votes at the next election, and to follow the rules laid down by the Department of Indian Affairs. Above all he must balance his people's present needs against long-term goals. It is very hard!

In this transition from a traditional mode which has stood the test of time for thousands of years to a system imposed by the immigrant society there is a need for the combined wisdom of the Indian people. Only the older and experienced people of our race can develop the essential guidelines. Somewhere, from the very roots of our history and heritage, the answers can be found in the experience of our survival. It is in the content, in the reality of poverty, discrimination, violent deaths and suicides among our young people, in the reality of hope and aspirations for the future that the Indian Ecumenical Conference was born. It is fitting that the site for the annual conference was chosen in the afternoon shadows of our sacred mountains at Morley, in the foothills of the Rockies.

One of the highlights of the Conference is the big pow-wow held on the Friday evening of the Conference week. At this time, in traditional fashion, outstanding leaders are presented peace pipes, buffalo robes, headdresses, and other Indian things. Some of the better known recipients have been Andrew Dreadfulwater, Cherokee, from the North West Territories; Clifford Hill, Creek, from Oklahoma; Ernest Tootoosis, Cree, from Saskatchewan; Ernest Willie, Kwakiutl, from Toronto; George Erasmus, Dogrib, and Eddie Box, Ute, both from Colorado; Stewart Etsitty, Navaho, from Arizona; Wilfred Pelletier, from Vancouver; Don Marshall, Mic Mac, from the Maritimes; the late Andrew Ahenekew, Cree, from Saskatchewan; and Jake Rabbit, George Ear, and Horace Holloway, Jr., Stoneys, from Morley.

Grand Entry of the Nakoda Pow-wow hosted every Labour Day weekend.

The pow-wow is enjoyed by young and old. The various dances are part of the religious conference because our society is a complete society. Our society does not separate the secular and the religious; we do not think of our worldly concerns one day and the vast creation of the Great Spirit the next. Every day is a day the Great Spirit has given us to enjoy.

I might paraphrase the Wisdom literature and thoughts of the Old Testament in terms parallel to the Red Man's sayings and thoughts.

Does not wisdom call,
Does not understanding raise her voice?
On the heights beside the way,
In the path she takes her stand;
Beside the gates in front of the town,
At the entrance of the portals she cries aloud,

To you O men I call
My call is to the sons of men,
O simple ones, learn prudence
O foolish men, pay attention
Here, for I will speak noble things,
And from my lips will come what is right [Prov. 8:1-6].

The religion, culture, and philosophy of my people has grown out of our identification with nature. The sayings of our elders are similar to the Wisdom literature.

Wisdom of Nature calls at all seasons,
When will you learn from her instruction,
Understanding speaks aloud and gives sound reasons,
When will you listen, hear and take discretion.

At the entrance of the forests wisdom hails,
At the entrance of the prairies she is at hand,
At the heights beside the mountain trails,
And in the valleys she takes her stand.

To you, "O brave" I call,
My call is to the sons of the Red men,
O brave warriors, hear all,
Walk the good path as the Great Spirit's men.

Part V
The New Trail

The Next 100 Years

Nearly every morning I take my hunting dogs and go out and spend some time among the hills, the valleys, and the woodlands of Stoney country—my home. And, whenever I go out, be it during the colourful fall, on frosty winter mornings, in the fragrance of spring, or early during the sun-drenched days of summer, I am always conscious of the mountains on the horizon. These sacred rock monuments remind me that the Great Creator is timeless, while the refreshing mountain springs and the wildlife that inhabit His hills remind me that He is generous and loving.

The legends of long ago tell how close my people have always been to these mountains. They tell how our braves sojourned in them in search of their calling. They remind us that these mountains are our sacred places.

Yesterday the mountains were covered with snow, and the snows were red with the fires of dawn; today they are wrapped in a film of mist; tomorrow they will be dressed in another natural garment. Their appearance is always altering—yet their reality never changes. They remain as they were in their creation.

The whiteman has carved his roads and railways across them and stopped their waters with his hydro dams. Yet the mountains remain—they are immovable. In some areas our mountains have been left untouched as yet by technology, development, and the accompanying pollution. In those areas, spirits of long ago still remain; the mountains retain their sacred trust as the dwelling places of the spirits.

My people are like the mountains. For a hundred years or more the invading immigrant society pushed the Stoneys this way and that. We were bullied and defrauded, our customs were ridiculed;

yet my people resisted and held on to their faith in our cultural traditions. When steadfastness was essential to our survival, as a people we have proven ourselves as immovable as the mountains. We have survived, but survival by itself is not enough. A people must also grow and flourish.

Today, we, the descendents of and heirs to a great people—the Great Spirit's people—are rediscovering the realities of our proud heritage.

In the past decade we have again begun to flex our muscles and test our capabilities in our world—a world we now share with a multitude of immigrants of various races, religions, cultures, and customs. We have begun to question injustice and resist discrimination and prejudice. Our voice is heard again across this Great Island. Sometimes the voice is one of anger when the hurts are inflicted on our children all over again. Sometimes the voice is one of joy when one of our people succeeds or when the immigrant society occasionally shows interest in our progress.

When I hear our refound voice, when I see our reawakened muscle, I am optimistic that during this second century of our enforced inclusion in the Canadian mosaic we will take our rightful place in modern society.

As I climb the hills and think of our proud heritage, our brave history, I seem to get new strength and courage as I look into the future.

Wakâ Tâga, the Great Spirit, has been generous to my people. Beneath the Stoneys' reserve lands—the lands which our grandfathers marked out for us and our children and our children's children—lies a great lake of natural gas. For nearly a century this lay unknown and unexploited. Today, when the need for fuel is urgent, it is being tapped to provide the energy for the nation's cities. The royalties from this gas, used wisely, can provide the energy to stimulate my people's rebirth.

But although the Stoney Tribe is receiving money from natural gas royalties at present, this will not last forever. The life of the gas reserves may be thirty years, or it could be forty. Other means of income and long-range plans have to be considered and developed for the benefit of the whole tribe while we have the capital monies to work with. When there is no more gas royalty money to rely on, we must be ready with programs to create employment, to ensure livelihood.

The wise Stoney elders have talked to me on many occasions

about the gas royalties, and about our treaty with the government and its importance regarding the future. As we approach the centenary of Treaty Seven, the Stoneys want some reassurance from the federal government that the treaty agreements and promises will be binding on both parties, the Canadian Government and the Stoney Tribe, in the centuries to come.

The treaty agreement was to be honoured "as long as the sun shines, rivers flow, and grass grows"; during this centennial year the Stoney Tribe, consisting of three bands—Bearspaw, Chiniquay, and Wesley—want reaffirmation by the government that our treaty rights will be upheld and honoured in the future.

After the gas wells run dry here at Morley, we do not want to have to turn to the government once again for their assistance and charity; this is when our treaty rights will be very helpful in securing from the government the necessary things for the survival of our people. At that time, all our traditional lands, except those now included in our reserves, will have been taken up by the immigrant society, and there will hardly be a place left for us to spread our blankets. This is why our wise elders want some reassurance from the federal government that our treaty will be honoured, so that our children and our children's children will have something, at least a land base, on which to make their living.

The question of our claim for the land on the Kootenay Plains is still before the courts. It may be decades before it is resolved. The Stoneys have been waiting a hundred years for this land; we are still waiting.

For thousands of years the Stoney people gained an education from the tribal elders which fitted them to live with pride and confidence on this Great Island. They learned the ways of the seasons, the ways of the animals and birds. They learned which plants and herbs would sustain their good health. They learned the ways of living together, respect for the needs of others, the sharing of the bounty of the hunt, and the meaning of prayer. They learned to survive in all seasons; they learned the importance of bravery and wisdom; they learned the responsibility of leadership. They did not build schools, as the whiteman does, but the Stoney educational system was suited to the requirements of a free and independent people living in a free land.

Then came an alien race with an alien culture and ways with which we had no experience. The acquisition of new knowledge to cope with our new environment was necessary.

In 1974 the elders of the tribes of Alberta met to discuss the future of Indian education and, after careful deliberation, made a joint statement:

> In order to survive in the twentieth century, we must come to grips with the whiteman's culture and with the whiteman's ways. We must stop lamenting the past. The whiteman has many good things, for example, his technology. Take them. Discover and establish the harmonies with the basic values of the Indian ways, and thereby forge a newer and stronger sense of identity. To be fully Indian today, we must become bilingual and bi-cultural. We have never had to do this before. We will thus survive, for we have always survived. Our history tells us so.[1]

The idea of the elder as one who is filled with wisdom has disappeared from the whiteman's thinking. Instead, he relies on science. Today the Indian people see the immigrant culture worshipping technology as though it were a god.

Technology is not wisdom. With technology it is possible to build things and build them bigger—machines and roads, bridges, dams, and buildings. With technology it is possible to drill deeper for oil and gas, make bigger mines for iron and coal, and exploit the soil and the forests more thoroughly. This can be good; but without the application of wisdom in its use, technology will only change our world into a vast quarry which provides material for great factories while the people live in cities which resemble mighty beehives. Only wisdom can harness technology so that man can build a better world where people can live in pride, freedom, dignity, equality, and brotherhood. My people must never loose their respect for the wisdom of the elders, wisdom which will balance all human activity. My people say: "If you destroy nature and the environment, you are destroying yourself. But if you protect the environment and safeguard the water, ultimately you are protecting yourself." Wisdom harnessed with technology can go a long way in creating a better social order, a world in which all creation can survive and enjoy life to the fullest.

Young Stoneys have begun to show an interest in a schooling in the immigrant culture, and this is good. They will need it. Society has changed very quickly in the past twenty years, and a sound schooling in the three Rs has become essential for survival. In my father's time this was not so. Education in the ways of the animals of the foothills was sufficient to live with integrity. Even for my generation, the need for a Western education was not so clearly defined. However, it is different now, and several younger Stoneys are in the process of completing a university education; there is no doubt that this tiny trickle will soon grow into a flood.

The real obstacle to the continued success of schooling our children is not teaching them to read, but making suitable reading matter available. White children are encouraged to read because their reading materials concentrate on the stories of the white racial heroes. Even if the hero is of another race, even if he is a rabbit or a horse, he expresses white values. If historical "fact" depends on a point of view, that point of view is always white in the books our children get to read. For the sake of our children we need a body of literature, history, and simple philosophy written from the Stoney viewpoint. The cost of developing this literature will be very high. Funding from the Alberta Cultural Centre is on a per capita basis, so, although we are grateful for it, it would cover our needs only if we were a much larger community. When funding sources think of Indian resource people—the storytellers and oral historians—they think of $20 a day. When the Indian people ask for help from white resource people, they need $200 a day.

The cost of schooling for our children is prepaid, by agreement in the Treaty. Our trustees, Queen Victoria and her heirs, saw to that. Even when the cost of school is added to the other treaty obligations which our trustees took upon themselves, the rental price for all our lands in perpetuity was very cheap. If we had had just one 1977 land developer as our adviser in 1877, the price would have been much higher. As it is, we have every right to expect that the price that was agreed upon—in education services, in health services, and in economic development—should be paid without argument and with first-rate goods.

Today, in schooling, we need the best available—plus. As a television commentator might say in the second period of a game when the home team is several goals behind, "We will have to play catch-up hockey." We will have to get some more production out of our front line—Indian teachers. We will require some different strategies—relevant curriculums. We will require some modifications of style—development of our literature and social studies texts. The training of our teachers can be done; the University of Calgary Outreach Program has proved that. The development of our own literature and social studies texts can be done; the Stoney Cultural Education Program has proved that. It may require massive funding for the next ten years, but it is the only way to put our school system back in the hockey game—and this hockey game is the future of our people.

My vision tells me that the first phase of the program is the development of the Stoney Education Centre. The building will include all the facilities necessary for the training of our young people in the skills required to advance them into a competitive position with all other young people. The curriculum will include programs in all the areas necessary for them to learn how to function comfortably in their world, a world which is bilingual and bicultural. The staff will be a mixture of the best teachers who can be provided from our own cultural resources and from the colleges, technological institutes, and universities of the immigrant society. The programs will be directed to meeting the needs of our own communities, to providing teachers, doctors, lawyers, nurses, carpenters, plumbers, electricians, mechanics, clerks, typists, accountants, managers, and all the other skilled personnel we need so urgently. Each program will also contain Stoney cultural input from our elders, which is a vital area of learning for our young people.

There is an urgent need for this Education Centre—one that is located within our own community with visiting expert teachers from the immigrant society. It is the only way in which we can integrate the wisdom of our culture with a knowledge of the technology of the other culture. We have experimented with the technique over the past five years in the Stoney Cultural Education Program, using poor buildings and improvised technology, with the assistance of teachers from the University of Calgary Outreach Program; we know that it works. We have had our first university graduates this year. We now need to put a full-scale program into operation. It will require a high level of funding, but with so much money spent on a school system which hasn't worked for so long, our trustees must look at alternatives which will produce results.

The economic development of our communities must also be studied in terms of our bicultural reality. Our non-Stoney advisers continually talk to us about economic viability and profitability. "Profit" seems to mean that after everyone has gotten all he needs, there is something left over that no one needs, so we put it in the bank. The idea of profits and banking is foreign to us. In traditional days, if we needed two deer for food, we did not kill ten! Is it this idea of profits that stimulates whitemen to build houses which are bigger than their families need, to buy more cars than they can use? My people were able to live in this country for thousands of years without reducing the size of the animal herds. The coming of the whiteman saw the buffalo destroyed in a decade. After only two centuries, the immigrant society is short of water, has an energy crisis, and experiences seasonal food shortages. A large section of the population, including most of the Indians, lives in poverty. Is this what is meant when the whiteman talks of economic viability and profitability—a few very wealthy people who have more than their share and many very poor people who have much less than their share? This is not the way of my people.

The Stoney people have thought of a way to use our grazing land for the benefit of all our people. *Wakâ Tâga*, the Great Spirit, the Creator, made this land for all his people. He created the earth and the grass, He arranged the seasons to give growth to men and animals and plants. Men can be a part of this natural rhythm and can even assist in making the harvest more plentiful by their work and their wisdom. The Stoney people need food—meat, vegetables, eggs, and milk—to sustain themselves. Now that we have bought some more fertile land east of the reserve and have the capital to develop it, it makes sense to raise cattle and hogs, to grow potatoes and vegetables to feed our own people. Starting with a small herd and small plots of grain and vegetables, we intend to develop a viable agricultural and ranching program. I use the word "viable" in the way that makes sense to us. "Viability" means "living" and this program will help the living of everybody. The Stoneys who look after the stock will earn wages. Some of our young people will learn the skills which are needed in a ranching enterprise. All our people will eat well from the production of meat and other food, which will be distributed through community-owned and community-operated stores and supermarkets. Any excess production can be marketed through the normal markets of the greater society. We call this program STAR because it stands for Stoney Tribal Agriculture and Ranching, and because the stars have always been a challenge and an inspiration to the best in men.

Our forests, which occupy more than half of our 100,000 acres of land, will be used to establish a viable lumber-based industry. Again, viability means better living for all of our people. Our people need houses and furniture to put in those houses. Not all our present families have good housing yet, and each year our young people start an average of twenty-five new families by marriages. Our new sawmill, which was nearing full production in the spring of 1977, can provide the lumber needed for a housing program, for a public building program, and for furniture production. These industries will provide employment for our young people as well as providing housing, furniture, fencing, and firewood for our people. All surplus production can be channelled into the markets of the greater society.

Already we have established a viable concrete product project. Stone and sand are readily available on our land; cement is brought in from a nearby cement plant. Again, the viability of the project is understandable to our people in terms of improving our living and providing worthwhile employment and income for our people. Everybody lives a little better! A number of our young people have learned the necessary skills quickly under the supervision of a competent whiteman who is sensitive to the cultural differences of our young people. More training for these young people in the Stoney Education Centre will improve their work performance.

I have touched briefly on commercial development in writing of the distribution of production from STAR. Such development must extend to more than agriculture. In the past century all the income of the Stoney people has been spent in retail and service enterprises operated by white people. While this has assisted in the growth of the nearby towns and villages, the Stoney Council must soon begin to develop viable retail stores and services within the community. Viability must be defined as improving the living standards of all our people. For example, most of the Stoney people cannot afford the luxury of washing machines and dryers in their own homes; they are dependent on laundromats, which are twenty or thirty miles away. So the construction and operation of a laundromat within the community must be an early project.

The past year has seen the construction and operation of a gas station with a convenience store in our community. It is very important for our people to have a place where gas and oil can be obtained, where food items can be purchased, and where some Stoneys can earn an income and offer a worthwhile service to their community. It may be difficult to place such an enterprise in the context of financial management (especially since it does not yet show a profit), but it fits very well into our ideas of viability. The quality of life has been improved for our people. This enterprise's success, in our terms, leads us to think about attempting other retail distribution of food, clothing, and various household needs. A supermarket would give worthwhile employment to more of our people and would provide services within the community which are now only available twenty or thirty miles away.

Certainly we must build a more balanced economy—one in which all money spent on services and supplies does not leave the community as it has in the past.

My people are often accused of not possessing the virtues of frugality and saving. This is not quite true. In traditional times, my people always preserved a part of the meat supply and much of the berry harvest; they dried the meat, made use of the winter refrigeration provided by the Creator, and mixed pemmican. That most of them have not saved money has something to do with the small cash incomes which they have had in the past, as well as with their lack of understanding of the other culture's banking system. While I do not suggest that the introduction of banking services in the community would produce an instant change, it would certainly allow the people to investigate the banking system in familiar surroundings. As they became more confident in their financial dealings and as their incomes improved to a point where saving was possible, I believe that they would apply their traditional attitudes toward food storage to the new concept of cash storage. This is what bicultural education is all about. Such learning could be further stimulated by a suitable teaching unit in the Stoney Education Centre.

The most promising economic possibility for our people could lie in the tourist industry. We have all the necessary assets and resources. Our land is midway between Calgary and Banff and has excellent access from the Trans-Canada Highway—which itself passes through the reserve. We are located in the beautiful foothills, and the reserve includes woods, open meadows, and lakes, all with the spectacular Rocky Mountains for a background. Many spots are ideal for horseback riding, hiking, golfing, and other tourist recreational activities.

The first stages of tourist development have been started with the Stoney Indian Park and the Stoney Wilderness Centre. The Park already offers tourist camping space and rental facilities, plus guides for riding, backpacking, and fishing. The Wilderness Centre, although newer, is more sophisticated in its operation and its goals. Built on the edge of Lake Chief Hector, the base camp has good facilities which emphasize outdoor living in traditional teepees (which my people still use in the summer). The idea behind the Wilderness Centre is a desire to introduce young people from the larger society to the philosophy and methods which have allowed the Stoney people to live in the wilderness. If the centre allows some of our guests to obtain insights into our values and our way of life, and at the same time provides employment for Stoneys in which they can use the skills they have developed over their lifetimes, then the centre is achieving its goal.

From this small beginning we are already planning conference facilities, motels, restaurants, and recreation areas for the future. There is a need for our people to be trained in many of the skilled areas which will provide employment opportunities as these schemes develop.

Opportunities could also be found for some of our people to employ their hunting skills. Much of our traditional hunting area has been taken up by Banff National Park. Hunting within the park boundaries is not allowed, and there are very few carnivorous beasts roaming the area. This absence of human hunters and scarcity of animal predators results in overstocking and the necessity, from time to time, of reducing the number of grazing animals so that a proper ecological balance can be maintained. Indian people could, and should, be represented in the Parks Branch to advise on the conditions of the game and the best method of reducing game population whenever this becomes necessary. Stoney hunters could be employed to thin the herds. If the meat produced in the reduction of herds were made available to Stoney tribal members, it would assist in providing us with the game we love to eat, but which has become more difficult to obtain by hunting since the establishment of Parks and the Wilderness Areas. Also, the skins of animals thinned from the herds could be an important contribution to the Stoney handicraft industry, which is particularly important to our women.

In the Stoney community, the first steps in economic development must be those which meet the needs of the Stoney community. The most important need is to break down the pervasive dependence on welfare by creating jobs, a step which will give our people the satisfaction of looking after their families. At first these jobs must draw on the present experience of our people, but gradually training must be available so that they can upgrade existing skills and acquire new skills. Leaders must be given the authority to select development projects which meet these criteria.

Our people have traditionally had an effective political system within our own communities. For thousands of years a Chief and his advisory council have looked after the interests of each band. The method has been concensus. This method has put a high value on getting the opinion of all band members before the Chief makes a decision. I think that this way of government will continue with our people for many years to come.

Modern technology is important to the governing process as the numbers of our people continue to increase. Already, we are making use of the telephone. Our new administration building will have audiovisual facilities built in. Council discussions will probably be taped for the records, and videotape and film slides will be used to keep tribal members in touch with community activities. We have also begun to discuss the establishment of broadcast facilities for our community. Closer communication will lead to greater involvement of the "grassroots."

Poor relations with the federal and provincial governments have caused difficulties in the past. Legislation which affects the Indian people has been passed through the provincial legislature with no input from the Indian people. Other countries have overcome this problem by making sure that native people are represented by their own legislators. One possible method is the New Zealand plan, whereby a number of seats are reserved in each election exclusively for Maori members, guaranteeing that the voice of the aboriginal people will be heard in the legislature. This or some other method could be used here in Canada to ensure that there is Indian representation in both the provincial and the federal parliaments.

I believe that by our own efforts, with adequate support from governments, we will be able to work our way out of the multitude of difficulties which face us now. The development of facilities and programs in education is the first phase for our emergence as a people. The training programs needed for social and economic development will be set up and administered within the community with input from the elders, who have the wisdom to integrate our cultural values into the curriculum. A long, hard look will be taken at the curriculum materials in our schools to assure that our children absorb knowledge which supports rather than undermines their identity. We must find the means of producing these relevent materials in sufficient quality and quantity to support a bicultural and bilingual program. A program of economic development which can be understood in terms of Stoney objectives will be developed to provide employment and to improve the living standards of our people.

So, as I run with my hunting dogs among the hills in the morning of a new day, the question comes ringing in my ears over and over again:"How do we, as the Great Spirit's people, build a path into the next hundred years?" And the answer comes loud and clear to me: "The Great Spirit has been our guide in the past, He is our guide today, and He will be our guide into the future." As I climb the hills and look over the valleys and think of our heritage, I seem to get new strength and courage as I look to the future.

As I stand on top of the hill which overlooks the beautiful Bow River Valley, with the sacred shining mountains in the background as a refuge, I am reminded of our proud heritage, the little babies in their moss bags, the beautiful maidens, the brave warriors, the medicine women, the wise elders, and the buffalo that roamed as monarch of the plains, the eagle that guarded the skies. They all speak of brotherhood and oneness with the universe.

As I look across the beautiful valley, it seems as if I am looking across the next one hundred years. I am reassured about the future because I have faith in the Great Spirit, the Creator, and I am reminded of the words of the Hebrew prophet of old and I repeat:

They that wait upon the Great Spirit shall renew their
strength,
They shall mount up with wings as eagles,
They shall run and not be weary,
They shall walk and not faint. [Is. 40:31].

The old path is a proven path to travel on. It has withstood the test of time, not only over centuries, but over thousands of years. This is the path my ancestors walked and it shall be the path my future generations will walk on and on and on. It is the path of the Great Spirit, the Creator.

Our proud history is unequalled and unsurpassed on this Great Island. Each of us can hold his or her head high, as one of the original people of this beautiful land, and say, "I am an Indian." The Stoney philosophy of living in harmony with nature and in accord with the creations of the Great Spirit will be the theme of many peoples, cultures, and languages who live on this Great Island in the future.

We are the Great Spirit's people! These mountains are our sacred places!

Morley townsite, c. 1970. The mountains remain, as they were in their creation.

Epilogue

Chief John Snow

128 Years Later

To begin, I want to recount some of my observations and predictions that I presented to the conference "One Century Later; The Native Peoples of Western Canada since the 'Making' of the Treaties," which was hosted by the Western Canadian Studies Conference at the University of Calgary in 1977. On that occasion I stated:

> One century later we are dismayed, frustrated, and hurt. One century later, we have become strangers in our homeland. Most of our land, our resources, and wealth are taken from us in the name of progress and civilization. One century later, we have become a poor people, a forgotten people in a strange and indifferent society. There is no meaningful redress for our land claims. There is no respect from the uncomprehending larger society for our treaty rights, hunting rights, fishing rights, and aboriginal rights. One century later, we as Indian people have almost lost faith in democracy in a land of democracy. We have been suppressed by government red tape, bureaucracy, and paternalism. We have experienced despair, loneliness, and hopelessness.
>
> No one seems to be really interested in the Indian and his problems. They are only interested in Indian land because it contains a wealth of resources: natural resources, water resources, mineral resources . . . A U.S. president once described an Indian reservation . . . " . . . [as] a land set aside for Indian people surrounded by land thieves." We know exactly what the president meant. One century later, many of our beautiful and living forests have been flooded. Huge hydro dams are built. In many cases no compensation was made for flooding our hunting grounds, sacred areas, and traditional areas. The motto seemed to be, if you step on the Indian without compensation, make a hydro dam, build a skyscraper, this is progress. In the name of progress there is no redress. In the name of progress we are becoming powerless.[1]

When I reflect on the subsequent twenty-five years that led to the 125th commemoration of Treaty Seven in 2002, sadly I have to report that those bitter words remain true today. I welcome this opportunity to reflect upon my life's work and to describe some of the events I was involved in over those twenty-five years.

As Chief of the Goodstoney–Wesley First Nation, I have been at the forefront of many challenges facing us in the modern world. I have been asked to speak out on many controversial issues facing my people. I was one of the Chiefs who opposed the federal government's 1969 "White Paper." The Chiefs and elders of Treaty Six, Treaty Seven, and Treaty Eight met in a series of meetings from 1969–1970 to draft a Treaty Indian position paper called the "Red Paper" to defend our treaty rights, which the federal government threatened to unilaterally eradicate in its' policy paper. As we prepared the "Red Paper," we remembered the Creator. Sacred pipe ceremonies and special prayers were observed by our people, including elders, ceremonial leaders, and chiefs. When the paper was ready, the Chiefs and elders of Alberta travelled to Ottawa, where I helped to present the Indian Association of Alberta's "Red Paper" to the late Prime Minister Pierre Elliott Trudeau and his cabinet, in Confederation Building in Ottawa in opposition to the "White Paper."[2]

Throughout the 1970s, up to the mid-1980s, I was honoured to host the Indian Ecumenical Conference, a continent-wide spiritual movement held at Stoney Indian Park at Morley, Alberta. There were thousands of Indigenous people who came from the four corners of this Great Island to rediscover our spiritual heritage, to renew our sacred ceremonies, and to listen to the traditional teachings of our wise sages. There were families, youth groups, adults, children, elders, and medicine people in attendance. Some of them stayed in the teepees provided by the Nakoda people and experienced living like our people once did in the old days: touching Mother Earth, feeling the forces of nature, the winds, the rains, and the warmth of the sacred fire that was kept burning for the duration of the Conference.

As a Chief, one of my responsibilities was to protect my people and the land or territory where we lived. I knew we once had a large traditional territory that we used in order to survive and to flourish as a people. After treaty was made in 1877, most of our traditional territory was taken and occupied by the encroaching civilization. Another of my many responsibilities as Chief was to get our traditional lands and our natural resources back. In 1971 I became the first Treaty Indian to address the Legislative Assembly of the Alberta legislature, pressing our concerns about the impact of a twenty-seven-mile lake created by the proposed Bighorn Hydroelectric Dam on the North Saskatchewan River. In subsequent years I have also raised the same issue with task forces and at board hearings, and have given interviews to the news media and magazines. We want to inform the Canadian public that we still have Aboriginal and Indian rights, hunting and fishing rights, rights to sacred sites—the sacred hot springs and vision quest areas—and the right to gather from the abundant natural resources—berries, herbs and medicinal plants, soapstone, and earth paints—that we use for our livelihood and to retain our spiritual tradition in our ancestral territory, despite the many laws and regulations that restrict our freedom to practise our traditional ways.

In order to protect and assert our treaty rights, I spearheaded the Stoney Nations' land claims research and initiated the Nakoda Learning Centre at the Nakoda Lodge. Our community now enjoys the benefits of one of the most comprehensive Native Studies libraries and archives in Canada. As a result of this research work, the Stoney Nakoda Nation has successfully negotiated two specific claims in 1990 and 1999 worth millions of dollars.[3]

On the national scene, I became very involved with the National Indian Brotherhood (NIB) under the leadership of the late Walter Dieter in the early organizational stages of the national coalition of First Nations. In 1981 the NIB was transformed into the Assembly of First Nations (AFN), which has grown in strength to represent the 640 First Nations across Canada on national issues of importance. In 1993 I served as senior adviser to National Chief Ovide Mercredi.

One of the most important events of the early 1980s was the repatriation of the Canadian Constitution proposed by Prime Minister Trudeau. Many of the Alberta First Nations were opposed to repatriation because it threatened our special relationship with the British Crown. The Treaty Nations of western Canada have a unique and sacred relationship with the British Crown arising from the sacred treaties signed in the 1870s. In 1976, during the 100th commemoration of Treaty Six, some of the Chiefs from Treaty Six and Treaty Seven travelled to London, England, to express our concerns directly to the Queen in Buckingham Palace and to lobby British parliamentarians.

Despite our strong opposition to repatriation, the 1982 Constitution Act was passed in both parliaments as required by law. There have been many books written by academics about the con-

One of our outstanding Native leaders when he was National Chief, Ovide Mercredi.
A child in his traditional regalia stands proudly beside him.

stitutional process, as well as extensive media coverage in newspapers and magazines, but the Native point of view is rarely expressed. I was a delegate to all the First Ministers Conferences (FMC) held during the 1980s, which were high on expectations but negligible in positive results that would protect our Aboriginal and treaty rights. I was privileged and proud to present the constitutional position of the Stoney Nakoda Nation to the 1983 FMC in a brief I called "The Right to be Indian."[4] I also challenged the Canadian government at the time, when I stated, "We, the original peoples, were placed on this Great Island to live according to the Creator's plan and in harmony with His creation. Will the Canadian Constitution blend its voice with the harmony that is our right and our destiny, or will it create discord in the song of our land?" So far, the Canadian government seems to have decided to create discord in the song of our land. Our land claims are still outstanding today.

In "The Right to be Indian," I argue that the federal government must honour and respect the terms of our sacred treaties as understood by our elders and not just rely upon the written text that was recorded by the Treaty Commissioners. The treaty promises and agreements were understood differently by our forefathers, and in some important instances the promises were not written down by the official recorders. Because of the different perspectives and understanding of the terms of treaty, equal authority must be given to our oral history as it has been passed down through our oral historians, the elders.

During the 1980s many planning meetings and negotiation sessions were held between the four national Aboriginal organizations, the provinces and territories, and the federal government at a series of First Ministers Conferences. But in the end, when the final FMC on Native rights was held in 1987, there was no agreement on any further constitutional protection for Canada's first citizens. It is interesting to note that where the politicians failed, it has been the unpredictable Supreme Court of Canada that has come to our defence in protecting some of our treaty rights, such as the right to hunt and fish, and in defining our Aboriginal title to this Great Island.

It has been a tough struggle for the First Nations to gain even minimal recognition of the great sacrifices and the significant contributions that we have made toward Canada's future growth and prosperity. I hope that our oral traditions and history will be told in the classroom books studied by future generations. We have a unique and special history to tell, to preserve, and to treasure as the first citizens of this Great Island. I hope that this second edition of *These Mountains Are Our Sacred Places* in some small way will serve to foster a better understanding of our Indigenous traditional values and philosophy as Canada enters the twenty-first century.

A pipe ceremony held on the Morley Reserve in 1991 with (left to right): Councillor David Bearspaw, Chief Bill Ear, Sr., Honourable Minister Tom Siddon, Chief John Snow, Sr., Chief Ken Soldier, and Chief John Ear.

Oral History

When I began to write *These Mountains Are Our Sacred Places*, I struggled within myself whether to put our sacred history on the written page and in a foreign language, English, rather than in our beautiful Nakoda language. Our history had always been an oral tradition, told in our Indigenous language in the spoken word, usually by the campfire. It is a living history passed on through the generations, from father to son or mother to daughter, in story or legend form. I did not want to break this tradition by transforming our history into writing. The history and the world view expressed in our oral tradition are very different, like day and night, from the history written by non-Indians.

In a way, I was forced to put my story on paper because many of our land claims are based partly on government archival records. In order to solidify our land claim, I had to write it on paper and present it to the governments or to their court systems. At that time, oral testimony as given by our elders was not accepted in the courts of Canada. Twenty-two years after this book was written, the oral history of our people was accepted by the courts as a result of the 1999 Supreme Court of Canada decision in the Delgamuukw case. I feel some vindication in knowing that the most important inspiration for my book was the stories and legends that I heard from the elders of my community.

At the age of seventy-two, I am still learning the legends, philosophies, and teachings of our ancient ones. My first language is the Nakoda language, the language that belongs to this Great Island. I learned English later in the residential school, but most of the Stoney people still speak the Nakoda language, although some of the young people do not. Through our language we learn about our legends, our religion, our oral history, and our belief systems. It is an Indigenous and beautiful history to tell others so that they, too, will journey with us according to our ways and see the world from a Native perspective. We interpret this history to mean that we are among the Creator's sacred creations, that our people are related to other beings and creation, and that we share the feeling of sacredness with them.

Our surroundings seem to come alive when history or legends are told by the living words of our elders. Our history is a record of our experiences and relationship to the earth, sun, moon, stars, the elements, the seasons, the winds, the waters, the fire, and the weather because they are all connected to each other and to us in our oral history. The elders know and talk about other forms of life—sentient beings and sacred beings—that dwell amongst us and journey with us in our human and spiritual travels in life.

One elder told me that he went to the mountains to visit the spirits there. Another told me that eagles possess spiritual powers that have helped our people over the centuries. The elders' stories relate to the surrounding environment and to nature's setting. The characters in their stories are alive and we can identify with them, whether they are animals or birds or rocks (or other elements the Creator has made) because we feel related to them. Indigenous people have a kinship relationship to Mother Earth and the whole of the cosmos. All creation has spiritual meaning in our Indigenous world view.

Our legends, as told by our ancient ones, must be preserved and studied. We need to continue to record our true history. We need to do our own research. We need to talk to as many elders as we can before they have all gone to the Spirit World. Elders with traditional knowledge, along with Indigenous youth and children, must come together to remember the stories. We must preserve these traditions, and future generations must continue this journey—knowing our traditions and oral history—if we as a people are to survive, grow, and flourish in the future. We must continue to speak our language. We must follow our culture, our customs, and our traditions, and learn about the ceremonies that were held in special places and the prayers that were said in sacred places. We must continue to pray for Mother Earth and to pray for all of Creation. This is our tradition and we must continue this tradition.

An Important Vision

A Nakoda elder, Norman Abraham, from the Bighorn Indian Reserve, helped me in my early years as a young chief of the Goodstoney-Wesley First Nation. He told me about the traditional roles of the elders and of the Chief in our Nakoda society. The elders, both men and women, are the keepers of our tradition, language, legends, and teachings. The Chief is like a father, and his family is the whole tribe. I was to care for the entire family—the tribe—and treat them equally and justly, just as you would your own family. Elder Abraham told me never to forget the Creator and the teachings and ways of our people. "Always pray to the Great Spirit to walk with you, guide you, protect you, and give you wisdom so you can lead our people along the good path." He gave me a sacred peace pipe and told me the importance of it in our Nakoda society. He taught me how to handle the pipe and how to use it in prayers and rituals as our medicine people have done through the ages.

To this day I still have that sacred pipe. I keep it in a very honourable place in my home, along with tobacco, sweet grass, and mountain sage, but I only use the pipe on rare occasions. In 1976 I took this sacred pipe on my trip to London, England. A delegation of chiefs went there to invite Her Majesty, the Queen of England, to come to Blackfoot Crossing in southern Alberta to commemorate the signing of Treaty Seven in 1877. She was unable to attend but offered to send her son Prince Charles, the heir to the British Throne, to take part in our centennial commemoration. I knew that the sacred pipe was important to our elders and Chiefs during the treaty-making days, so in keeping with our ancestors' tradition, I took the sacred pipe along so that our delegation could pray together and smoke the peace pipe while we were in London. It was important to make special preparations for the centennial of Treaty Seven, which is a sacred covenant, a treaty of peace and friendship, and a way to share the bounty of the land with the newcomers to our country.

Those were very busy times in London that summer. We had opportunities to attend various functions, special lunches, dinners, and speaking engagements to explain why we were there and to remind the British people and their government about the Sacred Treaty that was signed in 1877 with representatives of the British Crown.

Although our days and evenings were full of activity, I invited our delegation to one of four pipe ceremonies I conducted there. Most of the delegates attended that first gathering. We sat in a circle as I led the ceremony according to our custom and offered prayers in the Nakoda language. About half of the delegates also attended a second pipe ceremony. I held the third pipe ceremony by myself in a hotel room where my wife, Alva, a Quechan Indian, and I were staying.

I knew I had to have four pipe ceremonies, so I conducted a fourth ceremony very early one morning. As I initiated all four of these ceremonies, I was aware that our traditional people—the pipe holders, the medicine people, and ceremonial leaders—have always prayed for our mother, the earth, all of her children, and the whole family of Creation. Following that tradition, I offered prayers in the Nakoda language. I also prayed for a good treaty centennial. I prayed that our Sacred Covenant between the British people represented by the Canadian Government and the Indigenous people in the area covered by Treaty Seven (our treaty of peace and friendship, and the agreements and promises made to share the land and its bountiful resources) would be honoured by both parties in the years to come. I concluded by praying for a safe return of all the delegates to our homeland, North America, when our tour to England was complete.

When I concluded the fourth ceremony, it was very early in the morning—sunlight was just beginning to touch the earth—and after the pipe ceremony I went back to bed and fell asleep.

When I woke up, it was just like I'd come back from a long journey. I remember very vividly walking on a land that I was familiar with across the ocean on a gorgeous day. In my dream, I had a Vision. I was walking across the Stoney Indian Reserve just east of the Indian Ecumenical Conference grounds, known as the sacred grounds. It is just across the highway from where my brother Wallace and his family used to live. I was in the spirit world; I was moving westward, gliding in the air across time and across space. I saw Willow Creek, a crystal-clear stream that usually runs downhill into the Bow River. I remember the area very well because when I was a boy I used to ride my pony there. As I was walking, I was in the air but I could see the creek below. The creek was very dirty, murky, dark and purplish in colour, like sewage water backing up. It was flowing uphill instead of downhill.

Just then, I heard a most beautiful voice, very calm and soft-spoken, which said to me in my Nakoda language, seeming to refer to the water running against the natural flow: *"This is caused by Calgary Power."* I knew the voice was referring to the three dams built by the Calgary Power Company, which are causing the waters to flow unnaturally. It was strange that the water was flowing against the natural flow. The water kept whirling and bubbling up, looking very dirty and not fit for drinking.

As I crossed to the west side of Willow Creek, I touched the ground. Just then, a spiritual being caught up with me and walked with me on my left side. I was ecstatic and overwhelmed by the wonderful presence. I did not dare look at my companion face to face, but glanced over and looked at him from the side. He was an Indigenous man with long black hair down to his waist. His kind face resembled that of a prophet, a messenger, a very special human spiritual being. He was a young man in his late twenties or early thirties, with all the features of a North American Indian—high cheekbones, dark eyes, and a beautiful nose. His broad shoulders and strong-looking arms were copper coloured. He wore a tanned animal skin, a kind of soft rawhide that criss-crossed his body, with a large, thong-like strap on his left shoulder that widened as it came down to cover his waist. He was barefoot, and his legs were muscular and looked very strong, as though he could walk all day without tiring.

I looked at my feet and saw that I, too, was barefoot. We were walking westward to the Indian Ecumenical Conference grounds, the sacred grounds where many of our Indigenous people camped and took part in sacred gatherings. During the 1970s and early 1980s, many of our Indigenous people came there from across this Great Island to heal and to be healed, and to rediscover our culture, our language, our traditions, and the ways of our people. As I walked, I felt very light. I seemed to be walking in the air again, although I was touching the ground, and ahead I could see the sacred mountains.

We stopped for a moment. Two scenes appeared before us. Straight to the south of us was a scene much like a large mural that blended in with the area. In the scene were several tents, three large tents and a few smaller ones, and a man like Louis Riel, bearded and sitting by one of the tents on a chair with a table in front of him, with some papers on the table. My companion motioned to the mural and said to me in the Nakoda language, *"You don't belong there."* It was that same beautiful voice I had heard when I was gliding over Willow Creek.

Then, with an arm motion from where we were standing toward the rising sun, he indicated another large mural. Like the other mural, it blended in with the surrounding area. A teepee was there. I could see Chief Walking Buffalo standing in front of the teepee. He was wearing his native regalia and his famous buffalo horn headpiece. As I looked, Walking Buffalo came alive, moving, walking, and smiling as he appeared to be talking with the people around him. Also, the people around him were alive and moving about. I could not make out who they were but they were all Indians. Then my companion, gesturing toward the teepee, said to me in the Nakoda language, *"That is where you belong, and always remember that."*

After seeing the two scenes in my Vision, we continued our walk westward toward the Ecumenical Conference grounds. I felt as light as a feather. I still felt very light and seemed to be walking in beauty in a sacred land.

Just before we reached a small pond along the pathway, the

prophet lifted his head and looked toward the Conference sacred grounds and toward the sacred mountains and spoke to me again in the Nakoda language. "What you began here, don't ever stop." Then the prophet vanished.

When he spoke those last words to me, I thought the prophet meant my involvement in the Indian Ecumenical Conference, a continent-wide Indian spiritual movement, the hosting and bringing together of various Indigenous peoples of this Great Island for spiritual renewal. I thought he also meant my role in respecting and upholding the teachings of our elders and in encouraging our people to return to the sacred places of our land, to rediscover our original faith, and to renew the sacred teachings of our ancient ones. This was what I began in 1971, here in Morley, Alberta.

I shared my dream with my loving wife, Alva. She paused for a moment as though in deep thought, then she said to me: "Tell this dream to the elders when we get home. That's a beautiful dream." Since then I have shared this Vision with some elders and my family and friends, but I never shared it in print.

My Vision has been my inspiration over the years. The experience is a very important part of my history as I walk in life's journey on this Great Island. In my Vision I was on a pilgrimage with an Indigenous prophet. We walked barefoot on the sacred grounds and

Here I am standing, in 2005, at the edge of the area where my Vision took place. *(Photo by Barry Huddleston)*

saw the sacred mountains. The prophet gave me a message to pass on to coming generations. I am sharing this Vision in this Western Canadian Classics reprint of my book because it has inspired me throughout my life and has guided me in accomplishing many things.

My visit to London gave me inspiration to finish writing *These Mountains Are Our Sacred Places*. By the time it was ready for print, the planning for the commemoration and re-enactment of the signing of Treaty Seven at Blackfoot Crossing on the Siksika Reserve at Cluny, Alberta, was well underway. It was an opportunity for the First Nations of Treaty Seven and the British Crown, represented by Prince Charles as promised, to reflect upon the importance of this historic occasion. We wanted to remind the Crown and the Canadian public of the sacred treaty promises made one hundred years ago by their forefathers, many of which had not been fulfilled. We expressed some hope and optimism during this commemoration, and yet many of the social, economic, and political issues remain the same today. At the university conference in Calgary in 1977, I stated: "We as Indian people are beginning to rediscover our heritage, culture, language, and religion after one hundred years of being called savage, heathen, drunk, and lazy."

I feel the Vision I had when I was overseas in the old country gave me strength, courage, and direction in my future work as one of the Chiefs of the Stoney Nakoda Nation.

The North American Indian Ecumenical Conference

One of the highlights of my life was hosting the North American Indian Ecumenical Conference. The event was held annually from 1971 to 1985 in the Stoney Indian Park, a magnificent setting of hills, valleys, and creeks, with a buffalo herd grazing nearby amongst poplar, spruce, pine, fir, and willow. The Old Bow Fort Creek flows by the sacred grounds and in the background the Rocky Mountains tower over the camp. As I write on page 209 of this book, "These sacred rock monuments remind me that the Great Creator is timeless, while the refreshing mountain springs and the wildlife that inhabit His hills remind me that He is generous and loving." Indigenous and non-Indigenous people came from all over North America for the four- to seven-day-long Conference.

Indigenous peoples from Central and South America, New Zealand, and Hawaii, and Laplanders from the old country were all warmly welcomed. Many elders came to speak and to teach the traditions and spiritual ways of our people. In attendance were medicine people, ceremonial leaders, Chiefs, councillors, clergy, youth, and children. I was Chairman of the steering committee for the Conference for several years. We had an open agenda, and everyone had an opportunity to speak about various issues, including language, traditions, history, beliefs, philosophies, and the importance of keeping the sacred fires burning.

At the beginning of each Conference, the sacred fire would be lit and it would be kept burning through the entire Conference. On occasion a medicine man was there to help start the sacred fire as they did in ancient times by rubbing two sticks together. I have seen and admired these gifted people for their ability to start the sacred fire in a traditional style at the Conference.

Accompanying the lighting of the sacred fire, a pipe ceremony was always observed by our pipe holders and ceremonial leaders. Prayers were offered for Mother Earth and all her children: the whole of creation. Prayers were also offered for the seasons so that they would continue to bring renewal and beauty to the land. One of the elders would explain the meaning of the sacred fire that was so central to our gathering, telling those present to revere the fire as one would an altar. Garbage is not to be thrown on the sacred fire, but sweet grass, sage, tobacco, and other offerings are to be placed on it, offered with prayers. The smoke of the sacred fire will carry prayers to the Great Mystery, our Creator. The fire would burn day and night throughout the Conference with young people responsible for keeping the fire going.

Often people would gather around the sacred fire for prayers, meditations, telling stories, sharing experiences, and encouraging one another in the journey of life. Many of us felt the presence of God, the Creator, and were touched. We felt a deeper understanding of our faith as we sat around the fire.

I was inspired by the teachings around the sacred fire to write a poem called "The Sacred Fire":

Along the Sacred Fire we walked
and talked with our Great Creator,
By the Sacred Fire we heard
living legends of long ago,

Beside the Sacred Fire we shared
our stories and our dreams.

Around the Sacred Fire we stood
tall and proud as one people,
From the Sacred Fire we felt
the warmth and healing energy,
In the Sacred Fire we saw
new hope for the ages to come.

The Sacred Fire will always burn
within us as we journey on.
The Sacred Fire will always light
our path as we blaze new trails.
With the Sacred Fire we will
journey on to that final camp,
a most beautiful place.

Native traditional dancing, singing, and drumming have always been part of our cultural heritage, so pow-wows were held one evening and sometimes two evenings during the Ecumenical Conference. The pow-wows would begin outdoors with an impressive grand entry—a colourful pageant of singers, drummers, and dancers from various tribes in their regalia. A prayer would then be offered at the beginning of the pow-wow, which recognized the Great Creator in all things that we do.

One of the highlights of the Conferences were the pow-wows and the Native traditional dances held on the sacred grounds. During the Conferences we were also honoured to enjoy and appreciate a variety of Native dances we had never seen before. The Dene and Cree people from the Northwest Territories performed the Tea Dance; the Cherokee and Muskogee people from the Oklahoma area performed the Stomp Dance. Watching these dances made us aware of the beauty of our Indigenous dances across this land, and helped us appreciate the rich cultural heritage of our people.

My own family has always been involved in pow-wow dancing. Now, my grandchildren have taken up Native dancing and are on the pow-wow trail in Canada and the United States. Today, the spirit of the pow-wow has returned to our people, with a great number of Indigenous children and youth learning pow-wow songs and dances, making their own regalia, and rediscovering their culture and proud heritage. I know that the pride in their culture that these young people are discovering will be passed down and continue to be an inspiration for cultural and spiritual renewal in the years to come.

The Conference was a renaissance for Indigenous peoples after having been deprived of the freedom to worship the Creator and to practise our spiritual ceremonies, our culture, and our way of life for so many years. During the first half of the twentieth century, Canadian laws prohibited the sun dance, the potlatch, and other Native ceremonies. Although these laws were eventually lifted, the residual feelings of suppression, discrimination, and injustice continue today. There was a reawakening of Indigenous pride and culture when the Ecumenical Conference took root in the 1970s. Many participants at the Conference spoke about their personal experiences and one of the common themes that emerged was the impact and legacy of the residential school system imposed on Indian people in Canada starting in the 1880s to the 1960s.

During this time period, the Canadian government and the Christian Church established the residential schools and took full control of the education of the Indigenous people of this land. They took many children away from their parents and forced them into forms of schooling and religion that were foreign to their culture and way of life. The officials at the schools discouraged the students from speaking their mother tongue and deprived them of praying to the Creator, according to their custom. The years children spent in residential schools, and the years parents spent without their children, were very difficult ones in our history. When the strong bond

My grandchildren (left to right), Chrissy, Kyle, Mika, and Eli Snow in their traditional dancing regalia.

between parents and their children was broken, our families were never quite the same. The negative impact and effects of the residential school system are still felt in Indigenous communities today. However, we have survived and are exposing the true history of the residential schools for all to know.

The Conference was timely and very important because it had only been a decade since the Canadian Bill of Rights (1960) had given us the right to vote in federal elections and recognized us as citizens of our own country.

In the early 1980s I received a letter from Thompson, Manitoba, from a leader who had attended the Indian Ecumenical Conference in Morley, every summer. He stated that his group was not coming to the Conference that summer because they were hosting their own Conference. They had come together as a community to have their elders teach them about their language and the importance of Native spirituality. The Morley Conference ended in 1985, but whenever I travel, I continue to meet people who say: "Hey, I was at your Conference. I learned so much there. I have talked to my elders and we are organizing things at home and going back to our roots, going back to our language and the ways of our people." This was one of the purposes of the Ecumenical Conference, to return to our Native traditions. Native people who were caught up in modern times and did not know which way to turn were encouraged by the elders to go back to their roots, to their sacred places, to relearn the Native philosophy of life in harmony with nature and respect for the Creator's creation. This does not mean all Indians should return to the reserve or reservation; so many of them are already overcrowded. But, it is possible to retain our spiritual philosophy in modern times, wherever you are, be it on a reserve, a reservation, or in an urban setting.

Many talented, gifted, and outstanding Indian people who had experienced something unique in life attended the Conferences. One such person was the late Rev. Andrew Ahenekew, an Anglican priest who served his church well for over forty years. During the 1970s Andrew regularly attended the Ecumenical Conference, and the last summer he attended, he brought a special message to all of us. His message was simple, yet deeply spiritual. As we sat and talked on that beautiful summer evening, he said that, although he had been a missionary for forty years, something had been missing in his life. He said that the Conferences had helped him find what he was missing: he had found himself as an Indian. He was proud to be

Indian. He could be a Christian and still have a peace pipe and still be an Indian. He told me of his vision, a dream just like in the olden times. In Andrew's vision, a white bear appeared to him and told him to look for a certain plant and to boil it in water, and the water would come out a special colour. He could then use it as a medicine to heal people. Following his vision, Andrew found the plant and dug it out, including the root, and boiled it in water as he was instructed, and it came out exactly as the white bear had said it would in his dream.

So Andrew used the medicine to heal people. He had found his purpose in life and he became a medicine man according to Indian tradition. From then on, hundreds of people came to him to be healed. They brought him gifts of blankets, clothing, money, guns, sweet grass, tobacco, and other possessions. He healed many people using the medicine given to him in his dream. When people drank the medicine, it cleaned out their whole system, right through the bones, the joints, and the marrow. It gave them new strength, new life, and new hope.

This dream was part of Andrew's personal history, which he had experienced, which he believed in, which he lived, and it became his medicine in his healing ministry. Andrew also used a peace pipe and prayed in the name of Jesus Christ our Lord. He put together the best of two religions and it was real and powerful. Some of these gifts of healing can only be found in the sacred grounds, in the vision quest areas, and on the mountaintop—and in the sacred places of other Indigenous Nations—and only through a divine revelation of the Creator.

After a large gathering in 1985, smaller groups and families continued to come back to the sacred grounds for the next decade. From 1986 to 1987 smaller groups had their conferences on the sacred grounds. From 1988 to 1993, Rick Lightning from the Ermineskin Nation in Alberta organized small conferences at the site in memory of his late father, Albert Lightning. Albert was one of the elders who regularly attended the Ecumenical Conference and to set up his teepee for feasts and ceremonies. Albert, with the help of some young people, also made a medicine wheel on the sacred grounds. Even today some of the families who used to attend the Conference come back to see the sacred grounds, bringing offerings and offering prayers at the medicine wheel. The Indian Ecumenical Conference will long be remembered by our people as a very sacred event at which many have rediscovered our rich spiritual heritage.

The annual Indian Ecumenical Conference at Morley remains one of the landmark gatherings of the late twentieth century. It brought Indigenous peoples together on a continent-wide basis. We, as Indigenous people, had been drifting away from our original teachings, and the legacy of the Conference is that it encouraged our people to return to our cultural roots and heritage, and to rediscover the sacred teachings of our ancient ones, the keepers of wisdom, the caretakers of the land. We, the descendants, must continue the teachings and the work they have begun at the time of creation and through the ages. This philosophy, this teaching, and this work are most important if we are to survive as a people and continue to live on this planet Earth.

Traditional Teachings

I want to record some of the experiences I have had in the traditional Indian teachings. I learned the traditional teachings, the Nakoda language, and the special ceremonies from my parents, grandparents, and tribal elders. They taught me about our traditions and the sacredness of life and to respect all things the Creator has made. Once I heard an elder say that we must help our white brother before he kills himself and all of us. At the time, I thought it was a harsh statement, but I have come to understand the elders and their teachings. Another statement made by the elders was that modern man is a giant in technology but a dwarf in spirituality and, conversely, the Indian is a giant in spirituality but a dwarf in technology. In time, it came to me that we must help the non-Indian society learn about the values and the philosophies of Indian life.

Life is not only human life, but the life of the forest, the trees, the elements of nature, and so on. The elders were saying that unless modern society is in tune with those things, it will continue to destroy, to pollute, and to make bigger machines and greater weapons that eventually will destroy the planet Earth. The elders believe we must teach all of our brothers and sisters that life is sacred and very valuable and was created for a purpose. Everything is interrelated, and we must live in harmony in the renewal process of the seasons. The fundamental basis of our teachings is to respect the Great Spirit's creation—Mother Earth and her inhabitants—and to remember them in our prayers and our ceremonies.

One of the most important things in life is the family. When you return home, you feel the love and warmth of your family. Your family gives you courage, support, hope, and spiritual strength. Your home is a place of rest, a place to enjoy and raise your family, a place of shelter, and a place to pray with your family. To provide a good home for a family is a great responsibility. This is where a child is nurtured and nourished and where spiritual teaching begins. When a child is born, the elders say, bring up that child the right way. That child is lent to you by the Creator. Therefore, teach that child to be honest, courageous, and strong, and that the Great Spirit made all things.

We must encourage our families to provide a good family home, to preserve our traditions, and, above all else, never to forget our spiritual teachings and ceremonies. We need to remember that the Creator will help and protect our family through difficult times, just as He protects the little birds of the air and all other life. Our family is our greatest treasure, the beginning and the end of our journey in this life, but our spirit continues on to the final camp, a beautiful place where our loved ones have gone to live forever.

These were the teachings of our people in the olden days, but it seems in modern times we are forgetting these things and turning to scientific ways to explain our world. One of our most respected leaders, Chief Walking Buffalo (George Mclean), one of my grandfathers, put it this way:

Hills are always more beautiful than stone buildings, you know. Living in a city is an artificial existence. Lots of people hardly ever feel real soil under their feet, see plants grow except in flower pots, or get far enough beyond the street light to catch the enchantment of a night sky studded with stars. When people live far from the scenes of the Great Spirit's making, it's easy for them to forget His laws.[5]

I want to share some of my thoughts about spirituality and traditional teachings. In the olden days our people believed in the vision quest, they believed in dreams, they believed in visions. They believed the Creator communicated with us through dreams and visions and other things in Creation, so we must be aware and keep an open mind that respects our traditions and beliefs. Life has continued for many thousands of years with the Native people showing respect and praying for Mother Earth. It is our belief that even the birds sing praises and pray for the whole of creation because they, too, are spiritual beings in creation.

I have learned so much about the tremendous richness of Native spirituality from elders as they talked about things in our own language, from the Indigenous perspective. The teachings of the Nakoda people are always there when our elders speak. Spirituality is interwoven with every aspect of our society and our customs, and it is preserved in our language. Today I continue to learn new lessons as I listen to the legends that I originally heard as a child. I have learned the deeper meaning of life and insights into the ways of nature. I have come to understand that the spirits are all around us, and I continue to learn more about this philosophy.

I believe that to know our spirit is to discover who we are. Who are you? Where did you come from? Who are your parents? Who are your ancestors? Where did they come from? Who created them? When we visit other people, we often ask these questions first to find out if we are related. We want to connect with other people in a meaningful way.

According to oral tradition, we are taught that the Great Spirit, our Creator, created the red people, or Indigenous people, for a purpose and placed us on this Great Island, often called the New World by the immigrant invaders. I believe that when they say the "New World," they mean the Western Hemisphere. We, the Indigenous people of the New World, are taught that we are all one people and there is one Creator. We believe in the one Great Creator. Though we speak a host of languages and dialects, and observe diverse cultures, dances, songs, and ceremonies, and live in very different climate zones, we believe in one Creator, the Great Spirit, the Great Mystery (*Wakan Tonga*) who made this Great Island and all things surrounding it.

For thousands of years, our people lived off the land and its resources. Our traditional territory contains sacred sites, sacred mountains, vision quest areas, sun dance sites, sweat lodge sites, sacred hot springs, special places, herbal medicine areas, wild berry areas, and edible plant areas. To know our spirit is to know our sacred places and our sacred sites, our sacred waters, and the meaning of the sacred fire. These are the places where our people received their inspiration, knowledge of healing and medicine, traditional knowledge, and knowledge of the healing energy and power of Mother Earth. We have a lot to learn from our elders.

I believe that to know our spirit is to learn our legends, languages, songs, dances, and ceremonies. In our Nakoda–Sioux tradition, to know our Spirit is to know and respect the teaching and meaning of our sacred pipe and the ceremonial use of tobacco, sweet grass, sage, cedar, willow fungus, eagle feathers, and the other things we use in our fasting, prayers, and ceremonies. And to know our spirit we must learn and understand our traditions.

In the winter of 1986, while I was in Phoenix, Arizona, to receive an honorary Doctor of Divinity degree from Cook College and Theological School, I met a teacher friend of mine, a Native elder and Presbyterian clergyman, who shared a special story with me. It is a sad and yet an inspirational story about a family from the southwestern United States who moved to the city from the reservation. Since then I have shared this story of the successful Indian businessman with others because many of our Native people have had similar experiences while living in the city.

This successful Indian businessman and his family moved to a city to seek greater opportunities in the urban setting. He was a very well-educated man with a young, growing family. The man relocated his family to an urban area and initially did very well. They moved into a modern home that had all the luxuries that the urban area can offer.

He had a good family; he had a good job with a good income. He had two vehicles, attended church regularly, and was a member of elite organizations. He made a good living for a while until he began to experience family problems with his growing children. As they were growing up, they were getting into alcohol and drugs. When he experienced these problems he was frustrated and very depressed because everything seemed to be going wrong. Finally, the man gave up in desperation and he thought about the traditions and teachings of his people.

He said to himself, since all hope seemed to have gone: I am going back to the reservation and will search for the Indian God, if there is one.

He returned to his reservation. It was quiet and peaceful there. He walked in the desert wilderness like his ancestors did before him. The desert plants, trees, sands, and landscape were familiar to him and brought memories that he seemed to have forgotten. He saw the beauty and felt the presence of nature.

While walking, he heard a commotion nearby. He saw a bird making a lot of noise and flapping its wings on the ground. The bird seemed to be calling for help. He looked around and about halfway up the tree was a nest with little birds in it. At the bottom of the tree was a rattlesnake ready to go up the tree. Just then, a roadrunner came into sight and stopped at the base of the tree as if to say: "What is going on here?" The roadrunner fought the rattlesnake and killed it.

Then a thought came to the man. If the Creator so protects the little birds of the air, surely he will protect me and my family. After seeing this, the man was relieved and strengthened with renewed faith and courage to face the future. He went back to his family knowing that the Creator was in control, that the Indian God was still looking after his creation, and that He would help them and protect them.

After this experience in the desert wilderness, like many of our people who experience these things in nature's setting, the man went back to his family and began to rebuild his life and the problems he faced began to resolve themselves. This is a story with a deep spiritual meaning, a Native experience, a turning point in this man's life when he rediscovered the Creator in nature's setting.

This story is not an isolated incident but rather an illustration of many stories of many Indian people across this nation who have had similar experiences and are now returning to the sacred places and rediscovering our original faith and our rich spiritual heritage.

Fulfilling the Prophecy

An ancient prophesy foretells that a day is coming when Indigenous people will teach other peoples and other nations the importance of life. Life in this prophesy means the sacredness of life in the whole creation, not only human life but that of other beings, the elements, forces of life in nature and in the cosmic world. This prophecy tells of a day that is coming when Indigenous people who have special knowledge of nature and Earth's ecosystems will be respected and heard by all humankind.

The delicate and intricate life of the ecosystem must not be disrupted nor disturbed because it is part of the renewal process, which the Great Creator has made. If we begin to mar and destroy the rhythms and harmonies of Nature we are destroying the essence of life; ultimately we are destroying Earth and its inhabitants, including humankind. The Native philosophy/teaching has been to observe and learn from the laws and ways of Nature and live accordingly.

Our ancient prophecy tells us that a day is coming when

Indigenous people of this land will teach other peoples, other Nations about life: the importance of life in harmony with the cosmos. I believe that day has arrived. It is not only humankind that inhabits Earth. There is a host of other living beings who inhabit this world with us. The Creator made all things for a purpose according to our traditions and teachings.

Indigenous philosophy and teachings are about the sacredness of life. There is not one day set aside as holy. Every day is the Creator's day. Every day is holy and everything He made is holy or sacred. We are taught to respect all things that are the Creator's. We live in a world with other sacred beings. When you speak, honour them by speaking the truth. Do not tell a lie when you speak because the trees listen, the rocks listen, the waters listen, the winds listen, the animals and birds listen, indeed every word is heard by Mother Earth. In essence, all of creation is listening and hears you when you speak. So we are taught in our Native traditions to always speak the truth. When you speak truthfully, you honour yourself and all creation.

There is a tremendous difference between the world view of Indigenous people and that of modern civilization. As we walk on pavement, on ceramic floors, on cement, we never touch Mother Earth. When we walk in the forest and the wilderness, we can feel the presence of nature and we can become part of the cosmic world. The forests are very strong and can withstand the winds, the storms of life. The winds come, sometimes soft winds, sometimes a storm, but wind is part of our life. Each day, the wind gives us the breath of life, and this is the work of the Great Mystery.

So we need to look at the traditional teachings if we are to be in tune with Mother Earth and to know the ecosystems and the ways of nature. Our money-oriented society seems to have forgotten that we need all of life to sustain us. These are some of the lessons that Indigenous people can teach in this time of environmental destruction. To fulfill the prophecy of our elders, we must remain as the caretakers and keepers of the land and teach others about living in harmony with nature.

Only after the last tree
Has been cut down,
Only after the last river
Has been poisoned,
Only after the last fish

Has been caught,
Only then
Will you find that money
Cannot be eaten.
(Cree Indian Prophesy)

Today, there are fewer of our sages left, both men and women, across this Great Island, who still possess the traditional wisdom, the sacred teachings, and the ancient prophecies that have been passed down to us through the ages. And each year there are fewer and fewer sages left among our First Nation's people. Some of us first heard these Indigenous voices and teachings in our teepee by the sacred fire in our teepee village. These voices have become fainter with each passing generation, and we must listen to them before they disappear.

I realize that to fulfill the Indigenous prophecies of our Ancient Ones, we, the descendants who have inherited their voices and know these things, must now tell others our stories. We must ensure that we pass on these precious teachings to the coming generations. We know that the Sacred Circle of our traditional teachings will continue throughout eternity because this knowledge is given to us through nature by *Wakan Tonga*, the Great Creator. Now we must go out and share our Sacred Message with all the races of people in the Global Village. *We are the Great Spirit's people! These mountains are our sacred places!*

My granddaughter, Shenoa "Hannagose" Snow in the summer of 2005. The log cabin where I grew up was close to this rock outcropping. As a child, I would climb the rocks; they were my mountain. Now, my grandchildren play where I once did. *(Photo by Barry Huddleston)*

Notes

Chapter Two

1. Reverend James E. Nix, *Mission Among the Buffalo: The Labours of the Reverends George M. and John C. McDougall in The Canadian Northwest, 1860-1876* (Toronto: The Ryerson Press, 1960).

2. Nix, *Mission Among the Buffalo.*

3. Public Archives of Canada, MG 29/D8; Alexander Morris, Lieutenant Governor of the North West Territories, to Reverend John McDougall, June 20, 1874. Archives are hereafter cited as P.A.C.

4. Nix, *Mission Among the Buffalo.*

5. Public Archives of Manitoba, Alexander Morris Papers, Lieutenant Governor's Collection, Rev. George McDougall to D. A. Smith, January 8, 1874 (typed abstract). Archives are hereafter cited as P.A.M.

6. Nix, *Mission Among the Buffalo.*

7. *Ibid.*

8. Alexander Morris, *The Treaties of Canada* (Toronto, 1880), p. 272.

9. P.A.C., R.G. 10, Vol. 1160; Extracts from the Annual Report of the Deputy Superintendent General of Indian Affairs, William Spragg, March 18, 1874.

Chapter Three

1. Canada, Sessional Papers. Annual Report of the Secretary of State (1868-1873) and of the Department of the Interior (1874-1879). Hereafter cited as *Sessional Papers*, followed by the report number and the year of publication.

2. The official papers of both Lieutenant Governors Adam G. Archibald and Alexander Morris are on deposit in the Provincial Archives of Manitoba (Winnipeg). The correspondence covers the years 1870-77. The documents illuminate the day to day administration of the Indian Affairs Branch, and they contain frank accounts of the problems and circumstances surrounding the treaty negotiations.

3. Interview with Peter Wesley, Big Horn Reserve, Stoney Research Library, Tape E.H.; "E", Side 1, April, 1971. See also Tape W.F., "L", Side 1, May 23, 1971.

4. George F. G. Stanley, *The Birth of Western Canada* (Toronto: University of Toronto Press, 1975), p. 211.

5. P.A.M., Alexander Morris Papers, Lieutenant Governor's Collection, David Mills, Minister of the Interior, to the Lieutenant Governor of Manitoba, March 7, 1877.

6. P.A.M., Alexander Morris Papers, Ketcheson Collection, Alexander Morris to David Mills, February 19, 1877.

7. P.A.M., Alexander Morris Papers, Lieutenant Governor's Collection, David Mills, Minister of the Interior, to the Lieutenant Governor of Manitoba, March 7, 1877.

8. Peter Farb, *Man's Rise to Civilization As Shown by the Indians of North America From Primeval Times to the Coming of the Industrial State* (New York: Avon Books, 1968), p. 333.

9. P.A.C., R.G. 10, Vol. 3651; Telegraph from Anderson and Sproat to the Minister of the Interior, July 16, 1877.

10. Morris, *The Treaties of Canada*, pp. 171-72.

11. *Ibid.*, p. 245.

12. P.A.M., Alexander Morris Papers, Lieutenant Governor's Collection, Memoranda by W. J. Christie regarding Saskatchewan district Indians, October 29, 1874.

13. *Ibid.*

14. P.A.M., Alexander Morris Papers, Ketcheson Collection, Memoranda concerning Stoney Indians and Blackfoot Tribes inhabiting the western part of Saskatchewan Country in the North West Territories, c. 1876.

15. Morris, *The Treaties of Canada*, p. 262.

16. P.A.C., R.G. 10, File 8576, James F. Macleod, Commissioner, North West Mounted Police, to Hon. D. Mills, Minister of the Interior, July 26, 1877.

17. L. M. Hanks Jr. and J. R. Hanks, *Tribe Under Trust, A Study of the Blackfoot Reserves of Alberta* (Toronto: University of Toronto Press, 1950), pp. 7-14.

18. Ibid., p. 10.

19. Morris, *The Treaties of Canada*, p. 255.

20. *Ibid.*, p. 369.

21. *Treaty Number Eight, made June 21, 1899 and Adhesions, Reports*, et cetera, (Ottawa: Queen's Printer, 1966; reprinted from the 1899 edition), p. 12.

Chapter Four

1. P.A.C., R.G. 10, File 339151, Jonas Bigstoney to the Indian Commissioner, June 3, 1909 (Translated); also Interview with Lazarus Wesley at his home on the Morley Reserve, Tape W.F. "H", side 1, May, 1971.

2. John Nelson joined the Indian Department as Surveyor in May 1881. He was appointed as a permanent salaried officer in June, 1883.

3. *Sessional* Papers (No. 6) 1888, Report of John C. Nelson, In charge Indian Reserve Surveys, p. 279.

4. P.A.C., R.G. 10, Vol. 1625, W. Graham, Farmer, Stoney Reserve, to F. C. Cornish, Indian Agent Sarcee Agency, February 6, 1890.

5. Sessional Papers, (No. 4) 1880, Report of the Superintendent General of Indian Affairs, p. 81.

6. *Sessional Papers*, (No. 5) 1883, Report of John C. Nelson, D.L.S. Indian Reserve Survey, p. 219.

7. P.A.C., R.G. 10, File 339151, John Abraham to the Secretary, Department of Indian Affairs, May 31, 1909 (translated).

8. F. G. Roe, "The Extermination of the Buffalo in Western Canada," *Canadian Historical Review* XV (March 1934), pp. 1-23.

9. Peter Farb, *Man's Rise to Civilization as Shown by the Indians of North America From Primeval Times to the Coming of the Industrial State* (New York: Avon Books, 1968), p. 308.

10. P.A.C., R.G. 10, File 25940, R. W. Gowan to E. I. Galt, Assistant Indian Commissioner, May 3, 1880.

11. *Ibid.*

12. P.A.C., R.G. 10, Vol. 1635, Agents' Monthly Reports 1886-87, et passim.

13. *Sessional Papers*, (No. 4) 1880, Report of the Indian Commissioner, Edgar Dewdney, p. 80.

14. P.A.C., R.G. 10, Vol. 1623, Hayter Reed, Assistant Indian Commissioner, to the Indian Agent Sarcee Reserve, July 5, 1886.

15. *Ibid.*

16. *Sessional Papers* (No. 3) 1885, Report of Superintendent General of Indian Affairs, John A. Macdonald, p. xlviii.

17. *Sessional Papers* (No. 4) 1886, Report of the Superintendent General of Indian Affairs, J. A. Macdonald, p. xlviii.

18. *Sessional Papers* (No. 5) 1883, Report of T. P. Wadsworth, Inspector, Indian Agencies, p. 180.

19. *Sessional Papers* (No. 6) 1887, Report of the Superintendent General of Indian Affairs, J. A. Macdonald, p. lii.

20. P.A.C., R.G. 10, Vol. 1624, Hayter Reed, Assistant Commissioner, to the Indian Agent, Sarcee Agency, February 14, 1888.

21. P.A.C., R.G. 10, Vol. 1628, Report of Mr. Graham, Farmer on Stoney Reserve, July 1889.

22. *Calgary Herald*, October 9, 1886.

23. *Calgary Herald*, January 22, 1890.

24. P.A.C., R.G. 10, Vol. 1629, S. B. Lucas, Indian Agent, Sarcee Agency, to the Indian Commissioner, January 12, 1892.

25. P.A.C., R.G. 10, Vol. 1145A, Michael Phillips, Agent Fort Steele, to A. W. Vowell, Superintendent of Indian Affairs, Victoria, B.C., March 18, 1891.

26. P.A.C., R.G. 10, Vol. 1639, S. B. Lucas to the Indian Commissioner, July 27, 1891.

27. P.A.C., R.G. 10, Vol. 1626, Hayter Reed to Indian Agent S. B. Lucas, August 3, 1893, *et passim*.

28. Glenbow Public Archives, John Laurie Papers, file 22, unpublished manuscript, "Truce Between the Kootenays and the Stoneys."

29. *Ibid.*, Lucas, Agent, Sarcee Reserve, to P. L. Grasse, Farmer in Charge, Stoney Reserve, n.d. Cited in "Truce Between the Kootenays and the Stoneys."

30. *Sessional Papers* (No. 15) 1888, Report of the Indian Agent, Wm. Carnegy de Balinhard, Sarcee Agency, p. 103.

31. *Sessional Papers* (No. 14) 1893, Report of the Indian Agent, S. B. Lucas, Sarcee Agency, p. 179.

32. *Ibid.*, p. 83.

Chapter Five

1. The reactions of the Blackfoot Tribe are graphically recounted by Hugh Dempsey in *Crowfoot, Chief of the Blackfoot*, Hurtig, 1972, pp. 164-93.

2. Telegram dated April 4, 1885, from private papers of John McDougall, United Church Archives, Toronto.

3. *Calgary Herald*, August 19, 1885.

4. *Calgary Herald*, July 15, 1885.

5. C. E. Denny, *The Law Marches West* (Toronto: J. M. Dent and Sons, Ltd., 1939), pp. 202-203.

6. P.A.C., R.G. 10, File 22173, E. Dewdney, Indian Commissioner, to the Superintendent General of Indian Affairs, July 17, 1885.

7. *Ibid.*, E. Dewdney to W. C. de Balinhard, Farming Instructor, Sarcee Reserve, August 19, 1885.

8. *Ibid.*

9. P.A.C., R.G. 10, Vol. 1623, E. Dewdney, Indian Commissioner, to W. C. de Balinhard, Farming Instructor, Sarcee Reserve, August 19, 1885.

10. *Ibid.*

11. *Ibid.*

12. P.A.C., R.G. 10, Vol. 1635, W. C. de Balinhard to the Commissioner, November 2, 1886.

13. P.A.C., R.G. 10, Vol. 1625, Assistant Commissioner, to the Indian Agent, Sarcee Agency, November 18, 1889.

14. *Ibid.*, Assistant Commissioner, to the Indian Agent, Sarcee Agency, November 19, 1889.

15. *Ibid.*, Assistant Commissioner, to the Indian Agent, Sarcee Agency, March 14, 1890.

16. *Ibid.*, L. Vakoughnet, Deputy Superintendent General of Indian Affairs, to the Indian Commissioner, June 26, 1890.

17. P.A.C., R.G. 10, Vol. 1625, Hayter Reed to the Acting Indian Agent, Sarcee Reserve, October 28, 1890.

18. P.A.C., R.G. 10, Vol. 1145a, Hayter Reed to S. B. Lucas, Sarcee Agency, November 28, 1891.

19. P.A.C., R.G. 10, Vol. 1626, A. E. Forget, Assistant Commissioner, to the Indian Agent, Sarcee Agency, August 21, 1894.

20. P.A.C., R.G. 10, Vol. 1626, Copy of Resolution passed by the High River Cattle Association, September 11, 1894.

21. *Calgary Herald*, February 17, 1893.

22. P.A.C., R.G. 10, Vol. 1626, A. E. Forget, Assistant Commissioner, to the Indian Agent, Sarcee Agency, August 21, 1894.

23. P.A.C., R.G. 10, Vol. 1137, Circular No. 341, February 22, 1894.

24. *Ibid.*, Circular No. 237, February 9, 1891.

25. P.A.C., R.G. 10, Vol. 1626, Hayter Reed to Indian Agent, Sarcee Agency, December 8, 1892.

26. P.A.C., R.G. 10, Vol. 1625, The Commissioner, to the Acting Indian Agent, Sarcee Agency, February 10, 1891.

27. P.A.C., R.G. 10, Vol. 1626, A. E. Forget, Assistant Commissioner, to the Indian Agent, Sarcee Agency, October 4, 1894.

28. P.A.C., R.G. 10, Vol. 1628, Report of Mr. Graham, Farmer on Stoney Reserve, for October 1889.

29. P.A.C., R.G. 10, Vol. 1137, Memorandum No. 237, August 28, 1894.

30. John Laurie Papers, File 22, "Truce Between the Kootenays and the Stoneys."

31. P.A.C., R.G. 10, Vol. 1625, The Commissioner, to the Acting Indian Agent, Sarcee Agency, February 10, 1891.

32. P.A.C., R.G. 10, Vol. 1626, A. E. Forget, Assistant Commissioner, to Indian Agent, Sarcee Agency, July 20, 1893.

33. P.A.C., R.G. 10, Vol. 1137, Circular No. 878, June 16, 1893.

34. *Ibid.*

35. P.A.C., R.G. 10, Vol. 1626, A. E. Forget, Assistant Commissioner, to Indian Agent, Sarcee Agency, August 17, 1893.

36. *Ibid.*, May 14, 1894.

37. P.A.C., R.G. 10, Vol. 1137, Circular No. 454, July 30, 1894.

38. P.A.C., R.G. 10, Vol. 1638, F. C. Cornish, Indian Agent, Sarcee Agency, to W. Graham, Farmer, Stoney Reserve, May 15, 1890.

39. P.A.C., R.G. 10, File 121698-19, A. N. McNeill, Assistant Secretary, Department of Indian Affairs, to E. J. Bangs, Farmer in charge, Stoney Reserve, August 4, 1897.

40. P.A.R.C., File 772/31-2-3 C. P. (railway right of way).

41. P.A.C., R.G. 10, Vol. 1137, Circular dated December 28, 1892.

42. The government announced its intention of fining parents $2.00 per day if their children were absent from school without authorization. Glenbow Public Archives, file 4, Sarcee Indian Agency Papers, Gibbon Stocken, teacher, to S. B. Lucas, Indian Agent, December 3, 1894.

43. The incident is described, with many contemporary quotes, in a feature article by Fran Fraser, *Calgary Herald*, March 12, 1962.

44. The biographical material on Peter Wesley is based largely on material found in the John Laurie Papers, file 22, unpublished manuscript, "Peter Wesley, the Rebel."

45. Interview with Moses Wesley, Tape. W. F. "M," Side 2, April 2, 1971.

46. John Laurie, "Home of the Kootenay Plains", *Canadian Cattlemen*, August 1950, pp. 22–23.

47. Robert Smallboy, "Decision to Leave Hobbema," *The Western Canadian Journal of Anthropology*, I, No. 1, 1969, p. 118.

Chapter Six

1. P.A.R.C., File 27119-1, Vol. 1, Land Committee to the Indian Commissioner, January 11, 1898.

2. *Ibid.*, Land Committee to the Indian Commissioner, February 9, 1898.

3. *Ibid.*, A. E. Forget, Indian Commissioner, to E. J. Bangs, in Charge, Stoney Reserve, January 17, 1898.

4. *Ibid.*, A. E. Forget to the Secretary, Department of Indian Affairs, March 1, 1898.

5. *Ibid.*, Assistant Secretary, Department of the Interior, to J. D. McLean, Secretary, Department of Indian Affairs, June 1, 1898.

6. *Ibid.*, D. Laird, Indian Commissioner, to the Secretary, Department of Indian Affairs, January 30, 1901.

7. *Ibid.*, memorandum, S. Bray, Chief Surveyor, to the Secretary, Department of Indian Affairs, February 9, 1901.

8. *Ibid.*, memorandum, A. W. Ponton to the Secretary, February 16, 1901.

9. *Ibid.*

10. *Ibid.*

11. P.A.R.C., File 27119-1, Vol. 1, Memorandum, S. Bray, Chief Surveyor to the Secretary, Department of Indian Affairs, February 9, 1901.

12. *Ibid.*, W. W. Cory, Deputy Minister of the Interior, to D. C. Scott, December 13, 1920.

13. *Ibid.*, W. M. Graham, Indian Commissioner, to D. C. Scott, January 11, 1921.

14. The Department of Indian Affairs maintained a file (No. 37119-1) entitled "Surveys and Reserves—Stoney Agency, Vol. 1, 1898–1929" which dealt with the Morley Reserve. A separate file (No. 27119-2) entitled "Surveys and Reserves—removal [sic] of Stoney Indians From Kootenay Plains" was opened in 1909.

15. P.A.C., R.G. 10, File 339151; S. Bray, Memorandum for the Deputy Minister, March 18, 1909.

16. *Ibid.*, Secretary, Indian Affairs Branch, to T. J. Fleetham, Indian Agent, March 29, 1909.

17. *Ibid.*, T. J. Fleetham, to the Secretary, April 5, 1909.

18. *Ibid.*, John Abraham to the Secretary, Department of Indian Affairs, May 31, 1909, (translated).

19. *Ibid.*, John Abraham to the Secretary, Department of Indian Affairs, May 31, 1909, (translated).

20. *Ibid.*, J. D. McLean, Secretary, to Chief Jonas Goodstoney, June 11, 1909.

21. *Ibid.*, J. D. McLean, Secretary, to John Abraham, July 8, 1909.

22. *Ibid.*, memorandum, David Laird to Mr. Pedley, Deputy Minister, Department of the Interior, Indian Commissioner, June 23, 1909.

23. *Ibid.*

24. *Ibid.*

25. *Ibid.*

26. *Ibid.*

27. *Ibid.*, The Assistant Deputy Superintendent General of Indian Affairs, to P. G. Keyes, Secretary, Department of the Interior, July 7, 1909.

28. *Ibid.*, P. G. Keyes to J. D. McLean, October 6, 1909.

29. *Ibid.*, J. D. McLean to P. G. Keyes, December 9, 1909.

30. *Ibid.*, memorandum, S. Bray, Chief Surveyor, to the Assistant Deputy Superintendent General of Indian Affairs, August 30, 1909.

31. P.A.C., R.G. 10, File 368174, T. J. Fleetham, Indian Agent, to the Secretary, Department of Indian Affairs, November 10, 1909.

32. P.A.C., R.G. 10, 339151, John McDougall to the Deputy Superintendent General of Indian Affairs, March 31, 1910.

33. *Ibid.*, J. D. McLean to T. J. Fleetham, April 12, 1910.

34. *Ibid.*, T. J. Fleetham to the Secretary, Department of Indian Affairs, May 2, 1910.

35. *Ibid.*, R. W. Brock, Director, Geological Survey, to J. D. McLean, May 13, 1910.

36. *Ibid.*, Secretary, Department of Indian Affairs, to Reverend John McDougall, June 14, 1910.

37. *Ibid.*, Assistant Secretary, Department of the Interior, to J. D. McLean, September 28, 1910.

38. *Ibid.*, Assistant Deputy Superintendent General of Indian Affairs to P. G. Keyes, October 3, 1910.

39. *Ibid.*, memorandum; J. D. McLean to Duncan C. Scott, Superintendent General of Indian Affairs, n.d., [November, 1910], Map attached.

40. *Ibid.*, J. D. McLean to P. G. Keyes, November 21, 1910.

41. *Ibid.*, memorandum, N. O. Cote, Chief, Land Patents Branch, to W. W. Cory, Deputy Minister of the Interior, March 15, 1911. The timber limits mentioned were surveyed by a Mr. Frances, D.L.S., for a Mr. T. A. Burrows, who presumably held the lease to Timber Berth 1219, located immediately south of the Kootenay Plains. The nearest coal leases to the Plains were situated along the banks of the Bighorn River. They were likely registered soon after Martin Nordegg's discovery of coal seams throughout the North Saskatchewan River valley in 1909.

42. *Ibid.*, Acting Deputy Minister of the Interior to J. D. McLean, March 20, 1911.

43. *Ibid.*, J. D. McLean to J. A. Cote, March 30, 1911.

44. P.A.C., R.G. 10, File 339151, Amos Bigstoney to T. J. Fleetham, March 8, 1911.

45. *Ibid.*, Assistant Secretary, Department of the Interior, to J. D. McLean, June 10, 1911.

Chapter Seven

1. P.A.C., R.G. 10, File 339151, Albert Helmer, Chief Forest Ranger, to R. H. Campbell, Director of Forestry, Department of the Interior, July 12, 1911.

2. *Ibid.*, Assistant Secretary, Department of the Interior, to J. D. McLean, August 1, 1911.

3. P.A.C., R.G. 10, File 339151, Extract from Banff, *Crag and Canyon*, n.d. [June 1913?], enclosed by S. Bray, Chief Surveyor to the Deputy Minister, Department of the Interior, June 17, 1913.

4. Glenbow Public Archives, Tom Wilson Papers, File 19, T. E. Wilson to Forest Inspector E. H. Finlayson, December 25, 1916.

5. Interview with John Abraham at his camp on the Kootenay Plains, Stoney Research Library, Tape C.M. "A", June 3, 1971.

6. Glenbow, Tom Wilson Papers, File 2.

7. *Ibid.*, File 19, Moses House to Tom Eillision [sic], April 19, 1902, *et passim.*

8. *Ibid.*, File 19, Peter Wesley to Tom Wilson, March 27, 1903.

9. Interview with John Abraham, Stoney Research Library, Tape W.F. "L," Side 1, May 27, 1971.

10. Interview with Nat House at Bighorn Reserve, Stoney Research Library, Tape J.W. "A," Side 1, May 1971.

11. P.A.C., R.G. 10, File 339151, Helmer to Campbell, *loc. cit.*, July 12, 1911.

12. *Ibid.*

13. Glenbow, Tom Wilson Papers, File 14, Frank Oliver, Minister of the Interior, to Tom Wilson, April 7, 1908.

14. Order-in-Council, P.C. 2320, September 25, 1920.

15. P.A.C., R.G. 10, File 339151, J. D. McLean to J. K. McLean, D.L.S., August 24, 1911.

16. *Ibid.*, J. K. McLean to J. D. McLean, September 6, 1911.

17. *Ibid.*, J. K. McLean to F. Pedley, Deputy Superintendent General of Indian Affairs, September 9, 1911.

18. *Ibid.*, J. D. McLean to J. K. McLean, September 20, 1911.

19. *Ibid.*, J. K. McLean to J. D. McLean, September 29, 1911.

20. *Ibid.*, J. D. McLean to the Secretary, Department of the Interior, October 4, 1911.

21. *Ibid.*, L. Periera, Assistant Secretary, Department of the Interior, to J. D. McLean, November 13, 1911.

22. *Ibid.*, Glen Campbell, Chief Inspector of Indian Agencies, to the Secretary, Department of Indian Affairs, October 5, 1912.

23. *Ibid.*, Assistant Secretary, Department of the Interior, to the Secretary, Department of Indian Affairs, December 27, 1912.

24. *Ibid.*, L. Pereira, Secretary, Department of the Interior, to the Secretary, Department of Indian Affairs, October 9, 1913.

25. *Ibid.*, D. C. Scott, Deputy Superintendent General of Indian Affairs, to J. W. Waddy, Indian Agent Morley, October 16, 1913.

26. *Ibid.*, J. W. Waddy, Indian Agent, to D. C. Scott, Deputy Superintendent General of Indian Affairs, October 21, 1913.

27. *Ibid.*, D. C. Scott, Deputy Superintendent General of Indian Affairs, to Glen Campbell, Chief Inspector of Indian Agencies, March 17, 1914.

28. P.A.R.C., File 27119-2, J. W. Waddy, Indian Agent, to D. C. Scott, Deputy Superintendent General of Indian Affairs, December 28, 1914.

29. *Ibid.*, D. C. Scott to J. W. Waddy, January 14, 1915.

30. *Ibid.*, J. W. Waddy to D. C. Scott, January 22, 1915.

31. *Ibid.*, Scott to Waddy, January 30, 1915.

32. *Ibid.*, Waddy to Scott, February 9, 1915.

33. *Ibid.*, Jonas Benjamin, Stoney Indian, to D. C. Scott, February 9, 1915.

34. *Ibid.*

35. *Ibid.*, D. C. Scott to Jonas Benjamin, March 1, 1915.

36. *Ibid.*, R. H. Campbell, Director Forestry Branch, to D. C. Scott, April 1, 1915.

37. *Ibid.*, E. H. Yeomans to D. C. Scott, April 11, 1917.

38. *Ibid.*, memorandum to the Hon. Arthur Meighen, Minister of the Interior and Superintendent General of Indian Affairs, from W. W. Cory, Deputy Minister of the Interior, and Duncan Campbell Scott, Deputy Superintendent General of Indian Affairs, April 2, 1918.

39. *Ibid.*, D. C. Scott to Chief Wesley, June 29, 1918.

40. *Ibid.*, D. C. Scott to J. A. Markle, July 2, 1918.

41. *Ibid.*, C.P.R. Telegram, Wm. Graham, Indian Commissioner, to D. C. Scott, July 19, 1918.

42. *Ibid.*, R. H. Campbell, Director Forestry Branch, to D. C. Scott, July 22, 1918.

43. *Ibid.*, J. A. Markle to D. C. Scott, July 22, 1918.

44. *Ibid.*, D. C. Scott to R. H. Campbell, January 26, 1920.

45. The two bands subsequently were given reserves (commonly known as the Sunchild and O'Chiese) in the 1940s near Rocky Mountain House.

46. P.A.R.C., File 27119-2, J. B. Harkin, Commissioner of National Parks, to D. C. Scott, September 27, 1929.

47. *Ibid.*, M. Christianson, Inspector of Indian Agencies, to W. M. Graham, Indian Commissioner, November 27, 1929.

48. *Ibid.*

49. *Ibid.*, W. M. Graham, Indian Commissioner, to D. C. Scott, Deputy Superintendent General of Indian Affairs, December 2, 1929.

50. *Ibid.*, Morley Beaver on behalf of Chief Peter Wesley to the Department of Indian Affairs, October 26, 1934; petition enclosed.

51. *Ibid.*, W. Barr Murray, Indian Agent, to the Secretary, Department of Indian Affairs, November 16, 1934.

52. *Ibid.*, A. F. MacKenzie, Secretary, Department of Indian Affairs, to W. Barr Murray, Indian Agent, November 28, 1934.

53. The author could not obtain more precise information on the effects of the highways upon the Indian people because access was not granted to the files of the Province of Alberta Highway Department nor to the National and Historic Parks Branch, Department of Indian Affairs and Northern Development.

54. P.A.R.C., File 27119-2, W. Barr Murray, Indian Agent, to C. P. Schmidt, Inspector of Indian Agencies, September 20, 1938.

55. P.A.R.C., File 27119-2, Vol. II, M. Christianson, General Superintendent of Agencies, to the Superintendent, Reserves and Trusts Division, April 15, 1939.

Chapter Eight

1. Documents forwarded by D. G. Greyeyes, Regional Director, Alberta Region, April 1, 1971. Enclosure Exhibit "A": "Memorandum of Notes taken at Meeting of the Stoney Band of Indians held in the United Church on the Stoney Indian Reserve at Morley, Alberta, on Friday, March 16, 1946."

2. The National Parks Act of 1914 had greatly enlarged the Rocky Mountain Parks boundaries. As discussed elsewhere, the transfer of federal Crown lands to the Province of Alberta had also caused many difficulties.

3. See Note 1.

4. *Ibid.*

5. P.A.R.C., File 27119-1, Vol. III; Minutes of the meeting held at the home of Chief Enos Hunter on March 20, 1946. The Wesley Band at Morley was opposed to the purchase of the Coppock-Crawford ranches because they were too far from the majority of the band members to be of any immediate benefit. For example, it would mean hauling hay 25 or 30 miles from the ranches to the Wesley Band members living north of the Bow River.

6. P.A.R.C., File 27119-1; Vol. IV; enclosed memorandum drafted by John Laurie, n.d., [January 4, 1947].

7. *Ibid.*, R. A. Hoey to G. H. Gooderham, January 15, 1947.

8. *Ibid.*, enclosed memorandum drafted by John Laurie, n.d. [January 4, 1947].

9. *Ibid.*, memorandum to the Director, from D. J. Allen, Superintendent Reserves and Trusts, January 28, 1947.

10. *Ibid.*, R. A. Hoey to G. H. Gooderham, January 29, 1947.

11. *Ibid.*, G. H. Gooderham to the Director, Indian Affairs Branch, February 14, 1947.

12. The Province of Alberta refused to grant our researchers access to its files, and the federal Department of Indian Affairs released only certain files because its other correspondence could not be released without consent of the province.

13. P.A.R.C., File 772/30-3-144A., H. L. Keenleyside, Deputy Minister, Indian Affairs Branch, to Hon. N. E. Tanner, Minister of Lands and Mines, Alberta, October 2, 1947.

14. For some inexplicable reason, the reserve was never fenced and only recently (1971) has this particular point been brought to the attention of the Stoney Tribe by the Department of Indian Affairs.

15. P.A.R.C., File 772/30-3-144A., R. A. Hoey to G. H. Gooderham, September 16, 1947.

16. P.A.R.C., File 772/30-3-144A., N. E. Tanner to C. D. Howe, Acting Minister, Department of Mines and Resources, September 26, 1947.

17. *Ibid.*, G. H. Gooderham, Regional Supervisor of Indian Agencies (Calgary), to R. A. Hoey, Director, Indian Affairs Branch, Department of Mines and Resources (Ottawa), October 28, 1947.

18. *Ibid.*, G. H. Gooderham to John E. Pugh, Superintendent Stoney Sarcee Indian Agencies, October 18, 1947.

19. Interview with Peter Wesley at his home, Bighorn Reserve, Stoney Research Library, Tape W. F. "K," Side 1, May, 1971.

20. P.A.R.C., File 772/30-3-144A., G. H. Gooderham, Regional Supervisor of Indian Agencies, to R. A. Hoey, Director, Indian Affairs Branch, October 28, 1947.

21. P.A.R.C., File 772/30-3-144A, Report of John A. Pugh to G. H. Gooderham, November 6, 1947 (forwarded to Ottawa).

22. *Ibid.*

23. *Ibid.*, R. A. Hoey, Director, Indian Affairs Branch to G. H. Gooderham, Regional Supervisor of Indian Agencies, November 3, 1947 (airmail).

24. *Ibid.*

25. *Ibid.*

26. *Ibid.*, G. H. Gooderham to R. A. Hoey.

27. *Ibid.*, John E. Pugh, Superintendent, Stoney Sarcee Indian Agencies, to Indian Affairs Branch, Ottawa, November 25, 1947.

28. P.A.R.C., File 771/30-3-144A, Vol. 1, G. H. Gooderham to R. A. Hoey, November 18, 1947.

29. *Ibid.*, Indian Affairs Branch to N. E. Tanner, November 22, 1947.

30. P.A.R.C., File 772/30-3144A, Vol. 1, Gooderham to Hoey, *loc. cit.*

31. *Ibid.*, Deputy Minister, Indian Affairs Branch, to John Laurie, Secretary to the Indian Association of Alberta, February 6, 1948.

32. Interview with Nat House (a former Councillor for the Wesley Band), Stoney Research Library, Tape J.W. "A," Side 2, May 1971.

33. Interview with Killian Wildman at his home, Bighorn Reserve, Stoney Research Library, Tape J.W. "A," Side 1, May 1971.

34. Interview with John Abraham, Stoney Research Library, Tape C.M. "A," Side 1, June 3, 1971.

35. Province of Alberta, Order-in-Council 1321, December 16, 1947.

36. Government of Canada, Order-in-Council, P.C. 3242, July 17, 1948.

37. Hoey to Gooderham, *loc. cit.*

38. *Ibid.*

39. *Ibid.*

40. P.A.R.C., File 771/30-3-144A, Vol. 1, Deputy Minister, Indian Affairs Branch, to John Laurie, February 6, 1948.

41. Interview with John Abraham at his home, Bighorn Reserve, Stoney Research Library, Tape W.F. "L," Side 1, May 27, 1971.

42. *The Red Deer Advocate*, November 30, 1971; the article "Coal Revival Gives Nordegg New Lease on Life" discusses the activities of several coal companies and their exploration for coal reserves west of Rocky Mountain House.

43. P.A.R.C., File 771/30-3-144A, Vol. 1, Deputy Minister Indian Affairs Branch to John Laurie, February 6, 1948. The department files contain numerous newspaper articles depicting the desperate economic plight and deplorable housing conditions on the Morley Reserve. There is very little comment on the newspaper stories, but obviously the government was conscious of the adverse publicity being generated by the local press.

44. P.A.R.C., File 772/30-3-144A, Vol. 1, Keeleyside, Deputy Minister of Indian Affairs Branch, to John Laurie, February 6, 1948.

45. Glenbow Public Archives, John Laurie Papers, Minutes of the Annual Meeting of the Indian Association of Alberta at Le Goff Reserve, June 23–24, 1948.

46. *Ibid.*, Minutes of the Annual Meeting of the Indian Association of Alberta at Goodfish Lake Reserve, June 14-15, 1951.

47. Minutes of the Annual Meeting of the Indian Association of Alberta, June 20–22, 1955. The horses owned by the band freely roamed the plains; they were being captured by horse wranglers and shot by Forestry officials. The Stoneys argued that they were "really a form of money in the bank" because the animals could be sold to raise funds.

Chapter Nine

1. Alexander Morris, *The Treaties of Canada* (Toronto, 1880), p. 296.

2. Canada, House of Commons, Sessional Paper No. 27, 1 George V. A. 1911, Annual Report of the Indian Agent For the Stoney Agency, p. 127.

3. Mr. Justice Thomas R. Berger, Northern Frontier, *Northern Homeland: The Report of the Mackenzie Valley Pipeline Inquiry*, Vol. 1, (Ottawa: Ministry of Supply and Services, Government of Canada, 1977).

4. See E. Palmer Patterson II, *The Canadian Indian: A History Since 1500* (Toronto: Collier-Macmillan Canada Ltd., 1972), p. 171.

5. Each year the Department of Indian Affairs publishes a Register of Indian Graduates across Canada. In 1975, there were three graduates listed, but none were Stoneys. Three of our SCEP teacher trainees will receive their B. Ed., in 1977.

6. See *Statement of the Government of Canada on Indian Policy* (White Paper, 1968), presented to the 1st Session of the 28th Parliament of Canada by the Hon. Jean Chrétien, Minister of Indian Affairs and Northern Development.

Chapter Ten
1. The people hired for these positions were: Ian Getty, a history graduate from the University of Calgary; John Larner, a history teacher; Simon Waquon, a treaty Indian from Fort Smith; and Mavis Vogt, an executive secretary.

2. Morley was chosen for the base of operations because I was still Chief of my Band and treaty Indians are exempt from paying income tax only if they are working on an Indian reserve.

3. *Textbooks and the American Indian*, The Indian Historian Press, Inc., American Indian Educational Publishers.

Chapter Twelve
1. Statement of the Alberta Indian Languages Conference, Camp He Ho Ha, February 15-16, 1974.

Epilogue
1. From "One Century Later: Western Canadian Reserve Indians Since Treaty 7." (Vancouver: University of British Columbia Press, 1978) p. 2. See Chapter 1 for Chief John Snow, "Treaty Seven Centennial: Celebration or Commemoration?" pages 1-6.

2. *Citizens Plus*, a presentation by the Indian Chiefs of Alberta to the Right Honorable Pierre Elliott Trudeau and the Government of Canada, June 1970.

3. The Ghost Lake specific claim settlement was for $19.6 million. Settlement agreement dated "1999" is that signed on 29 July 1999, between the Stoney Tribe and Her Majesty the Queen in Right of Canada ($8.2 million).

4. A statement on the Constitution Act 1982, with recommendation, tabled at the First Ministers Conference, Ottawa, March 15-16, 1983.

5. Walking Buffalo spoke these words in 1958. The quote is taken from *Words of Power: Voices from Indian America*, edited by Norbert S. Hill Jr. (Golden, CO: Fulcrum Publishing, in association with AISES) p. 4. See also Grant McEwan's biography, *Tatanga Mani: Walking Buffalo of the Stoneys* (Edmonton: Hurtig, 1969).

Appendix

Text of Treaty Seven
Articles of a Treaty

Made and concluded this twenty-second day of September, in the year of Our Lord, one thousand eight hundred and seventy-seven, between Her Most Gracious Majesty the Queen of Great Britain and Ireland, by Her Commissioners, the Honorable David Laird, Lieutenant-Governor and Indian Superintendent of the North-West Territories, and James Farquharson MacLeod, C.M.G., Commissioner of the North-West Mounted Police, of the one part, and the Blackfeet, Blood, Piegan, Sarcee, Stony and other Indians, inhabitants of the Territory north of the United States Boundary Line, east of the central range of the Rocky Mountains, and south and west of Treaties numbers six and four, by their Head Chiefs and Minor Chiefs or Councillors, chosen as hereinafter mentioned, of the other part.

Whereas the Indians inhabiting the said Territory, have, pursuant to an appointment made by the said Commissioners, been convened at a meeting at the "Blackfoot Crossing" of the Bow River, to deliberate upon certain matters of interest to Her Most Gracious Majesty, of the one part, and the said Indians of the other;

And whereas the said Indians have been informed by Her Majesty's Commissioners that it is the desire of Her Majesty to open up for settlement, and such other purposes as to Her Majesty may seem meet, a tract of country, bounded and described as hereinafter mentioned, and to obtain the consent thereto of Her Indian subjects inhabiting the said tract, and to make a Treaty, and arrange with them, so that there may be peace and good will between them and Her Majesty, and between them and Her Majesty's other subjects; and that Her Indian people may know and feel assured of what allowance they are to count upon and receive from Her Majesty's bounty and benevolence;

And whereas the Indians of the said tract, duly convened in Council, and being requested by Her Majesty's Commissioners to present their Head Chiefs and Minor Chiefs, or Councillors, who shall be authorized, on their behalf, to conduct such negotiations and sign any Treaty to be founded thereon, and to become responsible to Her Majesty for the faithful performance, by their respective

Bands of such obligations as should be assumed by them, the said Blackfeet, Blood, Piegan and Sarcee Indians have therefore acknowledged for that purpose, the several Head and Minor Chiefs, and the said Stony Indians, the Chiefs and Councillors who have subscribed hereto, that thereupon in open Council the said Commissioners received and acknowledged the Head and Minor Chiefs and the Chiefs and Councillors presented for the purposed aforesaid;

And whereas the said Commissioners have proceeded to negotiate a Treaty with the said Indians; and the same has been finally agreed upon and concluded as follows, that is to say: the Blackfeet, Blood, Piegan, Sarcee, Stony and other Indians inhabiting the district hereinafter more fully described and defined, do hereby cede, release, surrender, and yield up to the Government of Canada for Her Majesty the Queen and her successors for ever, all their rights, titles, and privileges whatsoever to the lands included within the following limits, that is to say:

Commencing at a point on the International Boundary due south of the western extremity of the Cypress Hills, thence west along the said boundary to the central range of the Rocky Mountains, or to the boundary of the Province of British Columbia, thence north-westerly along the said boundary to a point due west of the source of the main branch of the Red Deer River, thence south-westerly and southerly following on the boundaries of the Tracts ceded by the Treaties numbered six and four to the place of commencement;

And also all their rights, titles and privileges whatsoever, to all other lands wherever situated in the North-West Territories, or in any other portion of the Dominion of Canada;

To have and to hold the same to Her Majesty the Queen and her successors for ever:—

And Her Majesty the Queen hereby agrees with her said Indians, that they shall have right to pursue their vocations of hunting throughout the Tract surrendered as heretofore described, subject to such regulations as may, from time to time, be made by the Government of the country, acting under the authority of Her Majesty and saving and excepting such Tracts as may be required or taken up from time to time for settlement, mining, trading or other purposes by Her Government of Canada; or by any of Her Majesty's subjects duly authorized therefor by the said Government.

It is also agreed between Her Majesty and Her said Indians that Reserves shall be assigned them of sufficient area to allow one square mile for each family of five persons, or in that proportion for larger and smaller families, and that said Reserves shall be located as follows, that is to say:

First, —The Reserves of the Blackfeet, Blood and Sarcee Bands of Indians, shall consist of a belt of land on the north side of the Bow and South Saskatchewan Rivers, of an average width of four miles along said rivers down stream, commencing at a point on the Bow River twenty miles north-westerly of the Blackfoot Crossing thereof, and extending to the Red Deer River at its junction with the South Saskatchewan; also for the term of ten years, and no longer, from the date of the concluding of this Treaty, when it shall cease to be a portion of said Indian Reserves, as fully to all intents and purposes as if it had not at any time been included therein, and without any compensation to individual Indians for improvements, of a similar belt of land on the south side of the Bow and Saskatchewan Rivers of an average width of one mile along said rivers, down stream; commencing at the aforesaid point on the Bow River, and extending to a point one mile west of the coal seam on said river, about five miles below the said Blackfoot Crossing; beginning again one mile east of the said coal seam and extending to the mouth of Maple Creek at its junction with the South Saskatchewan; and beginning again at the junction of the Bow River with the latter river, and extending on both sides of the South Saskatchewan in an average width on each side thereof of one mile, along said river against the stream, to the junction of the Little Bow River with the latter river, reserving to Her Majesty, as may now or hereafter be required by Her for the use of Her Indian and other subjects, from all the Reserves hereinbefore described, the right to navigate the above mentioned rivers, to land and receive fuel cargoes on the shores and banks thereof, to build bridges and establish ferries thereon, to use the fords thereof and all the trails leading thereto, and to open such other roads through the said Reserves as may appear to Her Majesty's Government of Canada, necessary for the ordinary travel of her Indian and other subjects, due compensation being paid to individual Indians for improvements, when the same may be in any manner encroached upon by such roads.

Secondly—That the Reserve of the Piegan Band of Indians shall be on the Old Man's River, near the foot of the Porcupine Hills, at a place called "Crow's Creek."

And, Thirdly—The Reserve of the Stony Band of Indians shall be in the vicinity of Morleyville.

In view of the satisfaction of Her Majesty with the recent general good conduct of her said Indians, and in extinguishment of all their past claims, she hereby, through her Commissioners, agrees to make them a present payment of twelve dollars each in cash to each man, woman, and child of the families here represented.

Her Majesty also agrees that next year, and annually afterwards forever, she will cause to be paid to the said Indians, in cash, at suitable places and dates, of which the said Indians shall be duly notified, to each Chief, twenty-five dollars, each minor Chief or Councillor (not exceeding fifteen minor Chiefs to the Blackfeet and Blood Indians, and four to the Piegan and Sarcee Bands, and five Councillors to the Stony Indian Bands), fifteen dollars, and to every other Indian of whatever age, five dollars; the same, unless there be some exceptional reason, to be paid to the heads of families for those belonging thereto.

Further, Her Majesty agrees that the sum of two thousand dollars shall hereafter every year be expended in the purchase of ammunition for distribution among the said Indians; Provided that if at any future time ammunition become comparatively unnecessary for said Indians, Her Government, with the consent of said Indians, or any of the Bands thereof, may expend the proportion due to such Band otherwise for their benefit.

Further, Her Majesty agrees that each Head Chief and Minor Chief, and each Chief and Councillor duly recognized as such, shall, once in every three years, during the term of their office, receive a suitable suit of clothing, and each Head Chief and Stony Chief, in recognition of the closing of the Treaty, a suitable medal and flag, and next year, or as soon as convenient, each Head Chief, and Minor Chief, and Stony Chief shall receive a Winchester rifle.

Further, Her Majesty agrees to pay the salary of such teachers to instruct the children of said Indians as to Her Government of Canada may seem advisable, when said Indians are settled on their Reserves and shall desire teachers.

Further, Her Majesty agrees to supply each Head and Minor Chief, and each Stony Chief, for the use of their Bands, ten axes, five hand-saws, five augers, one grindstone, and the necessary files and whetstones.

And further, Her Majesty agrees that the said Indians shall be supplied as soon as convenient, after any Band shall make due application therefor, with the following cattle for raising stock, that is to say: for every family of five persons, and under, two cows; for every family of more than five persons, and less than ten persons, three cows; for every family of over ten persons, four cows; and every

Head and Minor Chief, and every Stony Chief, for the use of their Bands, one bull; but if any Band desire to cultivate the soil as well as raise stock, each family of such Band shall receive one cow less than the above mentioned number, and in lieu thereof, when settled on their Reserves and prepared to break up the soil, two hoes, one spade, one scythe, and two hay forks, and for every three families, one plough and one harrow, and for each Band, enough potatoes, barley, oats, and wheat (if such seeds be suited for the locality of their Reserves) to plant the land actually broken up. All the aforesaid articles to be given, once for all, for the encouragement of the practice of agriculture among the Indians.

And the undersigned Blackfeet, Blood, Piegan and Sarcee Head Chiefs and Minor Chiefs, and Stony Chiefs and Councillors on their own behalf and on behalf of all other Indians inhabiting the Tract within ceded do hereby solemnly promise to engage to strictly observe this Treaty, and also to conduct and behave themselves as good and loyal subjects of Her Majesty the Queen. They promise and engage that they will, in all respects, obey and abide by the Law, that they will maintain peace and good order between each other and between themselves and other tribes of Indians, and between themselves and others of Her Majesty's subjects, whether Indians, Half Breeds or Whites, now inhabiting, or hereafter to inhabit, any part of the said ceded tract; and that they will not molest the person or property of any inhabitant of such ceded tract, or the property of Her Majesty the Queen, or interfere with or trouble any person, passing or travelling through the said tract or any part thereof, and that they will assist the officers of Her Majesty in bringing to justice and punishment any Indian offending against the stipulations of this Treaty, or infringing the laws in force in the country so ceded.

IN WITNESS WHEREOF HER MAJESTY'S said Commissioners, and the said Indian Head and Minor Chiefs, and Stony Chiefs and Councillors, have hereunto subscribed and set their hands, at the "Blackfoot Crossing" of the Bow River, the day and year herein first above written.

Signed by the Chiefs and Councillors within named in presence of the following witnesses, the same having been first explained by James Bird, Interpreter.

A. G. IRVINE, Ass't. Com., N.W.M.P.
J. McDOUGALL, Missionary.

JEAN L'HEUREUX.

W. WINDER, Inspector.

T. N. F. CROZIER, Inspector.

E. DALRYMPLE CLARK, Lieut. & Adjutant N.W.M.P.

A. SHURTLIFF, Sub Inspector.

C. E. DENING, Sub Inspector.

W. D. AUTROBUS, Sub Inspector.

FRANK NORMAN, Staff Constable.

MARY J. MACLEOD

JULIA WINDER

JULIA SHURTLIFF

E. HARDISTY

A. McDOUGALL.

E. A. BARRETT.

CONSTANTINE SCOLLEN, Priest, witness to signatures of Stonixosak and those following.

CHARLES E. CONRAD.

THOS J. BOGG.

DAVID LAIRD, Lieutenant-Governor of North-West Territories, and Special Indian Commissioner.

JAMES F. MACLEOD, Lieut.-Colonel, Com. N.W.M.P., and Special Indian Commissioner.

CHAPO-MEXICO, or Crowfoot, Head Chief of the South Blackfeet. his x mark.

MATOSE-APIW, or Old Sun, Head Chief of the North Blackfeet. his x mark.

STAMISCOTOCAR, Bull Head, Head Chief of the Sarcees. his x mark.

MEKASTO, or Red Crow, Head Chief of the South Bloods. his x mark.

NATOSE-ONISTORS, or Medicine Calf. his x mark.

POKAPIW-OTOIAN, or Bad Head. his x mark.

SOTENAH, or Rainy Chief, Head Chief of the North Bloods. his x mark.

TAKOYE-STAMIX, or Fiend Bull. his x mark.

AKKA-KITCIPIMIW-OTAS, or Many Spotted Horses. his x mark.

ATTISTAH-MACAN, or Running Rabbit. his x mark.

PITAH-PEKIS, or Eagle Rib. his x mark.

SAKOYE-AOTAN, or Heavy Shield, Head Chief of the Middle Blackfeet. his x mark.

ZOATZE-TAPITAPIW, or Setting on an Eagle Tail. Head Chief of the North Piegans. his x mark.

AKKA-MAKKOYE, or Many Swans. his x mark.

APENAKO-SAPOP, or Morning Plume. his x mark.

* MAS-GWA-AH-SID, or Bear's Paw. his x mark.

* CHE-NE-KA, or John, his x mark.

* KI-CHI-PWOT, or Jacob, his x mark.

STAMIX-OSOK, or Bull Backfat, his x mark.

EMITAH-APISKINNE, or White Striped Dog, his x mark.

MATAPI-KOMOTZIW, or the Captive or Stolen Person, his x mark.

APAWAWAKOSOW, or White Antelope, his x mark.

MAKOYE-KIN, or Wolf Collar. his x mark.

AYE-STIPIS-SIMAT, or Heavily Whipped, his x mark.

KISSOUM, or Day Light, his x mark.

PITAH-OTOCAN, or Eagle Head, his x mark.

APAW-STAMIX, or Weasel Bull, his x mark.

ONISTAH-POKAH, or White Calf, his x mark.

NETAH-KITEI-PI-MEW, or Only Spot, his x mark.

AKAK-OTOS, or Many Horses, his x mark.

STOKIMATIS, or The Drum. his x mark.

PITAH-ANNES or Eagle Robe. his x mark.

PITAH-OTISKIN, or Eagle Shoe, his x mark.

STAMIXO-TA-KA-PIW, or Bull Turn Round. his x mark.

MASTE-PITAH, or Crow Eagle, his x mark.

** JAMES DIXON, his x mark.

** ABRAHAM KECHEPWOT, his x mark.

** PATRICK KECHEPWOT, his x mark.

** GEORGE MOY-ANY-MEN, his x mark.

** GEORGE CRAWLOR, his x mark.

EKAS-KINE, or Low Horn, his x mark.

KAYO-OKOSIS, or Bear Shield, his x mark.

PONOKAH-STAMIX, or Bull Elk, his x mark.

OMAKSI SAPOP, or Big Plume, his x mark.

ONISTAH, or Calf Robe, his x mark.

PITAH-SIKSINUM, or White Eagle, his x mark.

* *Stoney Chiefs*
** *Stoney Councillors*

Introducing the Western Canadian Classics

F ifth House Publishers is pleased to present the Western Canadian Classics series, designed to keep the best western Canadian history, biography, and other works available in attractive and affordable editions. The popular and best-selling books are selected for their quality, enduring appeal, and importance to an understanding of our past.

Look for these Western Canadian Classics at your favourite bookstore.